Case Histories in Business Ethics

Is business ethics relevant to business?
How can studying business ethics change behaviour in business?
What's the connection between business ethics (or applied ethics generally) and ethical theory?

Case Histories in Business Ethics reflects upon, illustrates and extends the role of case histories (summaries of real cases) and case studies (which may be wholly or partly imaginary stories) in the teaching and studying of business ethics.

This volume features contributions from Lord Borrie, Sir Adrian Cadbury, Jon Entine and John Edmonds. It explores the role of case histories in developing and generating argument in business ethics, and shows that both better understanding and better practice in business ethics require attention to ethical theory as well as to case histories.

Also addressed is the use of case histories in engaging the widest range of student capacities, affective as well as cognitive, which directly affect the development of character. The connections between virtue theory and possible uses for case histories are also explained, as well as the potential use of new ways of developing case studies, such as through the use of information technologies, in the acquisition of virtues and transferable skills.

Dr Chris Megone is Senior Lecturer in Philosophy at the University of Leeds, where he teaches Ethics, Applied Ethics and Ancient Philosophy.

Revd Dr Simon J. Robinson is Senior Anglican Chaplain to the University of Leeds and Lecturer in Theology.

Case Histories in Business Ethics

Edited by Chris Megone and Simon J. Robinson

LONDON AND NEW YORK

First published 2002 by Routledge
2 Park Square, Milton Park, Abingdon, Oxon, OX14 4RN

Simultaneously published in the USA and Canada
by Routledge
270 Madison Avenue, New York, NY 10016

Transferred to Digital Printing 2005

Routledge is an imprint of the Taylor & Francis Group

Typeset in Sabon by Taylor & Francis Books Ltd
Digitally printed by Butler and Tanner

British Library Cataloguing in Publication Data
A catalogue record for this book is available from the British Library

Library of Congress Cataloging in Publication Data
Megone, C. (Christopher)
Case histories in business ethics / Chris Megone & Simon J. Robinson.
p. cm.
Includes bibliographical references and index.
1. Business ethics–Case studies. I. Robinson, Simon J., 1951– II. Title.
HF5387 .M435 2002
174'.4–dc21

2001048451

ISBN 0–415–23143–4 (hbk)
ISBN 0–415–23144–2 (pbk)

Contents

Notes on contributors vii
Acknowledgements ix

Introduction 1
CHRIS MEGONE AND SIMON ROBINSON

PART I
Theoretical approaches to business ethics **7**

1 Business dilemmas: ethical decision-making in business 9
SIR ADRIAN CADBURY

2 Two Aristotelian approaches to business ethics 23
CHRIS MEGONE

PART II
Topics and case histories **57**

3 Shell, Greenpeace and Brent Spar: the politics of dialogue 59
JON ENTINE

4 Whistleblowing: the new perspective 96
GORDON BORRIE AND GUY DEHN

5 The Rick and Bianca case history 106

6 *Challenger* Flight 51-L: a case history in whistleblowing 108
SIMON ROBINSON

7 Pain and partnership 123
JOHN EDMONDS

8 John Lewis Partnership: a case history 131
SIMON ROBINSON

9 Nestlé baby milk substitute and international marketing: a case history 141
SIMON ROBINSON

PART III
The role of case histories in business ethics **159**

10 The use of case histories in business ethics 161
CHRIS MEGONE

Index 175

Contributors

Lord (Gordon) Borrie is the Chairman of the Advertising Standards Authority and a Labour peer. Previously he was the founding chairman of Public Concern at Work and the Director-General of Fair Trading.

Sir Adrian Cadbury studied Economics at Cambridge University and joined Cadbury Ltd in 1952. He retired as Chairman of Cadbury Schweppes in 1989. He was a director of the Bank of England 1970–94, and chairman of the Committee on Financial Aspects of Corporate Governance 1991–5. He is President of the Birmingham Centre for Business Ethics and Chancellor of the University of Aston.

Guy Dehn is the founding director of Public Concern at Work and a practising barrister. He was previously legal officer to the National Consumer Council.

John Edmonds is the General Secretary of GMB, Britain's General Union. He is a member of the TUC Executive and the principal trade union spokesperson on European Affairs. He has been a member of the Council of ACAS and of the government's Skills Task Force. He is currently a member of the New Deal Task Force and a Trustee of NSPCC. GMB is affiliated to the Labour Party and John Edmonds is a member of the Labour Party Policy Forum.

Jon Entine is a writer and Emmy-award-winning television news reporter and producer who specialises in business ethics. He won a National Press Club (US) award in 1995 for 'Shattered image: is The Body Shop too good to be true?', published in *Business Ethics* magazine. He has contributed to several business and management books, most recently in W. Hoffman, R. Frederick, M. Schwartz (eds) *Business Ethics: Reading and Cases in Corporate Morality* (2001).

Dr Chris Megone is Senior Lecturer in Philosophy at the University of Leeds, where he teaches Ethics, Applied Ethics and Ancient Philosophy. Recent publications include 'Aristotelian ethics' in R Chadwick (ed.) *Encyclopaedia of Applied Ethics* (Academic Press of America, San

Diego, 1997), 'Persons and potentialities: an Aristotelian approach', in M. Kuczewski and R. Polansky (eds) *Bioethics: Ancient Themes in Contemporary Issues* (MIT Press, Cambridge, 2000) and S. Mason and C. Megone (eds) *European Neonatal Research: Consent, Ethics Committees, and Law* (Ashgate, Aldershot, 2001).

Revd Dr Simon J. Robinson is Senior Anglican Chaplain to the University of Leeds and Lecturer in Theology. Previous publications include *Serving Society: The Social Responsibility of Business* (1992) and *The Decision Makers: Ethics and Engineers* (1999).

Dr Elaine Sternberg is the author of many works on business ethics and corporate governance including *Just Business: Business Ethics in Action* (2000), *Corporate Governance: Accountability in the Marketplace*, and *The Stakeholder Concept: A Mistaken Doctrine* (1999). A former investment banker, she is Principal of Analytical Solutions, a London consultancy firm specialising in business ethics and corporate governance, and a Research Fellow in Philosophy at the University of Leeds.

Acknowledgements

This book is derived in part from a lecture series held at the University of Leeds in the autumn of 1995 under the auspices of the Centre for Business and Professional Ethics. Lord (Gordon) Borrie, Sir Adrian Cadbury, John Edmonds and Elaine Sternberg were amongst the contributors to that series and we are most grateful to them, both for the original lectures, and for all the work that they have done since to revise those lectures so as to bring them up to date for publication now. We are also indebted to Elida Gibbs plc, Barclays Bank plc and Yorkshire Electricity plc (as it then was) for the sponsorship which enabled that very successful lecture series to go ahead.

In working on the Nestlé case we have been helped by David Smith at the Council for Ethics and Economics in America, who has worked very hard on developing the internet and CD-Rom versions of that case history.

We have been encouraged by several editors at Routledge (now part of Taylor & Francis), including Stuart Hay, Michelle Gallagher and Gavin Cullen. But we would especially like to thank Francesca Lumsden for her energy in seeing the project to a close. Finally, we should like to thank our families for their support, especially in the final stages of this work.

The authors and publishers would like to thank the following for granting permission to reproduce material in this work:

The Biologist journal and Martin Angel for the reproduction of Angel, Martin V. (1995) 'Brent Spar: no hiding place', Biologist 42(4) in Chapter 3.

Shell UK Limited for the reproduction of the Brent Spar Timeline in Appendix 3 of Chapter 3.

Public Concern at Work for the reproduction of Chapter 4 and Chapter 5.

Chapter 4 is a revised version of a document originally published under the title *Whistleblowing to Combat Corruption,* PAC/AFF/LMP (2000)1. Copyright OECD, 2000.

Every effort has been made to contact copyright holders for their permission to reprint material in this book. The publishers would be grateful to hear from any copyright holder who is not here acknowledged and will undertake to rectify any errors or omissions in future editions of this book.

Chris Megone and Simon Robinson
Leeds, June 2001

Introduction

Chris Megone and Simon Robinson

In the last thirty years there has been a dramatic increase in the study both of applied ethics quite generally, and of business ethics in particular. Business ethics is certainly a branch of philosophy even if, as an interdisciplinary subject, it may also be seen as a branch of other disciplines such as business studies or management. Thus this increase has brought a different sort of student to the study of ethics, often students who are studying ethics as a small part of a business or management course, although there have also been some students, usually by far the minority, who take business ethics courses as part of a philosophy degree. One result of this growth in students of ethics from a different academic background has been the introduction of different tools for the study of the subject. As opposed to simply reading book-length studies of ethics, or learned articles, students have often been presented with case histories (accounts of real cases) or case studies (which may be wholly or partly imaginary stories) as a substantial component of their courses in business ethics. (Hereafter, case histories alone will be referred to, for brevity.)

One main reason for this has been that students on a management or business course have not always found it obvious that ethics should be a required component in their studies. In response to this worry, it has been thought that case histories can at least demonstrate the way in which ethical concerns are so often integral to business decisions. At the same time, the case history has also had a prominent role in other aspects of business education, so it may have seemed natural to extend its use into this new area. However, not a great deal of further thought has been given to exactly how case histories are to play a role in business ethics curricula.

In particular two issues arise. First of all, many business students, once satisfied that ethics has a role in business, are likely to see a course in ethics as something that should help their practice, help them to reach better decisions and conduct themselves better in the business context. So one question is how, if at all, the use of case histories can contribute to the achievement of that goal. Second, it is not entirely clear how the study of ethics through case histories is supposed to be connected to the study of ethical theories and ethical concepts, which is often supposed to have constituted the central part of the traditional philosophical study of ethics. Thus the question arises as to whether the student of business ethics can learn anything about such matters through the use of case histories, and indeed whether the student with a business background needs to make use of ethical theories or principles, or the analysis of concepts, in their study of business ethics.

This latter question has also arisen for philosophers, who may approach business ethics (or applied ethics in general) from the perspective of a study of ethical theory. Philosophers working in ethics often distinguish three branches of ethics: metaethics, normative ethics and applied ethics. Metaethics is taken to focus on the question of the reality or objectivity of ethical values, judgements or decisions. Normative ethics is taken to focus on the study of ethical theories such as consequentialism, deontology or virtue ethics, or of ethical concepts such as courage, justice or goodness. Applied ethics is then taken to address specific ethical problems such as whistleblowing or the requirement for truth-telling in business.

Given this division, two assumptions may then sometimes be made by such philosophers. The first is that these three branches of ethics are quite separate, and thus results in one do not impinge on any other. The second, which is really a consequence of the first, is that the traditional concerns of philosophical ethics really have no bearing on applied ethics. (Attributing these latter assumptions makes possible one explanation as to why applied ethics has had something of a Cinderella status within traditional philosophy departments.)

This has therefore left a challenge for those who have found it odd that the study of ethics can be so sharply compartmentalized,[1] and in particular that ethical theory could be thought so clearly distinct from the question of what it is right, or at least permissible, to do on particular occasions. The challenge has been to explain how the three branches of ethics bear on each other, and in particular how the study of ethical theories and concepts can help with decisions over practical problems. In the present context, that challenge presents itself in the form of a question as to how the study of such theories and concepts is to be related to the study of case histories.[2]

Against this background, the most general aim of the present book is to explore the links between ethical theory and ethical practice in the business arena. In one way, this very general aim has been achieved by bringing together the perspectives of those actively involved in business practice, directly or indirectly, such as Borrie/Dehn, Cadbury, Edmonds and Entine, and those of theorists such as Megone, Robinson and Sternberg.

However, this very general aim is achieved primarily through the focus of the book on case histories. The specific and central aim of the book is to reflect upon, illustrate and extend the role of case histories (and case studies) in the teaching and studying of business ethics. It explores and illustrates the role of case histories, first in developing and generating argument in business ethics and, second, in engaging the widest range of student capacities, affective as well as cognitive, and thus directly affecting the development of character.

In addressing the first role, the book examines the way in which case histories can be used for the purposes of both understanding and assessing competing theoretical perspectives in business ethics. At the same time, this approach also helps to show how both better understanding and better practice in business ethics require attention to ethical theory as well as to case histories. In addressing the second role – the engagement of affective as well as cognitive capacities – the book explains the connections between Aristotelian virtue theory and possible uses for case histories.

Furthermore, the book also draws attention to the potential contribution of new ways of developing case histories and examines their role in the acquisition of virtues and transferable skills. The particular focus here is on the development of case histories on CD-Roms and the internet. The book contains a chapter on the Nestlé baby milk controversy which has now been running for nearly thirty years. This chapter also points to both CD-Rom and internet versions of this case history. These have been developed by an independent academic, Lisa Newton, for the US-based Council for Ethics in Economics.

What is available, using these electronic resources, is an interactive case history including data from many different sources covering the whole 25-year history of the debate. The sources include documents and contributions from all parties to the debate, so a student can click onto paper documents, video interviews and taped contributions. The wealth of material available and the possibility for interactive use of both CD-Roms and the internet may enhance the opportunity for using case histories in the ways discussed in this book. There are, of course, dangers with such new materials. Students may be simply overwhelmed with the range of materials presented, so lose sight of the principles they are seeking to examine, or fail to engage imaginatively with different possible perspectives. Thus development of case histories via these new technologies will require care.

In order to explain the suggested roles for case histories, the book is divided into three sections. In the first section a number of theoretical approaches to business ethics are outlined. In the first chapter, Sir Adrian Cadbury, who chaired the committee that reported to the UK government on the Financial Aspects of Corporate Governance in 1995, indicates the broad theoretical outlines of his approach to ethical dilemmas in business. In so doing, he comments on the limitations of codes of ethics, some qualifications required of any 'stakeholder' theory and the fundamental importance of confidence and trust. In the second chapter, Megone presents two Aristotelian approaches with somewhat different emphases. First, there is an extended account of Sternberg's ethical decision model, which she has defended at length elsewhere.[3] In the second half of the chapter, Megone outlines Aristotelian virtue ethics and argues that this provides a theoretical framework, both for ethical decision-making in business and for understanding the role of case histories in business ethics.

Against this theoretical background, the second section presents four extended case histories, as well as a briefer one, each of which illustrates a particular area of business in which ethical issues arise. Each case is presented together with analysis of the ethical problem raised, analysis incorporated within the chapter or presented in a distinct chapter. Entine introduces reflection on business ethics and environmental concerns through an analysis and account of the Shell Brent Spar case. Dehn/Borrie's chapter discusses business ethics and whistleblowing, and Robinson both outlines and discusses a case which highlights this issue – the Challenger launch disaster. In addition, Dehn offers the briefer Rick and Bianca case which is related to the same topic. Edmonds contributes a chapter on business ethics and employment, which is then explored further through Robinson's account of the John Lewis case. In the final chapter of this section the Nestlé baby milk controversy is recorded by Robinson as an example of the ethical problems that can be raised by international marketing.

The first two sections can therefore be used together in a number of ways. The reader can consider in the abstract both how the theoretical perspectives on particular problems, defended by contributors to the second section, cohere with the more general theoretical approaches in the first section. But the case histories themselves can also be used to examine either the more specific or the more general theoretical approaches. However, the final section addresses specifically the question of the use of case histories with a chapter which argues that Aristotelian virtue ethics shows how case histories can be used in three distinct ways, and thus develop a student's affective capacities as well as his cognitive capacities when studying business ethics.

The present book differs somewhat therefore from other texts in business ethics. Typically, case histories are used to illustrate assertions or arguments in business ethics, or to stimulate debate about an issue in business ethics. This book examines that role, illustrating the link between case histories and more general theoretical approaches in business ethics; but it also explores the link between this role and more novel uses in improving students' development in business ethics. It argues that whilst case histories can be used for reflection on ethical theories, they can also be used to enhance skills in moral decision-making. Using cases for developing decision-making skills has been addressed narrowly in professional training and development for many years, but insufficient attention has been given to this ethical dimension and how the ethical virtues relate to such decision-making. As indicated, the final chapter brings together Aristotelian insights on the moral psychology of virtue and the nature of virtue acquisition so as to explain how case histories can have a role here.

In sum the text will address both the more traditional question of the relation between case histories and ethical theories, and that of a novel way in which the study of business ethics can be affective and not merely cognitive, and show how the use of case histories can be developed to link these two aspects. The case histories in the text should serve as exemplars for both cognitive and affective roles. The book also indicates how the interactive opportunities offered by the CD-Rom and internet website associated with cases like the Nestlé case may take this approach further.

Notes

1 One reason for finding it odd is that it was not a compartmentalization made by the great Greek ethicists, Socrates, Plato and Aristotle.
2 Even if it is admitted that there are connections between the three branches of ethics, a slightly weaker assumption might also be made: namely, that applied ethics is simply derivative from, or dependent upon, the other branches, so that students of these other branches can learn nothing from the study of applied ethics itself. This would leave the challenge as one of having to show how the study of case histories can have any bearing on the study of normative ethics or metaethics.
3 E. Sternberg (2000) *Just Business: Business Ethics in Action*, 2nd edn, Oxford: Oxford University Press.

Part I

Theoretical approaches to business ethics

Chapter 1

Business dilemmas

Ethical decision-making in business

Sir Adrian Cadbury

Why should it be that issues of company conduct and personal conduct in business seem now to be higher on the public agenda? Is it because our behaviour is now worse than it used to be? Well, in due course I will give you an interesting example of nineteenth-century behaviour which, in my view, is very similar to the sort of behaviour found today. So I doubt behaviour has changed that much. It seems to me that there are a number of strands to be identified in answer to this first question.

First of all, business has become more international and, by becoming more international, it is seen, I suspect, to be less accountable. Since it is spread across the world and no longer rooted in a single community, it is held to be responsible to no single jurisdiction. When, by contrast, I joined the Cadbury business, it had its main factory at Bournville and was very much part of that local community, which in turn was part of the city of Birmingham. There were very strong local pressures, providing instant feedback, more or less, on the actions and decisions taken by the company. So, in a sense, you had a force for governance operating on the spot, which doesn't really exist now when companies have their centres spread all round the world. However, the importance of accountability, the need particularly for large international corporations to be answerable, is quite undiminished. The ten largest corporations in the world directly employ between them 4.3 million people, and of course many more indirectly, probably at least twice that number, so the way they conduct their affairs does have considerable social and economic importance.

A second reason why governance has risen up the agenda has been the occurrence of disasters. The Exxon Valdez tragedy, Bophal, Maxwell, corporate collapses – all of these highlight this question of accountability. Take the case of Bophal, for example. Who actually was responsible? How do we try to ensure that that kind of disaster does not happen again?

Third, there is undoubtedly more interest shown by shareholder groups, and by governments themselves, in ethical and environmental issues. For example, we have had in the United States the passing of the Foreign and Corrupt Practices Act. (I always rather like that because it suggests to me the idea that corruption is something that is only foreign. Well, I doubt that is true!) But the very fact that governments felt that they had to intervene in what was essentially a matter of how far a business should go in buying business (a question to which we will return to a bit later on) – that is, I think, something new. Such intervention raises the problem for governments of trying to define limits on conduct, of settling what is acceptable and what is not acceptable, in a world where transactions are moving faster and becoming more complex all the time. It is very difficult for them to keep up.

Fourth, there are issues raised by deregulation of the utilities, as well as the increased public expectations of business, and growing media interest. All of these have pushed the questions of conduct, both company and individual, more to the fore. In the face of these levels of concern, there is, I would suggest, a lack of general agreement as to what the rules of conduct should be, both for companies and for individuals. On the individual side, for example, life is very competitive and pay is related to winning. We may possibly be seeing changing attitudes towards what is right and wrong in this kind of area. Consider a well-known quote from Ivan Boesky, 'Greed is alright, I want you to know that. I think greed is healthy. You can be greedy and feel good about yourself.' The interesting thing about that quote is perhaps not just that he said it, but that he said it at the commencement address for UCLA, to all those bright new students coming up to the university, prior to making their way in life. The message they got was that. That does make one think.

Well, if these are the reasons that have brought corporate governance to the fore, what should be the determinants of conduct? My object in this chapter is to look at the ways in which we should set about making those ethical choices. How are we to come to decisions in business in conditions, if you like, of ethical uncertainty?

By virtue of being Chairman of the Committee on the Financial Aspects of Corporate Governance for four years, I had the opportunity to become involved in matters of corporate conduct, both at the national and the company level, and both in this country and abroad (where there is very great interest in these matters). In particular, as a committee we had the task of drawing-up the Code of Best Practice which we addressed to the boards of companies in this country and, in the first instance, to those listed on the London Stock Exchange. One very proper question, therefore, is how useful are such codes? Does the production of a code of best practice actually help boards in their task of directing and controlling companies? And at the company level, what guidance can company codes give to managers who are faced with decisions which require some degree of ethical judgement?

The sort of company I always had in my mind was one widely spread overseas, where the manager in some outpost in the Far East or in Africa was faced on the spot with a decision which they had to take with nobody to turn to. What help were the sort of rules that we drew up within the company going to be to such a person? Thus my interest lies really in the interpretation of rules and their practical use as much as in the precise nature of the rules themselves.

It is worth noting that the majority of business decisions do have an ethical content. (Incidentally, there has always seemed to me a problem over how you fit this subject of business ethics into a business course, because there should not be a separate compartment for an ethics options that you can take or disregard, treating it as quite unrelated to everything else that is happening within the business course. It is really a thread which runs through all the functions and all the aspects of a business. For example, financial decisions might seem the most securely based on arithmetic and rules. Yet financial decisions very often require you to make some decision as between profit now and profit in the future, and to do that you have to give some weighting to the interests involved here and now, and to those in the future, so you end up with an ethical dimension to the decision. So it seems to me that, at the end of the day, there are very few business decisions which can be made on the basis of mathematics alone.)

One kind of decision to which I will refer has to be made in situations where there seem to be competing values, not cases where one course is clearly right, the other wrong. You may decide to do the wrong thing. That is entirely another matter, but in that case there need be no query in your own mind as to which course is right and which course is wrong. The difficulties come when in fact both courses seem right and we have to decide which of them is going to prevail.

Another difficulty for decision-making arises from uncertainty as to what the rules mean. We may have some rules, but we don't actually know how to interpret them in the particular case which confronts us. Another problem may stem from conflicting orders. We are actually being asked to do two conflicting things at the same time and we have to choose between them. The final kind of problem I'll address arises when there is a complex decision to be made. I will come to a clear example of a complex decision later on, where a number of interests are affected and you have the problem of how you are going to decide which of those interests count most and should therefore have the major say in the final decision.

This business of different shades of right and wrong takes me back to my grandfather.[1] He was deeply opposed to the Boer War and he bought the only paper in this country which, at that stage, was promoting the cause of peace and was against the war. He bought it to make sure that it was able to continue its good work. After buying it, he discovered that a great deal of the paper was taken up with racing tips and betting news and this worried him because, in addition to being opposed to the Boer War, he was actually opposed to gambling as well. So for a period he drastically cut this side of the paper's activities. The results on the circulation were disastrous and, no doubt to the enormous relief of those working on the paper and I suppose to that of the readers, he decided in the end that to promote a journal which was going to speak out against the Boer War was actually more important than giving some mild support to gambling. So he put the news back in and all went well.

Now, my question is, when we are faced with an ethical decision such as one of those above, how do we set about resolving it? I should perhaps at this point explain what I mean by ethics. I use the word to mean the guidelines or rules of conduct by which we aim to live. To reiterate, then, what should be the determinants of conduct?

Both companies and individuals work within frameworks. The company framework is set by the law and by regulations, which are not quite the same thing as the law, but which we have to abide by although they are not necessarily statutory. Thus companies are subject to control by the Board, and to the forces of shareholder opinion through the General Meeting. There are also pressures from peer standards and public opinion. In the case of individuals, obviously some of those determinants just mentioned also apply, but there is also the personal code of the individual concerned.

But who sets these rules and who enforces them? What we find is, if we look at different countries, thinking on the corporate level now, that in fact the frameworks are different in different countries. In Germany, for example, the Board would have a greater degree of control over conduct than it probably would have in the UK. In the US the law and regulation would have a greater role to play than it does in the UK, and so on. So we are all subject to certain rules, but the particular mix of those rules is different and they change. They change as expectations change. Of course, regulation is pretty straightforward. That is clear. What is less clear is how what we come to regard as accepted standards of conduct are established and maintained. So let's look at codes.

There are really four levels of code. There are international codes, national codes and company codes and, perhaps in between these, there are trade or professional codes. International codes constitute an interesting development and one that is relatively new. Recently there has been an Inter-Faith Declaration, a code of ethics on international business for Christians, Muslims and Jews.[2] This is something at the international level very much to be welcomed. There are others. There is a body called the Caux Round Table. There are the Minnesota Principles set out by a group in the United States entitled 'Toward an Ethical Basis for Global Business'. There is a relatively new organization called Transparency International which states:

> Transparency International (TI), the coalition against corruption in international business transactions is at present working on a special project dealing with the compilation of different corporate codes of conduct from multi-national enterprises and those published by institutions such as the Caux Round Table, ICC, and so on, as we believe these to be essential in the implementation of strategies against corruption.[3]

So, there are certain guidelines being produced at the international level that we can look towards. A second source of guidance is to be found at the national level. The Code of Best Practice, which our committee produced, is an obvious example.[4] I mentioned that it was addressed to UK companies, and we did indeed at the beginning of the report say that we hoped that all companies, whatever their size, whether public or not, would pay attention to the principles which we had set out there. But, in the first instance, that code was addressed to listed public companies – companies quoted on the stock exchange.

Third, it seems to me, there are the trade and professional codes. These are obviously very important in the professions and have been there for a long time. But there are others as well which are quite interesting. For example, there is an advertising code under which Benneton had one of its advertisements banned. We might not think of it as a professional code, but it is still a code.

Then, fourth and finally, there are company codes, each company drawing up its own particular code in different forms and, one hopes, discussing it so as to ensure that it is not just a top–down process, but that it does actually have some basis in the way people in the company think and behave. The Cadbury committee Code of Best Practice was not specifically dealing with ethical matters, but nevertheless there was an ethical content and, I felt, it was quite an achievement to get the committee to agree on the significance of this point. We said it was important that all employees should know what standards of conduct were expected of them.[5] We regarded it as good practice for boards of directors to draw up Codes of Ethics or Statements of Business Practice and to publish them both internally and externally.[6] We stressed the principles of openness, integrity and accountability. They go together. Openness on the part of companies within the limits set by their competitive position is the basis for the confidence which needs to exist between business and all those who have a stake in its success. So company codes should reflect this.

Returning to the Cadbury code for a moment, one of the other points we dealt with was the need for independent members of a board. We defined what we meant by independence in this particular context and what we were referring to was independence of judgement. We made this suggestion in order to help boards resolve conflicts between the interests of the executive directors and the interests of the company. This led to a misunderstanding, in my view, that somehow we were implying that outside independent directors were more ethical than executive directors. That was not the point. They can all be equally ethical. What we were saying was that the outsider has less direct interest in the business, is more disinterested, more objective. Thus on issues like take-overs, management buy-outs, directors' pay, top management succession – all things in which the executive directors have an interest – then the outsiders have a particularly valuable role to play. This is not a question of their personal virtue. It is a question of their objectivity.

In general, the response to the Cadbury report was very encouraging and two general points were established, quite apart from whether or not companies followed our recommendations. First, public companies now have to make a statement about their compliance with governance requirements and all have in fact to review the structure of their governance processes, and that in itself seems salutary. I also believe that we have helped to clarify responsibilities in an area where we found there was a good deal of confusion, namely, that between directors and auditors.

So, codes are one determinant of conduct, but I suggested that a second way in which standards of conduct were set was by peer pressure, and this can be seen if you look at the UK financial sector which, as a convenient shorthand, I will refer to as the City, although that is a simplification. The City was an example in the past largely of self-regulation, regulation through peer pressure. That regulation came about by the wide acceptance of those who worked in the City of what might be called the rules of the 'Club'. Of course confidence has a special importance in the financial sector – it is very much the basis of business there, not least because money can be made through breach of confidence, as with insider trading. So membership of the Club involved acceptance of the rules and code of the Club, and if individuals transgressed that code there was a very effective form of punishment, which could well involve exclusion from the Club, thus depriving them of their business. So there are certain advantages to this club-type of approach to setting out rules of conduct. First of all, the rules are known, certainly by the insiders, by those to whom they apply. They are certain and that reduces the ground for dilemmas. Second, such an approach is cheap, effective and adaptable. One of the problems with any formal form of regulation is that it will usually be behind the game. With self-regulation, the Club rules, the moment that a new issue appears the Club can almost immediately provide a rule to deal with it.

However, there is a danger to this approach, and that is that the rules may be one-sided in that they are based on the interests of members of the Club and not on the interests of those whom the Club is there to serve. I said at the outset I would give an instance of nineteenth-century behaviour, and there is a very interesting case relevant here called the Steam Loop affair. The Steam Loop was an invention which was designed to secure savings for users of steam via economies of fuel, water and power. A company was formed in 1890 to exploit it and Slaughter and May were the solicitors, both to the company and to one of its promoters. Now the promoters rigged the market for the issue of shares to ensure that they got a successful launch – apparently in those days this was a regular occurrence. To get the new issue off to a good start, you created an artificial premium on the opening transactions and that was what was done with the Steam Loop shares. Unfortunately, though, the promoters then fell out with each other and there was an argument about who in fact owned some of the shares. So this whole performance was brought before a judge. Slaughter and May did not really think anything of this, since it was accepted as the normal system by which you launched new issues. So they assumed there would be no problem in going before the law. As one of the defendants declared: 'you only have to ask anyone about new companies if it [that is, creating a false premium] is not a necessity'. The judge, however, took a remarkably different view, and what he said was:

> I do say that if persons, for their own purposes of speculation, create an artificial price in the market by transactions which are not real, but are made at a nominal premium merely for the purpose of inducing the public to take shares, they are as guilty of as gross a fraud as has ever been committed.

Slaughter and May were shocked and thought the poor judge simply out of touch with what went on in the City, so went to Appeal. It went to their Lordships and their Lordships thunderingly upheld the judgement. And William May later referred to the case as 'a magnificent miscarriage of justice'. Sadly, poor William actually went to his deathbed believing that he had been very hardly done by.[7]

Now I think that case is interesting in a number of ways. First of all, it shows a clash between two different sorts of rules. The rules of the Club in this case clash with the rule of Law and, interestingly, this time it was the rules of the Club which had actually got out of kilter with legal opinion as to what was right. Of course, the rules of the Club are based on what is acceptable to the members, to the insiders, not to those who are outsiders. So, in this particular case, what was in effect happening was that, in order to provide an efficient capital market for the flotation of shares, it was a regular practice for those inside the market to rig it. This was of course done to protect what they regarded as their interests – their own interests, and also the interest of having an efficient capital market, outweighing the fact that poor unfortunate outsiders not in the know paid over the odds for the shares. It was that inability to see that there was a conflict of interest between the members of the Club and the world whom the Club was there to serve that seems to me one of the problems about Club rules.

That limitation apart, this kind of approach, certainly within the City of London, broke down for other reasons. It broke down because with the Big Bang you had a very rapid expansion of numbers employed in this particular field. The smaller finance houses had been run pretty much on a partnership basis, with considerable personal influence lying with the partners at the top who took people on, talked to them and discussed practice with them. They in fact set the tone. When you had this rapid expansion of numbers, that system of standards completely broke down and there was nothing to put in its place. A second reason was that the boundaries between different types of finance activity were swept away and with that some of the Club rules went as well. Then, third, you had an influx of newcomers who did not share the same attitudes, the same values, the same aims and constraints as had applied previously. As I say, we are in a much more competitive world where winning at all costs may be the motto. A final reason was internationalization. Into that Club came banks from very widely different backgrounds who didn't share precisely the same values. So the Club approach may have some good points, but it does depend on there being a coherent group with shared values, and even then such a coherent group can get out of touch with the wider community.

Now I turn to specific examples of difficult managerial decisions, with a view to examining the role of rules and codes in such decision-making. It seems to me that the first of these dilemmas occurs when managers find themselves under conflicting pressures arising from what we may perceive as the role of business in society. The manager may be involved in cutting costs in his particular business, and also being asked to ensure that the unit he is responsible for continues to play its part in the community. He may be having to get rid of staff and, at the same time, being told that he needs to take up a certain number of trainees who are just leaving school or college. So you get these pressures and, if one thinks in terms of rules, the difficulty for the manager is to know exactly which rule to turn to. This can be expressed in terms of responsibilities. For example, Tom Clarke suggests three levels of responsibilities of business in society.[8] The first level is that of a company meeting its material obligations, to shareholders, to employees, customers, suppliers, creditors, paying its taxes and meeting its statutory duties. That level of responsibility of a company to society is clear-cut, easily defined. The next level up from that suggests that a company has an obligation to take account of the consequences of its actions – for example: that it must be prepared to go beyond minimum standards to ensure that it is making the most of its human resources; that it is not damaging the environment; that it is actually assisting the environment, and so on. We then come to a third level of obligation, which is much less clearly defined. This refers to the responsibilities companies have for the relationship between business and society in a wider sense. At this level, the question arises as to how far a business has a responsibility for maintaining the framework of the society of which it is a part and in which it operates. That seems to me to be a difficult area. These supposed levels of responsibility raise important but difficult questions for managers in large businesses, managers who are unclear how to apply company policy in the individual instances they are faced with. For example, should they employ this disabled person or not? What help are the rules then?

And this sort of problem applies also to the small business. How far should the owner/manager become involved in activities outside of just running the shop? The latter is a problem the individual has to face alone. In the former case, the company still leaves the judgement to be made by the individual, but obviously the clearer we can make our statements of company policy the easier it is for managers to make those decisions. The responsibility here lies with boards of directors – the responsibility to set policies in relation, for example, to recruitment, to redundancy, to the company's relationship with the community. But there is a danger here – namely, that boards will make statements and rules on such matters, which are duly minuted and passed down the line, and as far as the board is concerned it will have done its job.

It will not have done so in two ways. First of all, there is a duty if you set out policy, to follow it up and make sure that it is actually applied in practice. Discrimination in employment may not happen very often at board level but it certainly happens at the factory gate. So it is a job for the board to follow this through and see whether their policy is actually operating. The second duty is to ensure that policies are backed up by the system of rewards and discipline within the company, because the people in the company know perfectly well what is going on in practice. So if in fact it is the person who makes his or her budget who gets promoted, whereas the person who has followed the apparent directive from the top to do all kinds of other good things like training, is left where he is, everybody draws their own conclusion. The rule may state that training is just as important as profit, but if the 'budget-meeter' is promoted, and the trainer is not, at the end of the day it is by the actions of the company that the rules are judged.

One area where I think there are difficult managerial decisions to be made is where a decision is required as to what to do in this kind of situation in relation to major policy issues. The difficulty is the possible conflict between the obligations that arise at different levels. A second difficulty has just been indicated, though it is in its own way more straightforward. This is where there is confusion down the line as to whether a company means what it says. I have a very good example here. It goes back a bit and concerns a court action involving the General Electric Company in the United States. It has been reported as follows:

> For the past eight years or so, General Electric had had a company rule called Directive Policy 20.5, which read in part 'no employee shall enter into any understanding, agreement, plan or scheme, expressed or implied, formal or informal, with any competitor with regard to prices.' ... The trouble, at least during the period covered by the Court action and apparently for a long time before that as well, was that some people at General Electric, including some of those who regularly signed 20.5, simply did not believe it was to be taken seriously. They assumed that it was window dressing: that it was on the books solely to provide legal protection for the company and for the higher ups; that meeting illegally with competitors was recognized and accepted as standard practice; and that often when a ranking executive ordered a subordinate executive to comply with 20.5, he was actually ordering him to violate it. Illogical as it might seem this last assumption becomes comprehensible in the light of the fact that, for a time, when some executives orally conveyed, or re-conveyed, the order, they were apparently in the habit of accompanying it with an unmistakable wink. ... [Thus it was that when] asked by Senator Kefauver how long he had been aware that orders issued in General Electric were sometimes accompanied by winks, Robert Paxton, an upper level G.E. executive replied [as follows]. He had first observed the practice way back in 1935 when his boss had given him an instruction along with a wink or its equivalent, and that when sometime later the significance of the gesture dawned on him, he had become so incensed that he had with difficulty restrained himself from jeopardizing his career by punching the boss in the nose. Paxton went on to say that his objection to the practice of winking had been so strong as to earn him a reputation in the company for being an anti-wink man. But he for his part had never winked.[9]

Now, that is a comical story, but, as a result, senior executives went to jail, and the interesting point about this to me is that I suspect that, in a milder sense, this is all too commonly a managerial dilemma. Managers may know the rule but be unsure as to whether the bosses really *mean* it, or, as in this case, perhaps the managers are given two rules: meet your budget, sell those transformers; on the other hand, don't go entering into any collusion. In such a case a manager may be left to choose one or the other. This does seem to be something that can be avoided, so long as direction from the top and practical implementation are coherent.

A third dilemma is one on which I have touched already, namely, how far one should go in buying business. What inducement is it legitimate for an employee to offer to make a sale, or to complete a deal, and, on the other side of the same coin, what gift is it legitimate for me as an employee to receive? I think this area provides a good example of the limitations of codes when someone is faced with a decision here and now. Virtually every code I have ever seen outlaws bribery and corruption. But, of course, the whole point is what is a bribe? How do you define a bribe? When is a gift, given or received, a bribe? The situation which I have in mind has certainly happened within my own company around the world. It occurs when it is made perfectly clear to you by the official concerned that if a planning application or a production licence is to go through, then a certain payment to them is a condition of agreement. What are you to do?

Well, what I suggested within my former company were two rules of thumb. I said that (a) any payment made should always appear on the face of the invoice, that is to say it should be open and declared, and (b) any individual receiving a gift should be content to see that written up in the company newspaper. The object of this was to provide, what one might refer to as, culture free rules. When operating in Africa and parts of the Far East, the Middle East, and so on, the rules in these matters are different, and it seems to me (a) arrogant and (b) actually impractical to believe that one can impose a set of rules from here all around the world.

Thus the two tests were really quite simple. The first test was to ensure that all payments went through the books in some form and one hopes were audited and could be accounted for. Indeed, I can certainly think of one case, which seemed to me anyway from the outside to involve bribing the police force, that went through the books and was audited and accounted for. By contrast, once people are paying cash, then the whole situation is out of control, so requiring that payments be detailed on the invoice is one way of keeping a check on things even though some of the payments may not be exactly to your liking. That is another matter. The second test determines whether an individual feels compromised by the gift they have received. Now it might be that the threshold of concern, of compromise, can vary somewhat between individuals. A case of whisky is of absolutely no interest to me because I don't like whisky. I don't like gin either, so that's no good. That would have no effect at all in bribing me, but it might be very effective for somebody else. So this test will determine whether in fact an individual has been put under an obligation by the gift. The company newspaper test relies simply on the point that, if the thought that all your friends know you have received this gift doesn't worry you at all, then its receipt is acceptable.

The point therefore is that rules or codes will not settle what is to be done in cases like these. What may help are some simple tests to help determine how the relevant rule is to be interpreted in each particular case. The reasoning behind the tests suggested here, as a way of resolving this third problem of decision-making, really depends on the very simple idea that on the whole openness and ethical behaviour go together. Certainly the reverse is true, that actions are unethical if they will not stand the light of day. Thus open decisions, openly arrived at, may not necessarily be ethical, but they are at least open to debate, and the responsibility for them is clear.

Now the fourth dilemma concerns how far businesses have a responsibility for jobs, for the number of people they employ? This dilemma arises, for example, if a company has a branch factory running at a loss. Assuming that every effort has been made to stem the loss, the decision facing the company is to close the branch unit. Whose interests are going to be affected by a decision to close, and in what way? What weight should be given to each of those interests in coming to a conclusion, both as to the closure itself and the manner of it?

If the company has shareholders, then they will expect the business to be run efficiently and profitably. They expect a return on their investment and so their interest is in seeing the profit leak plugged as soon as possible.

The people most directly and most disadvantageously affected will be the employees who are going to lose their jobs, those who are working in that particular branch. Their interests must carry a high weighting in coming to any decision. However, when you consider other employees working elsewhere in the company, their interest is in stopping the loss. Their security of employment will be greater if the company's financial position is strengthened through the closure. The employee interest does not end there – what about future employees? Clearly, it is in the interests of future employees that the company should succeed, survive and be able to take on more workpeople at a later date.

When it comes to suppliers, they are likely to be disadvantaged by closure. Equally, the local community will be adversely affected by the job losses themselves and the reduction in local purchasing power. The interests of the wider community lie in the opposite direction. A loss-making business is a drain on society and so society in its broadest sense gains from the improvement in profitability consequent on closure. In addition, a closed factory unit is likely to attract some other kind of business taking advantage of a forced sale and so the loss of jobs may only be partial and temporary.

Weighing up whose interests will be affected, if it is decided to close a branch factory, is a necessary part of the decision-making process. Businesses cannot be responsible for creating employment. Their task is to serve their customers efficiently and profitably; jobs are a consequence of businesses carrying out that task. What destroys jobs certainly and permanently is the failure to be competitive. Analysing who is affected by a decision to close is a pointer to the ethical dimension in the closure decision, which lies in the way in which it is carried out.

Here, the interests of those who will lose their jobs is what matters and their interests are best served by giving as long a period of notice as is commercially feasible, providing training and counselling to assist those displaced to find alternative work, and helping to find a new occupier for the vacated premises. Corporate social responsibility is expressed in the manner in which the closure is managed, not in failing to face up to the decision itself if it becomes inevitable. I emphasize this because my concern is that pressures which are put on companies by well-meaning people in the name of ethics may have the effect of influencing us as managers simply to put off making disagreeable decisions.

Decisions can be more or less ethical in themselves and in the way they are executed, but our job as managers is to take them as best we can. Shelving difficult decisions is probably the least ethical course of all. Yet, somehow in this country, that is the direction which pressure groups take. I have seen companies which simply failed to grapple with their problems. They slid inexorably downwards and when they failed, the verdict often was that they were victims of bad luck and that they had done their best in the face of difficulties. But when a company actually tackles its problems, grasps the nettle and closes a plant, the bishops and community representatives descend and those in charge are in deep trouble. As managers, we are there to face trouble and to resist the temptation to postpone disagreeable decisions in the hope that something may turn up. It is not in society's interests that tough decisions should be evaded because of public clamour.

The final point I want to touch on is this. Does a company's ethical approach matter if all that shareholders are thought to care about is profit? First, thinking shareholders care about the company's reputation, because profit in the future may well be linked to reputation. Reputation is a valuable asset which takes time to build up and needs to be jealously guarded. More fundamentally, business ethics matters to society because distrust is a real barrier to the flow of information and of trade. Confidence is important as a basis for business, and so society as a whole is impoverished if business standards slide. If that slide results in increased regulation, then that is a costly and often inefficient alternative.

The ethical standards of companies matter to them on three grounds. First, if unethical practices are condoned or ignored within a company, no one then knows where the line between acceptable and unacceptable conduct is to be drawn and there will almost inevitably be a downward slide in standards, which is cumulative and may lead to disaster – as we have seen in one or two cases in the financial world.

The second reason is that I do not believe that businesses will be able to recruit first-class competent people of ability and integrity unless their standards of conduct are seen as being acceptable to those people and as high as those set by competing careers. Unless the standards within business are perceived to be the equal of standards elsewhere in society, businesses will not get recruits of the quality they need. That will not only be bad for business, it will be bad for society.

There is a final reason, which was highlighted by the Barings disaster. The danger is that the failure of Barings will be seen as a failure of controls. The answer to fraudulent or reckless trading will be thought to lie in a tightening of controls. What went wrong was that the financial controls were not tight enough, it will be said, so screw down the controls. Some tightening of controls was clearly necessary in that case, and if there is not a proper system of control in a business, or if people do not understand the control system, then the business has to be at risk.

But we must recognise the limitations of the control approach. The speed of information technology and the complexity of international transactions require controls, but they have a supporting not a primary role. You cannot keep pace with the gyrations of international currency markets through control systems. The standards of honesty, integrity and prudence of the people who are put in charge of dealings like those on the foreign exchanges must be the primary safeguard. The Barings' failure was more a failure in selection, training and mentoring than anything else. Companies need to recruit and train people in whom they have confidence and whom they can trust. It is confidence and trust that are real safeguards against fraud and disaster, and they can only be fostered and instilled on a sound ethical base.

Notes

1 I also referred to this in 'Ethical managers make their own rules', Sir Adrian Cadbury, *Harvard Business Review*, 1987, p. 69.
2 This was distributed as an inter-faith declaration entitled 'A Code of Ethics on International Business for Christians, Muslims and Jews' in the mid-1990s.
3 Private communication from TI to the author.
4 *Report of the Committee on the Financial Aspects of Corporate Governance*, London, 1992.
5 *Ibid.*, section 4.29.
6 *Ibid.*, section 3.2.
7 Laurie Dennet, *Slaughter and May, A Century in the City*, Cambridge: Granta Editions, 1989, pp. 98ff.
8 Tom Clarke, private circular distributed at original lecture.
9 Reported in John Brooks, *The Fate of Edsel and Other Adventures*, London: Victor Gollancz, 1964, pp. 146–8.

Chapter 2

Two Aristotelian approaches to business ethics

Chris Megone

In a volume concerned with teaching using cases, James Allen writes

> Humanistic education has to do not simply with states of mind or feeling, or scientific truth, or bodies of knowledge. It has to do with action. For by virtue of its subject matter, which is human experience ... it implicitly addresses the questions that underlie action: 'How should one act?' 'How should one live?[1]

As he goes on to observe, this raises the question whether right action can be taught. As if in response to this, a slightly earlier Hastings Centre report on the Teaching of Ethics in higher education includes the following claim:

> One goal frequently proposed for courses in ethics is missing from our list: that of changing student behaviour ... We have concluded that this is not an appropriate goal for a course in ethics.[2]

Whilst it would not be surprising to find writers on theoretical ethics in the latter half of the twentieth century disowning any goal of changing student behaviour, it is striking that a centre concerned with applied ethics should have taken such a view. For undoubtedly many of those who come to study applied ethics are practising professionals in various fields who are concerned about how to behave, not merely about a theoretical understanding of the ethical problems they face. In any case, in the history of philosophy the ancient philosophers, Socrates, Plato, and Aristotle, would have been surprised at the idea that the study of ethics was not concerned with behaviour. Thus Socrates states in the *Republic* that the purpose of his inquiry is to determine how one should live,[3] and Aristotle asserts at the outset of his *Nicomachean Ethics* that the aim of an inquiry into ethics is not knowledge but action.[4]

In the light of this debate between some moderns and the ancients, the aim of the present chapter is to present two approaches to business ethics which address, in different ways, the issue of the practical nature of applied ethics. They also provide a theoretical framework for reflecting on the use of case histories or case studies in working on business ethics. Both theories can be contrasted with Cadbury's views presented in the first chapter, and also considered in relation to the comments of Borrie and Edmonds on specific areas of business practice.

Both of these approaches can be seen as, to a greater or lesser degree, Aristotelian. One adopts certain Aristotelian ideas in its methodology, whilst the other is an explicitly Aristotelian account of virtue theory and its application to business ethics. They can be seen to address the question of the relation between ethical reflection and changes in behaviour in distinct ways. If the question of changing someone's behaviour is raised, one might at first think of two ways of achieving this. On the one hand, an agent's behaviour will be affected by his decisions, so one way to change it will be by changing those decisions. An ethical theory can bear on this by presenting a decision procedure, a method for working out the right thing to do. Utilitarianism might be thought of as, in part, offering something of this sort, and Sternberg's approach, the first that will be presented here, also offers a distinctive (but not Utilitarian) decision procedure. On the other hand, behaviour may also depend on motivation, and Aristotelian virtue theory addresses the way in which motivation may be acquired, or change, and thus alter behaviour, as well as the matter of practical judgement. Such a virtue theory may also be of further interest in suggesting that these two factors affecting behaviour, desire and judgement are not as sharply distinct as we might first think.

Sternberg's approach to business ethics

Sternberg's approach to business ethics, one of the most prominent and theoretically rich in the field, provides a clear and carefully defended decision procedure for reaching ethical judgements in business practice. What follows is a summary account of central aspects of her position, presented here so far as is possible in her own words.[5] In this presentation Sternberg both outlines her theory and explains how it applies to a particular problem, the controversial issue of executive pay. She also argues against a competing approach to business ethics.

As a preamble to putting forward her substantive position, Sternberg first disposes of 'the belief that there is no such thing as business ethics, that business ethics is either theoretically meaningless or impossible in practice'. She concedes that

> sometimes, of course, that criticism is wholly justified. [Thus if] 'business ethics' is taken to denote a separate business ethic, a set of ethical rules that apply exclusively in business and nowhere else, then there is indeed no such thing. Equally, most of the sanctimonious criticisms of

> business that pass as business ethics fully deserve to be dismissed. But that is because much of what masquerades as business ethics is nothing of the sort, having little to do with either business or with ethics.

By contrast, she argues, when properly understood,

> 'business ethics' is not an oxymoron. The notion that 'business ethics' is a contradiction in terms is, however, often espoused, both by those who are hostile to business, and those who would defend it. Critics of business typically point to examples of bad business behaviour; they imagine that since some business people are unethical, ethical conduct and business are incompatible. But that conclusion is unjustified. Just as the moral failings of individual sportsmen do not prove that sport is immoral, nor can the misdeeds of particular businesses or business people prove that business is necessarily unethical.
>
> The other common basis for doubting the possibility of business ethics is equally flawed. It is the belief that being ethical in business means pursuing some social welfare or environmental or religious end in place of owner value. According to this widely held view, the way for a business to be moral is to devote its resources to fulfilling 'social responsibilities' rather than to pursuing profits. Since, however, the essence of business is maximising owner value by selling goods or services, this view of business ethics is literally absurd: it makes refraining from business the condition of being ethical in business. This view is indeed oxymoronic, and cannot be right.

Sternberg is in a position to address this latter point more fully once she has presented her substantive view of a proper understanding of business ethics.

Central to this view is her claim that, 'properly understood, business ethics is about what *business* must do to be ethical. It is therefore important to be clear about exactly what business is.' It is this point that marks a central Aristotelian aspect of her position. Sternberg describes her approach as teleological, and in this connection she takes from Aristotle's work two main thoughts. First of all there is the idea that a definition of a human activity should be given in terms of its purpose. As she says 'One of the most distinctive features of this approach is that it identifies and explains human activities by reference to their ends/aims/goals/objectives/ purposes.'[6] The reason this is important depends on a second Aristotelian idea, namely, that we can assess the goodness of behaviour by reference to the defining purpose of that activity. As she says, 'Purposes are essential for evaluating goodness. Because of their very different purposes, the criteria of a good pillow are necessarily different from the criteria of a good knife.' Applying this to activities 'If the purpose of writing is to inform, then what counts as good writing will be different than if the purpose is to confuse or amuse.' Thus 'It is a central theme [of this approach] that what constitutes ethical conduct in business depends critically on business's definitive purpose.'[7]

Against this Aristotelian background, she now states her view of the purpose of business.

> The specific objective which is unique to business, and which distinguishes business from everything else, is maximizing owner value over the long term by selling goods or services. Actual commercial enterprises, of course, often do much else: they collect taxes and support charities and constitute social environments. But it is only in virtue of maximizing long-term owner value that they can be recognized as businesses. It is the objective of maximizing long-term owner value that differentiates a business from a village fête or a family, a government or a game, a hobby or a club.
>
> The principles of business ethics are those which must be respected for the purpose of business – maximizing long-term owner value – to be possible. Since long-term views require confidence in a future, and confidence requires trust, the conditions of trust must be observed. Equally, owner value presupposes ownership and therefore respect for property rights. In order not to be ultimately self-defeating, business must therefore be conducted with honesty, fairness, the absence of physical violence and coercion, and a presumption in favour of legality. Collectively, these constraints embody what may be called '*ordinary decency*'.
>
> Furthermore, since business is more likely to achieve its definitive purpose when it encourages contributions to that purpose, and not to some other, classical '*distributive justice*' is also essential.[8] Just as 'ordinary decency' is distinct from vague notions of 'niceness', this concept of justice has nothing to do with modern attempts to redistribute income on political grounds. What distributive justice requires is simply that within an organization, contributions to the organizational objective be the basis for distributing organizational rewards. Though the term 'distributive justice' may be unfamiliar, the underlying concept is widely recognized. It is implicit in the commonly accepted view that productive workers deserve more than shirkers; when properly structured, both performance-related pay and promotion on merit are expressions of distributive justice.
>
> The key to business ethics is very simple: *business is ethical when it maximizes long-term owner value subject to distributive justice and ordinary decency*. If an organization is not directed at maximizing long-term owner value, it is not a business; if it does not pursue that

> definitive business purpose with distributive justice and ordinary decency, it is not ethical.

Having laid out the essence of her position, Sternberg is now able to claim that

> Understanding business and business ethics in this way helps to overcome one of the fundamental obstacles to business ethics: the mistaken notion that business ethics is necessarily inimical to business. It does so in three ways. First, when business ethics is properly understood, it becomes clear that it has nothing to do with unproductive 'do-gooding'. Quite the contrary: business ethics positively requires that owner value be maximized, subject only to respecting distributive justice and ordinary decency. Those values, in turn, are not incompatible with business operations, but are necessary for business's existence as an activity. Finally, what business has to maximize is not current period accounting profits but long-term owner value. Unlike short-term profits, owner value necessarily reflects the indirect, distant, and qualitative effects of a business's actions. When, therefore, business is understood as maximizing long-term owner value, it becomes entirely plausible that business performance should be enhanced by ethical conduct.

Having noted this connection between ethical conduct and good business, she adds a caveat.

> While it is generally true that 'good ethics is good business', it is important to highlight the limitations of that slogan. It does not mean that ethical conduct is the same thing as business success, or that the one guarantees the other. If a lucrative but illegal contract has to be refused, or honesty costs the business an important deal, acting ethically can lead to business losses; doing the right thing can sometimes cost dear. Business success does not follow automatically from acting ethically. Conversely, business success is no guarantee of ethical conduct. At least in the short run, spectacular rewards can sometimes result from doing the wrong thing, in business as elsewhere. But while it may be disturbing to see the wicked prosper, their doing so does not undermine the moral basis of business ethics; that relies neither on the ability of ethical conduct to generate business success, nor on a cost-benefit analysis. 'Good ethics is good business' is an observation about business ethics, not a moral justification of it.

Sternberg then addresses a second obstacle preventing business ethics being taken seriously:

> [This] is the notion that business ethics is an optional extra, a bit of fashionable trimming irrelevant to most businesses. But this is a mistake: business ethics cannot be safely ignored by any business. Business ethics is vital not because it is trendy – though business can ill afford to ignore anything, however silly, which seriously influences the markets in which it operates. Rather, business ethics is necessary because ethical choices are unavoidable.
>
> Ethical questions do not just arise when an organization faces catastrophic disasters or when it contemplates philanthropy. Rather, ethical issues permeate businesses' everyday, ordinary, routine activities. Hiring and firing, choosing suppliers, setting prices; establishing objectives, allocating resources, determining dividends ... ethical judgements are fundamental to them all. The choice facing business is not whether, but how, to address ethical issues. The challenge is simply to make the ethical component of business decision-making explicit so as to make it better.

Having noted the prevalence of ethical issues in business activity, Sternberg highlights the importance of improving ethical decision-making:

> Failure to recognize and properly address ethical problems can lead to very substantial charges, both legal and financial; being unethical can cost a business its very life. Many of the most dramatic business failures and the most significant business losses of the last decade were the result of unethical conduct: consider the fates of Barings and BCCI, Polly Peck and the Robert Maxwell group. Normally, 'bad ethics is bad business': the short-term gains which may be won by unethical conduct seldom pay in the end.
>
> And that is because a business that ignores the demands of business ethics, or gets them wrong, is unlikely to maximize long-term owner value. In a free market, the most productive staff, the finest suppliers and the cheapest and most flexible sources of finance can do better than to stay with a business that cheats or treats them unfairly. Equally, discerning customers are unlikely to be loyal to a business that offers dangerous or unreliable products or grudging, unhelpful service. In the long run, unethical business is less likely to succeed.
>
> Even in the short run, businesses whose conduct is unethical, or who do not understand the requirements of business ethics, can operate at a distinct disadvantage. Many standard business problems have unsuspected ethical elements, which businesses without a proper moral framework typically fail to recognize. High fault levels, high 'shrinkage', high turnover of staff and suppliers, employee illness, anxiety and absenteeism, low productivity and low repeat business are among the many business difficulties that typically result from uneth-

> ical business conduct; unsatisfactory behaviour by stakeholders often results from unethical treatment of them. When the underlying ethical questions are ignored, it is usually not the problems, but the business that goes away.

She then goes on to argue that if the ethical component of business decision-making is not correctly addressed, which occurs when the principles of business ethics are not properly understood or are ignored, then

> even attempts to be ethical can be bad for the business. Business is constantly entreated to support all sorts of charitable causes, and to foster social welfare in all its many guises. But though such demands are frequently made in the name of business ethics, they parade under false pretences. If a business's attempts to do good are not to be self-defeating, a proper understanding of business ethics is essential.
>
> That is because when business ethics is properly understood, it becomes clear that it has nothing to do with fulfilling 'social responsibilities'. Business is ethical, not hypocritical, if it only pursues 'social responsibilities' when they maximize long-term owner value. This does not mean that a business cannot or should not behave in socially responsible or environmentally friendly ways. It may well be that selling 'green' products will help attract 'green' consumers and investors and lenders, and that saving energy will save money. And to the extent that such actions do help maximize long-term owner value, they are wholly compatible with business. If, however, a 'socially responsible' act does not contribute to the business objective, then it is wrong – ethically as well as financially – for a business to perform it.
>
> It may well be protested that this is a strange conclusion; it may indeed seem like the very antithesis of an ethical position. But that is so only when business ethics is interpreted oxymoronically, when being ethical in business is deemed to require sacrificing business to other ends. There are, however, several reasons why it is wrong for business to pursue 'social responsibilities' independent of their effect on owner value.
>
> The main reason is that using business resources for non-business purposes is a kind of *theft*: it is an unjustified appropriation of the owners' property. Despite what might be called the 'Robin Hood Syndrome', taking assets from business owners to give to others is simply stealing. That the diverted resources are applied to ends which are commonly regarded as laudable, or as 'social responsibilities', does not make the act of diverting them any less larcenous. However worthy the charity being helped, if employees use company time and telephones to solicit contributions rather than to do business, they are cheating the business's owners. So are business managers when they

use business funds for 'socially responsible' but unauthorized non-business purposes.

They are also guilty of an offence akin to prostitution. Just as prostitution occurs when sex is proffered for money rather than love, so it exists when business pursues love – or 'social responsibility' – rather than money. Business managers who eschew maximizing long-term owner value, and direct their firms to any other goal, are as much prostitutes as artists or sportsmen who sell out for financial gain. In each case, the activity is perverted, and the 'right, true end' is neglected in favour of some other, extraneous objective.

But there is another, equally serious objection to the 'social responsibility' approach to business ethics. Not only does it divert resources from business achievement, but it diverts attention from the need to conduct business ethically. If business ethics is gauged by business support for worthy 'causes', then the focus shifts away from the way that business behaves in its own everyday, ordinary activities. The 'social responsibility' doctrine puts saving the whale ahead of treating employees fairly or customers honestly. But making charitable donations, however large, is no substitute for ensuring that all the business's stakeholders are treated with distributive justice and ordinary decency: everywhere, every time, by everyone in the business.

At this point Sternberg turns to a response to her argument which rests on an appeal to 'stakeholder theory'.

It may now be protested that much of this criticism of the 'social responsibility' doctrine is misguided. Once upon a time it might have been assumed that the purpose of business was maximising long-term owner value, but that is true no longer. Now, corporations are normally *expected* to be pursuing a myriad of objectives, social and psychological, political and economic; doing so can therefore hardly be considered a misappropriation of investors' funds. And this is partly true. Corporate purposes are properly determined by the corporate shareholders, and need not include business at all. To the extent that the corporations' owners have authorized their agents to pursue ends other than maximizing long-term owner value, those agents are wholly entitled to do so. But shareholders are seldom consulted.

Instead, 'stakeholder theory' has just become the new orthodoxy.[9] The stakeholder view maintains that business should be run not for the financial gain of its owners, but for the benefit of all who have a stake in the operations of business: for its employees and customers, its suppliers and its lenders, the community and the government. Stakeholder theory typically holds that business is accountable to all

> its stakeholders, and that the role of management is to balance their competing interests.

However Sternberg now provides reasons to reject this alternative theory.

> There are many things to be said against this view, but the first is that whatever else it may be, it cannot be an explanation of *business*. To understand why, consider an enthusiastic environmentalist who, critical of the pollution and waste caused by the motorcar, endeavours to remove from his own vehicle those properties that he finds most offensive. Being a handy sort of chap, he reduces the cumbersome passenger compartment to an open air slimline seat; he replaces the noisy engine with a silent chain drive; he eschews expensive, polluting petrol in favour of sustainable human energy. His contrivance is elegant and efficient, and better than a motorcar for many purposes. But whatever its merits, the one thing the new vehicle emphatically is not, is an improved motorcar: it is not a motorcar at all. By stripping away the essential features of a motorcar, the enthusiast has transformed what was once a car into something else altogether; he has, in fact, re-invented the bicycle.
>
> In like fashion, an organization whose objective is anything but maximising long-term owner value is not – cannot be – a business, because it lacks the definitive feature of a business. What qualifies an organization to be a business is just the objective of maximizing long-term owner value; however valuable organizations seeking other ends may be, they are not businesses but something else.
>
> It may be objected that this is playing with words. But it is not. What matters is not what the activity of maximizing long-term owner value is called, but what it is. If people prefer to reserve the word 'business' for mixed-purpose commercial organizations and their composite doings, so be it; maximizing long-term owner value will just have to be given a different name. Whatever it is called, however, the activity of maximizing long-term owner value is a vital part of modern life, which needs both to be understood and to be conducted ethically. And it is that indispensable activity which is the subject here.
>
> So whatever stakeholder theorists are offering, it is not an improved form of business. But perhaps it is something different and better, a superior form of corporate governance, for instance. Unfortunately, it is not that either: what stakeholder theory recommends does not even make sense. However widely accepted it is, and however useful the term 'stakeholder' may be as a collective name for those whom the business needs to take into account in its deliberations, the stakeholder approach is fatally, fundamentally, flawed.

First, it is based on a mistake. Starting from the fact that business is affected by and affects certain groups, stakeholder theory concludes that business should be accountable to them. But this cannot be right. Business is affected by gravity and by terrorists, and it affects the Gross National Product, but it is not, and logically could not be, accountable to them. That business must take many factors into account, does not give them any right to hold it to account. Nor does the fact that various groups are affected by business give them any right to control it. In asserting otherwise, the stakeholder approach undermines both the property rights that owners have in their assets, and the duty that agents (business employees) owe to principals (the business owners). As the property of its owners, a business is properly accountable only to them.

A second fundamental defect of the stakeholder approach is that it destroys accountability. This is a particularly ironic failing in a theory intended to promote ethical conduct. But by replacing direct answerability to owners with a notional trusteeship on behalf of competing stakeholders, the stakeholder approach makes accountability so diffuse as to be effectively non-existent.

Accountability to multiple masters can function only if everyone involved accepts a common purpose which can be used for ordering priorities. But the stakeholder approach to business conspicuously lacks such a criterion. By substituting a vague notion of 'balancing interests' for a measurable standard of financial performance, stakeholder theory provides no basis for ranking or reconciling the normally conflicting interests of stakeholders. Are their interests all strictly equal? Are some more important than others? If so, which are they? And when, and by how much, and why? Since stakeholder theory offers no substantive business purpose, it provides no guidance at all as to how such conflicts are to be resolved or how decisions are to be made.

And consequently, it also provides no effective standard against which businesses or business managers can be judged. When maximizing owner value is abandoned in favour of balancing ill-defined stakeholder interests, business managers are left free to pursue their own arbitrary ends. Stakeholder theory encourages arrogant and unresponsive managements, and fosters extravagance re salaries, perks and premises. Stakeholder theory permits resistance to takeover bids that would benefit shareholders, and promotes the pursuit of empire-building takeover bids that make little financial sense. Stakeholder theory indulges exploitation by lenders, and inferior performance by employees and by suppliers. So it is highly unlikely that the stakeholder approach would improve moral conduct.

Why then is it so popular? Because it appeals to those who believe that it is possible to get something from nothing. Specifically it appeals to those who would like to enjoy the benefits of business without the discipline of business. Many of the most prominent advocates of stakeholder theory have indeed been those with most to gain from avoiding accountability: business managers[10] who would like to have the power and prestige and perks of office without the responsibility. Stakeholder theory also appeals to the promoters of worthy 'causes' who believe they would be the beneficiaries if business profits were diverted from business owners.

But they are wrong: nothing comes from nothing. The wealth that they want from business will not be available if the essential business objective of maximising long-term owner value is forsaken. In the spurious expectation of achieving business behaviour that would in some vague way be 'nicer', the stakeholder view sacrifices not only property rights, and accountability, but also the wealth-creating capabilities of business strictly understood.

Having addressed 'stakeholder theory', Sternberg now returns to the ethical decision model she is proposing. She notes how her model is supposed to aid employees who already have their own character and moral outlook.

The relation between an ethical decision model and individuals' moral judgements is rather like that between a map and a sense of direction. However good one's sense of direction may be, simply knowing where north is cannot indicate where the terrain will be rocky or where the bridges are or what the best route is in unfamiliar territory. But equally, without a sense of direction, the information provided by a map will be of less use. Just as a map adds to rather than detracts from the value of a sense of direction, so an ethical decision model builds upon individual moral commitment. The purpose of a business ethical decision model is to provide information about what constitutes acceptable conduct in business; it clarifies the right way to handle ethical issues when they arise in the context of *business* activities.

In a similar way, she argues, the ethical decision model is a valuable tool for management.

A business ethical decision model can help employees do the right thing when acting in their business capacities. In helping business to make informed decisions, business ethics is rather like risk management, or management accounting. Of course, businesses can and do

> operate without such tools. Small businesses often dispense with formal accounting systems altogether, and even large firms can survive in favourable circumstances ignorant of exactly where their costs arise, or which of their activities are profitable. But a business without management accounts suffers from a serious handicap: it lacks a fundamental management tool, as basic to directing business as a compass or a map is to navigation. Operating without such aids may be more adventurous, but is unlikely to be as effective: it is easier to hit a target whose location and identity are known. Like management accounting, business ethics provides greater awareness of what is important in business activities, and can therefore improve business performance. Properly understood, business ethics is not an extraneous anti-business option, but a rigorous, analytical business tool.
>
> And that is because the ethical decision model identifies which problems businessmen actually need to address in their business capacities, and offers a way to resolve them. The Model indicates what information is relevant to ethical decision-making; it organizes that information so that it will be more productive in leading to a decision; and it specifies the ethical principles to be employed in deciding what is right. The Model introduces conceptual clarity and structure to matters which are too often clouded by emotion and moral fervour. It thereby provides a way of managing and resolving ethical problems in business.
>
> A model cannot, of course, eliminate ethical problems or the complexity of real situations. A decision-making framework can, however, promote consistency of decisions over time and place and individual decision-maker, and can encourage learning from experience. Furthermore, it can help to overcome 'moral muteness'. Having little practice in dealing with specifically moral matters in business, and lacking an accepted vocabulary for doing so, many business people feel uncomfortable with ethical issues, and are reluctant to take a stand. By providing the necessary concepts, and legitimizing the discussion of relevant moral issues, an agreed ethical framework can eliminate the time-consuming and destructive need for second-guessing management.

But what does the Ethical Decision Model look like? Sternberg now argues that the model she proposes, which is built on her analysis of the nature of business, consists of five straightforward steps. She illustrates these steps by applying the model to the issue of executive pay.

> The critically important first step in tackling all issues of business ethics is clarifying exactly what is at issue. In the forms in which they

are commonly posed – by the media, by demanding interest groups, by disgruntled stakeholders – ethical questions often seem perplexing, either trivial or intractable. But one reason why the answers frequently seem so elusive is because, in many cases, the questions themselves are fatally flawed. Like 'When did you stop beating your wife?', many questions of business ethics need to be unpacked before they can be sensibly answered.

Consider the media favourite, 'What should top executives be paid?'. As stated, the question potentially raises any number of issues – of psychology and public policy as much as of morality. The popular dispute may, indeed, not even be about pay at all, but about political ambition or economic redistribution or psychological motivation. Such questions are interesting and important, but they are not questions of business ethics. Failure to recognize the specific matter at issue is a major source of confusion in resolving ethical questions, both in business and elsewhere.

Broad rhetorical questions must therefore be analysed to determine exactly what is being asked. A useful start can sometimes be made by considering what the solutions are assumed to be. If, for example, as is often the case with respect to executive pay, the alternatives are different forms of regulation, then the issues are ones of ethics and public policy, not of business ethics. In contrast, the questions that actual businesses need to resolve are normally very limited and specific ones, which must be considered with a view to practical action. Though obscured in the general form, the questions 'Should Smith be paid more than Jones?' and 'Does Bloggs deserve a rise?' are not only more directly relevant to real businesses and much easier to answer, but may well not give rise to any particular ethical perplexity.

The first step, then, in addressing any question of business ethics, is simply to identify what is actually being asked. And that may be made clearer by determining: Who is asking? What has prompted the issue? What precisely is at stake? Who will be affected by the outcome? What sort of decision or action might be called for? Why are there differing views? Over what period – short, medium or long term – is the decision to apply? Who is responsible for taking, implementing, reviewing the decision? How long is available for making it? What objective is being sought?

Having analysed the question, the second step is to determine whether it actually is a problem for this business; if it isn't, then there is no business ethics issue for this business to resolve. The inquiry has three parts: Is the issue relevant to *business*? Is it relevant to *this* business? And is it a *problem* for this business?

The first question is the most basic: does the issue relate to maximizing long-term owner value? Unless it does, there is no business concern at issue, and nothing to be evaluated in terms of distributive justice and ordinary decency. When, for example, questions arise as to how or in what way business should pursue such goals as social welfare, environmental activism or personal development – or indeed any objective other than maximizing long-term owner value – the way to handle them is clear. The proper response is not to agonize over the proposals' individual ethical merits, but simply to point out that such activities are not legitimate for business as business. They can only be justified for business to the extent that they contribute to maximizing long-term owner value.

If an issue is relevant to business, however, the question still arises as to whether it actually is an issue for any particular firm. A sole trader without any employees does not have to agonize over the comparative merits of complicated remuneration schemes. Even if a concern is relevant to a particular firm, it remains to be determined whether it represents a problem. The matter may, for example, be easily soluble through the application of ordinary business criteria: if the business is making losses, it may be that no one gets a rise. Or the ethical issue may not be problematical simply because it is subject to legal or regulatory constraints. When there is a statutory wage ceiling, a law-abiding firm is bound by its limits.

Once the question has been established, the next (third) step is to identify the constraints which may limit solutions. Business decisions are constrained not only by law and regulation, but also by contractual, cultural, economic, physical and technical considerations. Even though the principles of ethical conduct are constant over time and place and industry, what businesses actually can do is crucially affected by their individual circumstances.

Contractual commitments represent a fundamental constraint on business conduct because contracts, like laws, should never be broken lightly. Indeed, so critically important is trust to business, that business should normally respect legitimate expectations whether they are based on formal contracts or promises or less stringent forms of unwritten understanding. If, therefore, a business has contractually committed to award its senior executives discounted share options, it cannot unilaterally shift to a more politically acceptable scheme until the contracts expire.

The [fourth] step is to see how alternative solutions measure up against the three key conditions of maximizing long-term owner value and respecting distributive justice and ordinary decency.

Assessing a proposal's potential effect on long-term owner value is a straightforward business calculation. All the potential costs and consequences, including those which are distant and delayed and indirect, must be weighed against all the potential benefits. The judgements of distributive justice and ordinary decency which a business must make are, in comparison, reasonably simple; unlike assessments of owner value, they are not normally ones of degree or extent.[11] Alternatives either do, or do not, satisfy the conditions; those which do not are not ethical for the business.

Executive remuneration will satisfy ordinary decency if it has been determined fairly, represented honestly, involved no physical violence or coercion, and complied with the law. And it will satisfy distributive justice, if the remuneration is proportional to the executive's contribution to maximizing long-term owner value. If those two conditions are met, then the remuneration is ethical, no matter how large the absolute amount may be. This is a point which both critics and defenders of high pay have failed to grasp. High pay is not unethical because it excites envy or satisfies greed; the 'going rate' and differentials, materiality and executive motivation are equally irrelevant to the moral status of business rewards.

It is important to remember that business remuneration is not a gauge of human dignity, or a reward for moral character. It is simply a payment for services rendered. What determines what those services are worth to a business, and accordingly how much it should pay for them, is the contribution that the services make to owner value. That in turn depends on both the quality of the employee's actual performance and the firm's specific circumstances. For a shirker, £5000 a year can be too much pay; £5 million can be too little for an innovator who has added many times that amount to owner value.

Differentials, as they are traditionally understood in Britain, are irrelevant. If widening differentials in pay reflect widening differentials in the contributions made to owner value, they are justified ethically as well as economically. High pay rises can even be perfectly compatible with redundancies. When traditional functions are no longer useful, and managing change requires increasingly sophisticated management skills, it will be right to pay top executives more while shedding unnecessary staff.

Another widespread error concerning executive pay, is that it is immoral because it rewards executive greed. But employees' motives affect the ethics of remuneration only insofar as they affect owner value. Whether executives are motivated by greed, or indeed by things other than money – by intrinsic interest in the job or, more commonly and more dangerously, by lust for power – their motivation has no bearing on what constitutes just remuneration.

References to the 'going rate' are equally irrelevant. The 'going rate' is simply the market price of a category of worker. Whether or not it should be paid requires comparing that price with the contributions to owner value expected from the worker. Unless the contributions exceed the cost, paying it will not be justified – ethically or financially.

Sadly, the essential importance of distributive justice and ordinary decency has also been missed by the defenders of high pay. Executive remuneration cannot be justified by the fact that it represents only a small part of total expenditure. Although when compared to turnover, pay is often immaterial, this does not mean that it is necessarily merited. And if profits are the basis for judging materiality, then *any* positive remuneration will be ruled out when the business is losing money. What makes remuneration just is not how it compares to sales or current period accounting profits, or how much it leaves over to pay other workers: what matters is whether it properly reflects the employee's contribution to owner value.

And on that basis, sadly, much executive pay is indefensible. The executive whose compensation increases while the value of the company he manages declines, is indeed being rewarded unfairly. Some of the discrepancies arise from time-lagged compensation, and the exercise of (irrevocable, unconditional, one way and often subsequently adjusted) options awarded in palmier times. All too often, however, the measures used even for performance-related pay are simply too 'loser friendly'. But that is a matter for business owners to correct.

This leads Sternberg to the fifth and concluding step in her model: identifying the right course of action for the business.

Once the relevant question and constraints have been identified, and alternative proposals have been assessed, the ethical answer should be clear. The business should choose that alternative which is likely to contribute most to long-term owner value, so long as it satisfies distributive justice and ordinary decency. If either of those conditions is not met, then even if the proposal appears to maximize long-term owner value, it should not be adopted. But equally, satisfying distributive justice and ordinary decency is not enough. The morally right course of action for the business must satisfy all three conditions: it is that which aims at maximizing long-term owner value *while* respecting distributive justice and ordinary decency.

Typically, the hardest part of ethical decision-making is not applying the principles of distributive justice and ordinary decency, but determining which action will actually maximize long-term owner value. But however difficult it may be to project outcomes, estimating long-term owner value cannot be avoided: it is the core not just of ethical decision-making, but of business as such.

As has been indicated, Sternberg's account is Aristotelian in specifying the definition of business in terms of its purpose, and in then determining the proper conduct of business by reference to that definitive purpose. As has also been noted, on this sort of account the effect of studying business ethics on behaviour will depend on the way in which attention to the decision model guides an agent's decisions.

In the second half of this chapter an alternative Aristotelian approach to business ethics will be presented, one which addresses the issue of the practical nature of applied ethics in a different way, and one which also provides a distinct theoretical framework within which to consider the use of case histories in applied ethics. This second approach is an Aristotelian virtue theory. It differs from Sternberg's analysis in giving virtues, rather than a decision model, a central role in the theory. One result of this is that the approach focuses on motivation, and its acquisition, as well as judgement or decision-making. Both the account of the acquisition of virtue and the discussion of practical judgement have implications for the role of case histories in the study of business ethics. These will be explained in the final chapter of this book. A second result of considering business ethics from the perspective of virtue theory may be a slightly different view of the purpose of business from that put forward by Sternberg, one in which the goals of business are constrained by Aristotle's conception of a worthwhile life, namely, a life of virtue.

Aristotelian virtue theory and business ethics

There are many fuller treatments of Aristotelian ethics than that which follows.[12] Likewise what follows is far from a complete account of the repercussions for business ethics of such a virtue theory. The primary aim of the present outline is to state enough about the theory, as interpreted here, to indicate both the thrust of its recommendations for ethical decision-making in business and the basis it provides for reflection on the use of case histories in the study of business ethics.

Once the account has been laid out, three main claims will be made regarding its significance. First of all, it will be suggested that, on this sort of approach, business ethics is simply a branch of virtue ethics as a whole, but that nonetheless it is relevant to know the purpose of the activity of business in order to clarify how some of the virtues apply in that area. Second, it will be argued that this account of virtue ethics may itself have a bearing on what the internal goal of business is. Third, it will be suggested that this account provides a useful framework for consideration of the way in which virtue is acquired. It is here that the account is relevant to the use of case histories in business ethics.

Two key questions

Aristotelian virtue theory focuses on two key questions. The first is: 'What kind of life should one live?', or in Aristotle's terms 'What is the *eudaimon* life, the happy life?' The second is, 'Does virtue pay?', or in Aristotle's terms 'What, if anything, is the connection between a life of virtue and *eudaimonia*, or happiness?' In taking up these questions as central to any ethical theory, Aristotle was following his predecessors, Socrates and Plato, but they remain crucial questions today.[13]

In order to show that the virtuous life is at least a necessary condition for achieving *eudaimonia*, or happiness,[14] if not a sufficient condition, Aristotle needs to give an account both of *eudaimonia* and of virtue which is adequate to explain the role of virtue in the *eudaimon* life. Thus in investigating his two main questions, Aristotle will need to provide deeper understandings of both virtue and *eudaimonia*. It might be asked, in the present context, why an account of Aristotle's approach to virtue need focus on what he says about *eudaimonia*. The latter discussion is important in that for Aristotle it is a constraint on an account of virtue that it vindicate, so far as is possible, the view that virtue pays, in his terms the view that virtue has a role in the *eudaimon* life. To appreciate the strength of the Aristotelian account of virtue, it is necessary to understand the relation it bears to his view of *eudaimonia*. In addition, the relation between virtue and *eudaimonia* also has a bearing on Aristotle's view of the purpose of business. Since *eudaimonia* is the ultimate goal of human life, whatever goal business has which distinguishes it from other activities, the pursuit of that goal must be consistent with the pursuit of *eudaimonia*. The effect of this point will be clearer once the relation between virtue and *eudaimonia* is clarified.

The nature of *eudaimonia*

In the *Nicomachean Ethics* (*NE*), Aristotle begins with an investigation of *eudaimonia*. Starting from the idea that in all (rational) actions agents aim at some good,[15] he argues that it is at least worth investigating whether there is not an ultimate good of all an agent's actions. He then points out that there is in fact widespread agreement that there is such an ultimate good, as all call it *eudaimonia*. But this appearance of agreement is misleading. It is in fact a purely verbal agreement, since people then disagree about what *eudaimonia* consists in. These differing views provide the basis for further investigation of what *eudaimonia* is.[16] Thus, some think it wealth, others a life of pleasure, others a life of honour or public esteem, others still that it is an active life of ethical virtue or, lastly, the life of contemplation.[17] Whilst he does not rule out the possibility that each of these factors, or lifestyles, may make some contribution to *eudaimonia*, he does think that, as an answer to the question 'What is *eudaimonia*?', some of the suggestions can be dismissed.[18]

Eudaimonia cannot be the life of wealth, since *eudaimonia* is an ultimate good, but wealth is simply a means to an end. It is worth having for what it can be used to acquire, not for its own sake. Nor is *eudaimonia* the life of pleasure; pleasure may be an ingredient of a worthwhile life, but to pursue pleasure alone is to live the life of a beast, to ignore crucial aspects of our human nature. Here Aristotle relies on the idea that what is good for a thing depends on the kind of thing it is (an idea seen above in Sternberg's remarks about good pillows and good knives). Nor can it be the life of honour or public esteem. One reason for this is that honour is not worth having in itself. It is only worth having if the bestower is a good judge.

This leaves the possibility that *eudaimonia* is the active life of ethical virtue or the life of contemplation. There has not, of course, as yet, been any positive argument that either of these possibilities is in fact correct. All Aristotle has done so far is rule out certain rival possibilities.

In *NE* I, 7, Aristotle pursues the investigation further by suggesting that attention to the function, or characteristic activity, of a human being may help clarify the nature of *eudaimonia*. In effect, Aristotle's argument here rests on the idea that what is good for a thing depends on the kind of thing it is, the point already implicitly appealed to in ruling out the life of pleasure. Aristotle is suggesting that in determining the ultimate human good, it will be helpful to attend to human nature. It may at first be thought odd to suggest that human nature has anything to do with a function or characteristic activity. Aristotle makes the comparison with flute-players or sculptors, who clearly have the function, or purpose, of playing the flute, or sculpting. In these cases it is plausible that a good flautist is one who does this well and that what is good for a flautist, qua flautist, is what enables him to play the flute well.[19] But it may be thought that humans, as such, lack any characteristic function or purpose.

In broad outline, Aristotle's response here depends on the idea that not merely artefacts or artificial categories of activity, but all natural kinds, including humans, have functions or purposes.[20] This response rests on his idea that in the case of any natural species one can distinguish between changes that their members undergo which are the changes that good members of the kind exhibit, and those which defective members manifest. Clearly acorns, for example, can change in many ways, but a good acorn will, when in appropriate light, soil and climate, develop into a sapling and then a medium-sized tree, and finally a fully grown oak. Such a fully grown tree will, in turn, be capable of producing many more acorns and thus optimally contributing to the persistence of the species and the recurrence of the cycle. This approach (according to which some changes in natural kind members are open to teleological explanation) accords with common-sense ways of thinking.[21] When we buy plants from a garden centre, we believe that if we put them in the advised conditions, and the plant itself is not defective, then they will develop in certain characteristic or normal ways, the ways good members of the kind develop. The same sort of beliefs are still widely held with regard to animals and, finally, to humans. It is widely accepted, for example, that there are norms (of an evaluative kind) regarding the times at which humans should develop the capacity to read, write and manage certain arithmetic calculations, as well as regarding human physical development.

Aristotle's view can be put in terms of potentials. Instead of thinking of a member of a natural kind as a medium-sized object, an acorn, or a sapling, say, one can think of it as a bundle of potentials. But out of all the potentials to change that are in that bundle, there is a subset of changes which a good member of the kind manifests, or actualizes. His further claim is that these potentialities are the essential properties of the kind, the potentialities that make an entity the kind of thing that it is. This is the thing's nature. So in the human case, human nature is that set of essential potentialities which good members of the kind realize. When a human being realizes those potentials he is realising his function or characteristic activity. So, Aristotle suggests, just as what is good for an acorn, qua acorn, is that which enables it to realize its essential potential, what enables it to become a fully developed oak, so what is good for a human is the realization of his essential potential.

Aristotle's further suggestion, in this same short passage in *NE* I, 7, is that human nature is constituted by the potential for a fully rational life.[22] It is that (large) subset of potentialities, the set which is realized in the fully rational life, that constitutes the human essence. On this view, then, the human good, the *eudaimon* life, will be one in which an agent fully realizes all those capacities which contribute to a maximally rational life. The concept of rationality should not be understood narrowly here. For the Aristotelian, rationality is not simply a matter of intellectual prowess. The rational life takes in both practical and theoretical rationality. Desires and emotions are subject to rational development as well as beliefs. Thus a very complex set of potentials, including those for language, for imagination, for relationships with others, as well as for such things as drawing conclusions from evidence or from premises, all these and more are part of a fully rational life.

On the basis of this line of argument, therefore, Aristotle, reaches the conclusion that the *eudaimon* life is the fully rational life. If, therefore, he is to establish any connection between such a life and the life of ethical virtue, or that of contemplation, he needs to show that the ethically virtuous life is indeed fully rational. (For present purposes the life of contemplation can be set to one side.) To understand his position it is necessary to turn now to his discussion of ethical virtue.

The nature of virtue

In *NE* II, 6, Aristotle offers a definition of ethical virtue: 'Virtue is a state of character concerned with choice, lying in a mean, i.e. the mean relative to us, this being determined by a rational principle, and by that principle by which the man of practical wisdom would determine it.'[23] This definition has five key components. First, virtue is a state of character. Second, it is concerned with choice (preferential choice – Aristotle is using a technical term, *prohairesis*, here). Third, it lies in a mean. Fourth, that mean is determined by a rational principle, and, fifth, that rational principle is the principle of a practically wise man (*phronimos*). Prior to introducing the definition, Aristotle has also discussed the way in which ethical virtue is acquired. An explanation of his views on acquisition, and of the five components of his definition, will illuminate his analysis.

Aristotle's account of the acquisition of virtue informs his proposed definition. He notes that virtues do not exist by nature. His key point in making this claim is that they are not necessary human properties, since clearly we can also acquire vices.[24] However, we are adapted by nature to receive them; in other words, the potential for virtue is a necessary property, and that potential is realized as a result of habituation or practice.[25] The role of habituation or practice is a crucial insight within Aristotle's account of the acquisition of virtue. He compares the acquisition of virtue to learning to be a builder or a musician. 'Men become builders by building ... so too we become just by doing just acts.'[26] How exactly is virtue acquired through practice? Once again only an outline of the idea will be possible here. Part of Aristotle's point is that habituation or practice has a cognitive role.[27] This is connected to the fact that there is a difference between doing just acts, and doing just acts as the just agent does them.[28] A child will first behave justly because he is told to do so ('share your sweets with your friends!'). In this case the child knows this is the just thing to do only in the sense that he has been told by someone that it is just. In a certain sense the child has purely external knowledge at this point. He does not yet 'see' the point of sharing the sweets.

Aristotle's claim is that such internal knowledge can only come through practising just acts. It cannot be learnt except through action. Burnyeat has suggested a parallel with skiing. If I am told by a friend that it is worth going skiing, then I may know that skiing is worthwhile in an external sense because I treat my friend as a reliable judge. But I cannot acquire the internalized knowledge that skiing has a point without doing it. There may indeed be several stages to the internal knowledge that is acquired through practice. For example, in the first instance, after actually doing it, I may know that skiing has a point only in the rather vague sense that I enjoy the activity, without having any clear idea what I enjoy about it. Through more practice, more skiing, I may become able to articulate more precisely what it is that makes it worthwhile. In the same way, after at first being guided to share sweets, a child may in time come to enjoy doing so without yet being able to articulate exactly what makes it enjoyable. Such articulation may become possible only after more practice (and, perhaps, also some reflection). At the end of this process of practice (together, in the later stages, with reflection), the agent will have internalized knowledge of the sort that is necessary to do just acts as the just agent does them – to the right people, at the right time, in the right way, for the right reason. However, the key point at present is to note that such knowledge can only be acquired through practice (practice is a necessary condition of its acquisition).

Practice also has another role in the acquisition of virtue. Virtuous action requires that the agent have the right desires. These are acquired and reinforced through practice. Consider the child sharing sweets. In the first instance, when guided by a parent, the child may want to share the sweets only in the sense that he wants to do what his parents tell him. In due course that child may want to share the sweets because he sees this sharing as having a point, perhaps because he values the shared activity, say. The child now has a different desire, a different motive for the action. But acting on such a desire also comes to reinforce it, to strengthen its motivational force, and thus to make it a more stable part of the agent's character. (This is an idea perhaps reflected in the modern 'psychologist's "law of effect": positive reinforcement of an action raises its probability of occurrence in the future'.)[29]

This discussion of the acquisition of virtue casts light on the definition Aristotle offers. Aristotle asserts that to do a just act justly – that is, as a just person does it (as contrasted with a small child, say, doing a just act because it is told to do it) – certain conditions must hold. 'The agent must also be in a certain condition when he does [it]: in the first place he must have knowledge, secondly he must choose the acts and choose them for their own sakes, and thirdly his action must proceed from a firm and unchangeable character.'[30] He goes on to claim that these latter two conditions are achieved through practice.

This brings us then to the first two features of his definition. Virtue is a state of character (*hexis*). This is a settled disposition of the mind. (Not all such dispositions are unchangeable, in the sense of fixed. In his remark above Aristotle is only referring to the state of character of a perfectly virtuous agent). A disposition of the mind is (roughly) a settled tendency to believe certain things and desire certain things. It is in virtue of this that when an agent has a character it is possible, to some degree, to predict his behaviour. And it has just been indicated, above, how repetitive practice contributes to such stability. Second, virtue involves preferential choice (*prohairesis*); a virtuous agent chooses the relevant acts for their own sakes. In order to choose an act in this way, the agent must not simply want the object of choice. A small child may want a drink, driven by thirst. By contrast to choose a drink, in this Aristotelian sense, the agent must see some point, something worthwhile, in the drink, and choose it for that reason. As has just been seen, in order to want something in this way an agent must have acquired knowledge through practice.

So virtue, for Aristotle, is (thus far) a settled disposition of desires and beliefs, but the agent must have desires and beliefs of a certain sort, the sort necessary for choice. Roughly, he must believe that certain objectives are worthwhile and he must desire those objectives because they are worthwhile. (In the simple case of drinking just described, the agent must want a drink because of its health-giving properties, for example, and desire it because of those properties.) The remaining three aspects of Aristotle's definition now fill out this account.

First, the virtuous agent's choices must lie in a mean. Aristotle's doctrine of the mean is another complex matter, but in outline his claim here is that the agent's motivations and actions must be appropriate. In order to be appropriate they must lie between extremes. Most important here are the agent's desires (which motivate). In the case of courage, for example, the agent's desires associated with fear must be appropriate. The agent must neither desire to flee danger too much (associated with cowardice) or too little (associated with rashness). If the agent has appropriate desires (and connected appropriate beliefs), he will be motivated to perform appropriate actions.

In general, then, the doctrine of the mean suggests therefore two things. First, there are certain actions and feelings which the virtuous person does and feels at the right time, to the right extent, for the right reasons, and so on. Second, there are two ways to go wrong here: namely, not to do those actions and feel those feelings when one should, or to the extent one should, and so on; and to do those actions and feel those feelings when one shouldn't, or to an extent one shouldn't, and so on.[31]

Choices and actions in a mean will be guided by a rational principle. This fourth feature of the definition is important for Aristotle since it is, in effect, here that his claim is made that virtues are indeed characteristics of the fully rational agent. How does rationality enter into his account? In brief, rationality begins to come into practice once an agent has reached the stage of 'seeing' the point of an activity, or objective. At that point the agent does not simply desire that activity, or objective, but desires it for a reason. The development of practical rationality then has two aspects. One involves reflection, first as to exactly what the point of objectives or activities is. As noted above, it is possible to enjoy an activity without quite knowing why. Then there is the need to reflect, or reason, as to how worthwhile one objective is as against another. A fully virtuous agent will have an all-things-considered grasp of what is valuable which enables him to judge exactly what is worth doing in the circumstances. But there is also a further aspect to practical rationality. Practical reason also requires that the agent's desires are guided by reason in the sense, crudely, that their strength matches the agent's view of the value of their objective. The fully rational agent will not have rogue desires motivating him to pursue objectives of lesser worth, or value, than others he could pursue.

Finally, Aristotle notes that the rational principle, which determines the mean (or appropriate) action, is the principle a man of practical wisdom would use to guide his action. Once again a lot could be said here. For the purposes of outlining the Aristotelian position it may be enough to say that practical wisdom is an intellectual virtue. It is the intellectual virtue that enables the agent to form the appropriate judgements as to what is, all things considered, worth pursuing, and also to determine the appropriate means to achieve that objective. However, since a rational agent's desires are for objectives that are desired because of the point which that agent sees in them, this intellectual virtue also interacts with the virtuous agent's desires. A little more will be said about practical wisdom in the final chapter of this book.

In sum then, on Aristotle's account, virtue is a stable disposition of the agent's beliefs and desires, where the beliefs include a fully rational conception of what is worth pursuing, and the desires are formed so as to pursue just such an objective. The motivations, preferential choices and actions of such an agent will thus lie in a mean, a mean which reflects rationality in the sense just explained.

To reinforce the plausibility of this account, Aristotle goes on to argue that it applies satisfactorily to those states of character most would consider to be ethical virtues. For example, he argues that courage fits this definition. It is a stable disposition of the mind which gives the agent a tendency to choose and act courageously. It lies in a mean between cowardice on the one hand and rashness on the other, and this can be further explained in terms of the wayward beliefs and desires held by those in these vicious states. Likewise temperance might be held to be a state of character lying between self-indulgence and asceticism, generosity one that lies between meanness and prodigality.

Rather than explore the details of this approach further, it is time to consider its application to business ethics. What this complex account of the nature of virtue has done thus far is to explain the relationship between virtue and *eudaimonia*, and thus vindicate the belief that virtue pays. Aristotle has shown that the ethically virtuous agent will be fully rational and, thus, that the ethically virtuous life is (at least) a constituent of the *eudaimon* life, since the *eudaimon* life is the fully rational life. This is an important achievement methodologically, since establishing the truth of this widely held connection serves, for Aristotle, to support the plausibility of both the account of virtue and that of *eudaimonia*. The establishment of the connection also has implications for the application of the theory to business ethics.

Aristotelian virtue theory and business ethics

What then are the implications of an Aristotelian virtue theory for business ethics? In what follows, three main implications will be outlined. First, the general nature of such a virtue theory's outlook for ethical questions in business will be explained. Second, the bearing of such a theory on the purposes of business will be indicated. Third, the importance of the remarks regarding the acquisition of virtue will be highlighted.

A virtue theory of the sort presented applies in the same way to all areas of life. The right action on any occasion will be that act which the virtuous agent would do, the act which involves the exercise of the relevant virtue in the circumstances. To that extent, business ethics is not distinct, from this perspective, from any other area of ethics. However, it is certainly possible, within this perspective, to acknowledge Sternberg's claim that to act virtuously it is important to know the purpose of the activity one is engaged in. This is not because, within this theory, the analysis of the virtue of justice differs from one activity to another. [32] It will always have a specific definition conforming to the generic definition of virtue discussed. However, its application will depend on the nature of the activity. For example, nursing is concerned with improving the health of patients, so a just nurse will need to be aware of that purpose in order to determine what justice requires in this area. Behaving justly as a nurse will require that agent to attend to the medical needs of patients (among other things, perhaps), in order to determine how to allocate care. By contrast, just treatment of those engaged in business requires attention to the purpose of business. If, for example, the purpose of business is to maximize long-term owner value by selling goods and services, as Sternberg maintains, then a just agent will need to attend to the contribution employees make towards that goal in allocating rewards. For this reason, too, that is, because specific activities have specific goals, particular virtues may be more prominent in some activities than in others. The virtue of courage may be more prominent in the life of a soldier or a policeman, the virtue of self-control more important to an athlete (in virtue of the demanding training and diet athletes normally follow). Nonetheless, the virtue theorist, especially one committed to the unity of the virtues, like Aristotle, will hold that the key to appropriate action in any area, and thus in business, will be the acquisition and relevant display of all the virtues.

The nature of business will, then, have a role in determining which virtues are likely to be most prominent for those engaged in this activity, even if Sternberg's suggested goal is not accepted as absolutely correct. Thus, given the purpose of business involves the production of value (for the owners) by selling goods and services, in Aristotelian terms the virtues of 'friendliness' (concerned with keeping contracts and similar obligations to others), truthfulness and justice will, as Sternberg implies, be prominent. As Sternberg argues above, business needs to be conducted with honesty and fairness. And justice is the virtue which governs the allocation of rewards and burdens in relation to the employee's contribution to the achievement of the goal of business. But other virtues may be relevant too. A virtue such as courage may be required in negotiating a contract, or in whistleblowing on injustice. Temperance (self-control) may also be required of an employee to ensure he adopts a lifestyle that enables him to contribute optimally to his work (for example an employee whose contribution of physical effort to an enterprise is crucial for the success of the whole). It may be a marginal issue whether this latter is considered a matter of business ethics, or ethics conceived more broadly, but, as has been indicated, within virtue ethics such sharp distinctions are not easily made.

It is sometimes objected to a virtue account of the sort given that it is of very little practical use.[33] The advice to do that act which exercises the relevant virtue in the circumstances leaves open the question which virtue is relevant, and also what is required in order to exercise that virtue on this occasion. But the Aristotelian theory does provide more resources. It gives an account of the nature of specific virtues which indicates the kind of considerations that one who has that virtue will attend to. It also gives an account of what virtue is, and how it is acquired, which indicates that part of acquiring the virtue of justice, say, will involve coming to have relevant beliefs such that the agent can identify when it is in question. For example, the child will learn that it is a matter of proportionate distribution and start to learn the sorts of consideration that bear on appropriate proportion (who made the cake, whose cake it is, who was invited to the party, and the like).

Furthermore in *NE* IX, 2 Aristotle has a long discussion of rules in connection with the topic of friendship. In this passage he does seem to suggest both the possibility of discerning many general rules that govern what is owed to different classes of people, and thus make more explicit the nature of justice. He also appears to emphasize the importance of that task. Having noted that it may be laborious, he adds 'Yet we must not on *that* account shrink from the task, but decide the question as best we can.'[34]

Aristotle specifically denies that it is possible to produce precise guidelines in matters of conduct:

> But this must be agreed upon beforehand, that the whole account of matters of conduct must be given in outline, and not precisely ... matters concerned with conduct and questions of what is good for us have no fixity, any more than matters of health. The general account being of this nature, the account of particular cases is yet more lacking in exactness.[35]

If, for example, justice in allocating rewards in business should be proportionate to the contribution to the goal of the business, it may be difficult to determine exactly how to compare the contribution of the inventors of a medicine, those in the patenting department and those who market it. So the Aristotelian theory has the resources to give fairly detailed practical advice without specifying a mathematically precise formula by which to determine solutions to ethical questions. Further suggestions will be made in the last chapter concerning the development of judgement on such matters.

Virtue theory and the goal of business

The second important feature of this Aristotelian approach to note here is the bearing it has on the internal purpose or goal of business. For this theory holds that there is an ultimate good, *eudaimonia*, which is (at least partially) constituted by the life of virtue, and which should be the goal of all other activities. This idea is hinted at in *NE* I, 7 when Aristotle argues that it would not make sense for carpentry or shoemaking to have a goal, if human life as such had none.[36] The thought here seems to be that, although clearly the internal goal of carpentry is woodwork, and of tanners shoemaking, these goals cannot be thought of as ultimate ends. So the pursuit of these ends only makes real sense in so far as they contribute to some further end, the goal of human life as a whole. Thus, by the same token, although business clearly has an internal goal which distinguishes it from other activities, that goal has to be made sense of, and partially determined, by the contribution of that activity to the ultimate goal, *eudaimonia*.

This same idea can be seen in Aristotle's *Politics* I, 8–10, when he comes to discuss commercial activity directly. In the earlier part of this book of the *Politics*, Aristotle has elaborated further his ideas about human nature, touched on above. He has argued here that to fully realize that nature, and thus achieve *eudaimonia*, a human being must live in a state or community, and take an active part in the life of that state.[37] It has already been noted that, for Aristotle, wealth is a means, not an ultimate end. Putting these thoughts together, it can now be seen that material goods are necessary, as a means, if an agent is to live a *eudaimon* life. Not only do material goods provide the necessaries for survival, they also provide humans with the leisure, the freedom from other concerns, needed to develop so as to live a fully virtuous life.

So the acquisition of material goods via commercial activity is necessary, but Aristotle now distinguishes two types of commercial activity.

> So one type of the art of acquiring property is by nature a part of the art of household management, in that either there must be available,

> or it must contrive itself that there is available, a supply of those things which go to make up a store of goods which are essential for life and useful for the association of state or household.[38]

This commercial activity is contrasted with another type which has no definite limit regarding the amount of wealth it can produce, while the skill of acquiring wealth within household management has a definite limit.[39] Of these two Aristotle goes on to say:

> There are two sorts of wealth getting, as I have said; one is a part of household management, the other is retail trade: the former is necessary and honourable, while that which consists in exchange is justly censured: for it is unnatural.[40]

Once again it is only possible in the present context to be brief about the ideas here.

Aristotle is distinguishing two possible types of commercial activity. Both are concerned with the acquisition of wealth, but one has a limit and the other does not. But he appears to be arguing that to undertake the activity of business for the purpose of maximizing wealth, without limit, is a mistake since it is contrary to what is needed for the proper development of human nature. (This is what is meant by 'unnatural' here.) On the other hand, it is perfectly compatible with such proper development (the development of virtue) to sell goods and services for the purpose of acquiring that quantity of wealth that is needed to lead a virtuous life. (This means that when undertaking the activity of business the proper aim is not just to sustain the business, but to produce what is required to allow those engaging in the business the leisure for the virtuous life, and the wherewithal for such virtues as generosity.)

In other words, Aristotle presents an argument here which appears to challenge Sternberg's view that the proper purpose of business is to *maximize* long-term owner value by selling goods and services. The internal aim or goal of business should be to seek to produce sufficient value for those engaged in the activity, by selling goods and services, to enable those people to lead a virtuous life. Since there is an ultimate end, *eudaimonia*, to which other activities are subordinate, the internal goal or purpose, when engaged in business activity, must be constrained by that ultimate end.

One possible reply here might suggest that Aristotle's remarks are not concerned to show that the internal goal of business itself contains a limit, but to point out that the time devoted to business activity must depend on the role of such activity within a *eudaimon* life. On this view, when an agent is engaged in business the internal aim for all the time he is so engaged should be to maximize long-term owner value, but a proper conception of *eudaimonia* will limit the time spent in business activity as opposed to other pursuits – relaxation, socializing with friends, or family life, for example. Thus, it might be said, the activity of flute-playing has as its internal goal making high quality flute music, and this goal as such sets no limit to the quality or quantity of flute-playing the agent engages in. But the amount of flute-playing the agent actually pursues should nonetheless be limited in proportion to the contribution that this activity makes, within the particular agent's life, to *eudaimonia*, the ultimate end.

But in the case of business, Aristotle can be seen as suggesting that the internal goal of the activity has a limit built into it for two reasons. First of all, as has been noted, Aristotle appears to distinguish two possible commercial activities with wealth as an internal goal, and to argue that only one has the appropriate wealth-making goal. To undertake the activity of business with the internal aim of maximizing wealth (long-term owner value), in other words in pursuit of wealth without limit, is contrary to human flourishing, and so not to be engaged in. To pursue the activity of business with the internal aim of producing sufficient owner value for human flourishing, in other words in pursuit of wealth with a limit, is necessary for human flourishing. Aristotle could be construed, on this interpretation, as suggesting that one commercial activity should be pursued, but another, business, should not be pursued at all. It seems more plausible to see him as advocating that business should be engaged in when it is undertaken with its internal goal properly understood, namely, with the internal goal of producing sufficient owner value for flourishing.

The second reason in favour of this interpretation is that Aristotle specifically contrasts wealth, as a goal of an activity, with health as the goal of medicine, by noting that health has no built-in limit when understood as such a goal. 'For the art of medicine aims at unlimited health.'[41] Health is worth having for its own sake, it is not a means to an end, so as such there is no limit to the extent it is worth pursuing when engaged in medicine. (This will be true of anything that is worth having for its own sake, so might apply also to the quality flute music which is the goal of flute-playing.) By contrast, wealth is a means to an end, so is only valuable to the extent that it is necessary for the ends that are constitutive of *eudaimonia*. Thus, it is possible, in principle, to attain sufficient wealth; and that is therefore the limit on the goal of business.[42]

Why does the internal goal of maximizing wealth, when undertaking business, threaten a virtuous life, it might be asked, since undertaking commercial activity with the internal aim of this objective is at least compatible with producing what is needed for a virtuous life? First, if an agent aims, when undertaking business, to maximize wealth, that threatens his ability to recognize that wealth is a means to *eudaimonia*, not an end in itself. The agent needs to recognize that the value of wealth is limited by its contribution to *eudaimonia*, so unlimited quantities are not worth pursuing. In a similar vein, pursuit of unlimited wealth threatens the virtue of temperance, since it is liable to give the agent the capacity to indulge in immoderate and unnecessary sensual pleasures (food, drink, sex, etc). It threatens also the virtue of generosity, since it may encourage the agent to care too much about wealth (the vice of meanness), or too little, encouraging the agent to waste his wealth (prodigality).[43] Finally, the pursuit, in business, of maximizing wealth may, by encouraging the agent to consider it as an end in itself, also lead him to devote undue time and energy to this activity, rather than seeking the necessary leisure time for the development of virtue, and of *eudaimonia*.[44]

Business ethics and the acquisition of virtue

The third point to highlight about this virtue theory as an approach to business ethics is that it does not focus only on providing a decision procedure. The account of virtue also emphasizes the importance of appropriate desires and emotions if an agent is to be capable of fully virtuous action. Furthermore, Aristotle draws attention to the significance of practice in the acquisition of the appropriate desires and emotions, and thus of virtue.

For those who come to study business ethics (or any area of applied ethics) with a view to improving their behaviour, the first of these points is of great significance. Aristotle drew attention to the fact that in order to behave virtuously it is not enough to make the correct decisions, or judgements, by pointing out that apart from the states of character which we term virtue and vice, there are also others, including *encrateia* and *acrasia*.[45] In the immediate context, the *acratic* agent is the most relevant case. For an *acratic* is someone who reaches the correct decision as to what to do, but fails to do it. A typical example is the person who finds himself still at work late, decides the best thing to do now is to go home and spend important time with the family, but finds himself still at his desk writing one more memo and missing the train that gets him in before the children are asleep. Once the case of the *acratic* is recognized, it is clear that in order to change behaviour it may not be enough to give an agent the right decision procedure.

The Aristotelian account of virtue indicates that the virtuous agent is distinct from the *acratic* because he has the appropriate desires and emotions as well. Aristotle is well aware, though, that even though desires are in his view subject to reason, in a way quite comparable to that in which beliefs are, their acquisition differs in a significant way from the acquisition of belief. While beliefs may usually (if not invariably) whither away once the believer realises that their content is false, an agent's desires will not immediately whither once the agent comes to believe their object is of little value. This is one of the important aspects of Aristotle's work on the acquisition of virtue. His insight is that desires change over time through practice. Thus, a student of business ethics who wishes to change his behaviour will have to recognize the importance of practice in achieving that.

This last point about the significance of an Aristotelian virtue theory as an approach to business ethics can be explored further in the context of reflecting on the value of case histories in that study. Thus it too will be addressed further in the final chapter of this book.[46]

Notes

1 James Allen, 'The Use and Abuse of Humanistic Education', in C.R. Christensen and A.J. Hansen (eds) *Teaching and the Case Method* (Harvard Business School, Boston, 1989), p. 51.
2 *The Teaching of Ethics in Higher Education* (The Hastings Centre, Hastings on Hudson, New York, 1980).
3 Plato, *Republic*, 352 d1.
4 Aristotle, *Nicomachean Ethics*, I, 3, 1095 a4.
5 This account draws directly on Sternberg's contribution to the Leeds lecture series. For contractual reasons the essence of this lecture has had to be presented, with the author's agreement, within the body of this chapter through quotation by the editor rather than directly. All quotations from Sternberg are from the Leeds lecture unless otherwise specified. A full account of Sternberg's position is available in her *Just Business: Business Ethics in Action* (2nd edition, Oxford University Press, Oxford, 2000; 1st edition: Little, Brown & Co. London, 1994 Warner paperback 1995; 'Introduction: What Makes This Book Distinctive' available online at *http://ssrn.com*).
6 E. Sternberg, *Just Business: Business Ethics in Action* (1st edition, Little Brown & Company, London, 1994; subsequently '*JB*1'), p. 4.
7 E. Sternberg, *JB*1, p. 4.
8 This is the third Aristotelian aspect of Sternberg's approach since she cites his account of distributive justice, see E. Sternberg, *JB*1, p. 80.
9 For a much fuller discussion of stakeholder theory, and criticism of arguments that supposedly support it, see Elaine Sternberg, *The Stakeholder Concept: A Mistaken Doctrine*, The Foundation for Business Responsibilities, 1999; available online from the Social Sciences Research Network on *http://ssrn.com*.
10 Cf. 'The Business Roundtable', *Corporate Governance and American Competitiveness*, March 1990, p. 13 (though they repudiated it in 1997); available from The Business Roundtable, 200 Park Ave, NYC 10016.
11 It is only in the unlikely case that all the alternatives both satisfy distributive justice and ordinary decency, and are projected to have equal effects on maximizing long-term owner value, that degrees of distributive justice or ordinary decency might be taken into account.
12 I have presented the account put forward here in more detail in my 'Aristotelian Ethics' in Ruth Chadwick (ed.) *The Encyclopaedia of Applied Ethics* (Academic Press of America, San Diego, 1997) Vol. 1, pp. 209–31.
13 It is still pertinent to investigate whether there is at least a common shape to a life worth living. And it is still important to consider why we should be moral, and whether the moral or virtuous life has any part in such a worthwhile life. Thus it is still generally assumed that if an act can be shown to be unjust or unfair it should not be undertaken; but the question 'What's the point of being just?' can still be raised. And if it cannot be satisfactorily answered, then it

might at least seem questionable whether an act's being just gives sufficient reason for doing it, or an act's being unjust rules out doing it.

14 In what follows I retain the Greek term *eudaimonia*. Whilst 'happiness' is often given as a translation, modern readers need to be aware that the term may have some misleading connotations, at least in so far as it is taken to connote a mere feeling. If we think of the notion of true happiness, as contrasted with some passing feeling, that might give a better sense of what Aristotle has in mind.

15 Aristotle, *NE*, I, 1 1094 a2. (All quotations from the *Nichomachean Ethics* in this chapter are from Sir David Ross's translation, Oxford University Press, Oxford, 1925.) For example, when a rational agent eats an apple he does so because of the good (or apparent good) he sees in doing so. This good might be the apple's flavour, or the health he will gain through eating it, to mention just two possibilities.

16 Aristotle assumes that, at least provisionally, widely held views or the views of wise predecessors can be supposed to have some truth in them. See, for example, *NE*, VII, 1 1145 b2–7.

17 I use the term ethical virtue to pick out characteristics such as courage, justice, temperance, which would normally be thought of as virtues nowadays, and which are manifest in courageous, just, temperate (and so on) acts. Aristotle's term for virtue, *arete*, is applied to any human excellence, including intellectual excellences, so that for him ethical virtues are a subset of all the virtues.

18 The arguments that follow are given in *NE* I, 5 1095 b17ff.

19 *NE*, 1, 7 1097 b27–30.

20 The interpretation of this passage is a disputed matter, and the account given here, which takes his ethics to rest in a significant way on his metaphysics can only be asserted, rather than fully defended, in the present context.

21 A fuller account of these ideas is given in C. Megone, 'Aristotle on Essentialism and natural kinds: Physics II:1', in *Revue de Philosophe Ancienne*, (1987) Vol. 6, 2.

22 *NE*, I, 7 1098 a4ff.

23 *NE*, II, 6 1106 b36ff.

24 I understand by nature properties to be essential properties and take it that essential properties are not merely necessary properties, but also properties that play an explanatory role, but in the present context it is the fact that an actualized virtue is not a necessary property that matters. See Megone, op. cit., fn. 21.

25 *NE*, II, 1 1103 a26–8.

26 *NE*, II, 1 1103 a36.

27 This and other features of Aristotle's view have been well discussed in M. Burnyeat, 'Aristotle on learning to be good', in A. Rorty (ed.) *Essays on Aristotle's Ethics* (University of California Press, Berkeley, 1980).

28 *NE*, II, 4 1105 b5–8.

29 See R. Nozick, *The Nature of Rationality* (Princeton University Press, New Jersey, 1993), p. 19.

30 *NE*, II, 4 1105 a33–5. Aristotle need not think that all characters are unchangeable, even if he is understood here as saying that a virtuous character must be unchangeable, rather than simply settled. It may be that the fully virtuous character would be one from which the virtuous agent would have no inclination to change.

31 I am grateful to Roger Crisp for suggesting this way of explaining the doctrine.

32 As, indeed, Sternberg agrees: she states explicitly that the values involved in business ethics apply to the whole of the moral life: there is no separate 'business ethic'.

33 This is another large issue. For further discussion, see C. Megone, 'Aristotelian Ethics', op. cit., pp. 228 ff.
34 *NE*, IX, 2 1165 a35–6. I owe this point to Roger Crisp.
35 *NE*, II, 2 1104 a1–5.
36 *NE*, I, 7 1097 b30.
37 *Politics* I, 1–3. Aristotle's idea here is that the development of rationality requires upbringing in a community. This idea requires a good deal of unpacking, but it includes thoughts such as that language acquisition cannot be achieved alone, and that the acquisition of virtue requires guided upbringing. There are many ways in which the development of the capacities that contribute to a fully rational life requires interaction with others.
38 *Politics* I, 8 1256 b26–30.
39 *Politics* I, 9 1257 b23–31.
40 *Politics* I, 10 1258 a39–b3.
41 *Politics* I, 9 1257 b25.
42 I am grateful to Elaine Sternberg for discussion of these matters. The points made here may not be conclusive, and the relevant passages of *Politics*, book I, are worthy of a paper-long treatment in themselves.
43 *NE*, IV, 1 1119 b24–9.
44 For some remarks on the importance of leisure, slightly contrasting in tone, see *NE*, X, 7 and *Politics* II, 9 1269 a35, II, 11 1273 a35 ff.
45 *NE*, VII, 1 1145 a17ff. Aristotle's classic discussion of *acrasia* follows in subsequent chapters of book VII.
46 I am most grateful to Roger Crisp, Simon Robinson, Nick Seel and Elaine Sternberg for very helpful discussions of some of the material in this chapter.

Part II

Topics and case histories

Chapter 3

Shell, Greenpeace and Brent Spar

The politics of dialogue

Jon Entine

There exist more than 6,500 offshore oil and gas installations around the world, many of which provide a facility for tankers to load oil into their holds. The North Sea is home to a majority of the world's heavy deep-water steel platforms. Of the approximately 600 rigs, operating in the North Sea and North Atlantic, about fifty will reach the end of their useful life by 2006. Because some of the equipment and the sludge contained within could pose serious environmental consequences, plans to decommission these rigs raise ongoing and conflicting economic and environmental concerns.

These issues came to a head in 1995 with Greenpeace's guerrilla campaign against Shell UK Limited and its attempt to sink Shell's floating storage buoy, the Brent Spar. Like the Exxon Valdez incident, it brought into focus some of the imposing problems mankind faces as the world population (and its tonnage of industrial by-products) continues to soar. Given the media interest, the nature of the scientific controversies involved, and the likelihood of future conflict, the Brent Spar incident has been cited as a classic lesson in stakeholder management and the importance of dialogue in crisis management. On close examination, however, the lessons of Brent Spar are far less clear. Provocative questions remain about what groups were legitimate stakeholders, what constitutes dialogue, and whether dialogue is the appropriate management strategy when the ethical divide remains so wide. This ambiguity is magnified by ongoing disputes over the factual record of the Brent Spar incident. Competing factions continue to spin the media record and the complicated scientific issues.

The only clear result is that the brouhaha has scarred the reputations of many of those involved, including Shell, Greenpeace, the scientific community, various European governments and the media. The controversy raises archetypal issues often found in contemporary controversies that pit corporations against social activists. Among them:

- The contested use of science: risk assessment/cost–benefit analysis, 'junk' science, environmental politics;
- The role of the media;

- Stakeholder reputation management and 'greenwashing' by corporations and social activist groups;
- Academic and popular historical revisionism;
- The problematic role of 'dialogue' in stakeholder conflict resolution.

Background

The North Sea and North East Atlantic have been the site of significant industrial activity since the 1960s. Just over 25 years ago, on 18 June 1975, UK North Sea oil was first brought to land after six years of exploration and development. It was shipped from the small Argyll Field and brought ashore by tanker to BP's Isle of Grain refinery in Kent. Since 1975, over 2 billion tonnes of oil and 1,381 billion cubic metres of gas have come ashore. Today, there are over 200 fields in production on the UK Continental Shelf – and production is at record levels. In 1998, 132.6 million tonnes of oil and 95 billion cubic metres of gas were produced.

Shell built and in 1976 put online an offshore facility, the Brent Spar, which stood between the coasts of Scotland and Norway in the Brent field in the northern North Sea. Brent Spar was installed to allow early production from the Brent field in advance of the pipeline to Sullom Voe, Shetland Islands, Scotland, being installed and commissioned. But even after the pipeline came into use, the Spar was retained as an alternative offloading facility and as back-up to the pipeline in times of shutdown. Brent Spar remained in full use for 15 years, finally ceasing operation in 1991. After the completion of an oil pipeline to the mainland at Sullom Voe in the late 1970s, and after three years of operation, Shell put the Spar storage buoy into standby status but maintained it in the event that problems developed with the pipeline. Over time, Shell (and the rest of the hydrocarbon industry) concluded that the costs of such precautions outweighed the benefits, although it had not yet resolved the best environmental and economical way of handling redundant platforms.

The Brent Spar was unlike most other installations in the North Sea. Under regulatory guidelines, all but the largest rigs were to be decommissioned by being brought to shore and dismantled for reuse or recycling. However, very large steel and concrete structures, such as the Brent Spar, are considered difficult or even dangerous to remove. Like an iceberg, most of the Spar's bulk – six huge storage tanks – lay beneath the water's surface. As a result, these leviathans are handled on an individual basis, although there remains a general presumption of total removal when possible (some 80 per cent of structures are completely removed). (Note: In July 1998, at the OSPAR Ministerial meeting in Portugal, the section of the Convention governing the disposal of offshore installations was reviewed and a new regulatory framework – Decision 98/3 – was instituted which bans any disposal at sea of offshore structures.)

Disposing of a North Sea platform that was 40 stories high and weighed over 14,000 tons was not a simple problem. Shell perceived the challenge as getting Spar out of the water or even just raising it higher without posing undue risk to humans or the environment. As the Spar was originally designed, it was built on its side, and then floated over deep water where it was ballasted so that it turned upright. When this was done, some of the tanks, essential for its mechanical strength, were overstressed during installation, which could have made it unsafe to 'reverse engineer' the installation process to get the buoy out of the water. Then later, during operation, the tanks fractured. While this did not threaten its safety when it was floating vertically, it was feared that if the process were reversed it would fail structurally. (Indeed, when it was eventually dismantled, it was cut off in sections while still being held vertically.)

In seeking to decommission Spar, Shell invoked the 1958 Geneva Convention on the Continental Shelf, which includes within its geographic scope the North Sea. Article 5 (5) states that 'any installations which are abandoned or disused must be entirely removed'. Consultative guidelines developed by the British government then in effect required Shell to prepare a formal plan for the dismantling and ultimate disposal that included the views of 'those interested parties ... who may be affected by the abandonment programme'.

Shell commissioned an Impact Hypothesis document and a Best Practicable Environmental Option document produced by Rudall Blanchard Associates. Overall, it undertook some 30 studies to determine what to do with the giant buoy, eventually refining the options to:

1 Continue to maintain the rig at a cost of $9 million a year;
2 Refurbish and then reuse the buoy which would cost $135 million over three years;
3 Dispose of the rig in the oil field, which Shell had already ruled out;
4 Sink the rig in deep water for $18 million, the most economical choice;
5 Dismantle the rig vertically (which would require a deepwater dismantling area) and dispose of it on shore, or;
6 Dismantle the rig horizontally (which would require shallower water than the prior option) and dispose of it on shore for $69 million.

Shell was at least somewhat aware of the public-relations-related concerns that would accompany its decision to become the first company to decommission one of its rigs. Shell had long prided itself (and indeed was thought of by many environmentalists) as being among the most environmentally sensitive natural resource companies. After four years of thorough investigation, and in consultation with many scientists, Shell chose what it concluded was the most environmentally responsible and economical disposal option: tow the Spar from the North Sea to sink it in a deep water channel in the North East Atlantic. Some scientists, such as Martin V. Angel at the Southampton Oceanography Centre (UK), believed that the criteria of evaluation did not address the right questions, since strong emphasis was placed on the structural integrity of the seabed rather than its direct environmental impact. This was an operating 'ethic' for hydrocarbon companies who were far more fearful of causing a geological disaster than an environmental one.

As it turned out, Shell and the government acted with little public consultation or disclosure and did not solicit the opinions of critical 'public interest' groups that had been monitoring the decommission debate for some years. Although Shell had historically demonstrated sensitivity to environmental issues, it rejected liberal stakeholder theory canon that the 'natural environment' held status as a stakeholder in company operations and fortunes. It also vociferously resisted the idea that public interest groups, who were publicly hostile to the natural resource industry as a matter of course, had a right to be involved in the review process. Greenpeace, the world's largest environmental lobby, had been campaigning for years against ocean dumping of any kind. As a consequence, Shell did not consider Greenpeace and other radical groups representative stakeholders and, therefore, did not include their (unsolicited) comments in the list of consultees, which was stipulated by the then UK government.

Shell asked the British government to approve its plans in September 1992. After scrutiny by government scientists and following extensive consultations, the UK's Department of Trade and Industry (DTI), which clearly saw Brent Spar as a test run for future decommissionings, endorsed the plans in December 1994. Shell was issued with a deep-sea licence to dispose the Brent Spar to a site 2,300 metres under the surface, about 240 kilometres north-west of the Hebrides on the North Feni Ridge. Meanwhile, under the Oslo Convention, all other appropriate European governments were notified and none objected. The UK government announced its approval on 17 February 1995.

The announced support by the British government of Shell's application attracted little media interest until Greenpeace, accompanied by a number of German and UK journalists, boarded the Spar for the first time on 30 April 1995. The occupation fired an immediate public debate pitting Shell and the UK government against Greenpeace. The environmental group, which had first become involved in an ocean dumping issue when its ship *Rainbow Warrior* intercepted a radioactive waste dumping vessel in the Atlantic in the summer of 1978, was on record as being opposed to any ocean disposal as unethical. (Ironically, years ago, Greenpeace disposed of the wreck of the *Rainbow Warrior* at sea to form an artificial reef for marine wildlife.)

Greenpeace complained that its perspective had not been included in the decision-making process – indeed the DTI refused to accept its written protests. Shell defended its lack of consultation with Greenpeace on the grounds that Greenpeace had definitely admitted that its goal was to reverse the disposal choice, not to participate in risk–benefit environmental and economic analysis. Greenpeace escalated its allegations, charging that Spar was a 'toxic time bomb' of drilling mud, oil residues and radioactive waste that could seriously damage the marine environment – an allegation disputed by Shell and questioned by most independent scientists and oceanographers. Greenpeace also asserted that allowing the use of the ocean as a free repository would signal that it was acceptable for companies to pass on the externalities of its operations. Its proposed alternative: onshore dismantling of Brent Spar.

The occupation

Greenpeace, noted for its confrontational tactics, sprung into action, helped along by a Shell misstep. Because of a narrow weather window, Shell chose to scuttle the Spar just before the Inter-ministerial meeting on the North Sea. This handed Greenpeace, whose membership had gone into decline, a golden opportunity for a high profile campaign. Greenpeace invoked broad ethical principles as well as specific environmental objections in launching a vigorous international campaign against Shell and its plan. Greenpeace initiated boycotts of Shell products in several European countries. In Germany, for example, where Shell's sales fell by between 20 and 30 per cent in the area around Hamburg during the crisis, protestors threatened to damage 200 Shell sites. Fifty were subsequently damaged: two firebombed and one raked with bullets.

Just before midday on 30 April 1995 activists, accompanied by a number of journalists, occupied the rusting and deserted platform. The audacity of the occupation, carried out at sea, attracted immediate media attention. Greenpeace claimed an impending ecological disaster. Daily postings on a special Internet website were enhanced after the second week by satellite phone/fax/e-mail equipment that enabled the occupants to talk directly to journalists. However, the main story did not break until 22 May when, after a failed night-time attempt, police and security men began evicting the activists under injunctions granted by Scottish courts. Greenpeace began offering direct television feeds to broadcasters around the world.

Shell evicted the protestors and began blasting high-powered cannons to fend off reoccupation by Greenpeace. Videotaped by Greenpeace vessels nearby, scenes of what appeared to be water cannons directed at Greenpeace helicopters were flashed around the world, making headline news. The drama was captured on video arranged by Greenpeace, and distributed by satellite. (According to Shell, independent eyewitness accounts suggest that the Greenpeace helicopter deliberately dipped into the water spray for the benefit of the Greenpeace camera.) The confrontation incited more protests including the firebombing of Shell stations already mentioned.

In the coming weeks, even as Shell began towing the Brent Spar out to sea, the media continued to cover the stand-off. BBC aired live interviews on board the Greenpeace ship *Altair* reporting on the 'daring' exploits of the protestors. Each report deepened the perception that Europe's largest company was using highly aggressive tactics against a dedicated band of highly moral men and women.

Although it had historically placed a strong emphasis on the environment in its public relations strategy and was deeply concerned about the long-term impact on its reputation, Shell was unable to counter the negative made-for-TV images manufactured by Greenpeace. With feelings running high, Shell's attempt to gain public support by arguing the scientific merits of its position largely through the print media, lost ground.

The confrontation brought to the surface simmering tensions between environmental organizations and the mainstream science community, which had remained supportive of Shell's plans throughout. In contrast, activist groups throughout Europe rallied by the German chapter of Greenpeace elicited the support of left-leaning European politicians and journalists. Worker representatives on Shell's advisory board in Germany wrote to Greenpeace to express their 'concern and outrage' at Shell's plans to 'turn the sea into a trash pit'. The company's situation was not helped by the fact that different country managers took a variety of stances. Under considerable local pressure, the head of Shell Germany said the first he knew about the disposal plans was from the media, while the head of Shell Austria pronounced the plan 'intolerable'. The Danish environment minister was the first to support the Greenpeace stance. When the German Chancellor, Helmut Kohl, protested to the British prime minister at the June G7 Summit, it was evident that the issue was spiralling out of Shell's control; Greenpeace was setting the public agenda on this issue.

After a nine-day trip, on 19 June, as the Brent Spar reached its final destination, two further activists were dropped onto Brent Spar to disrupt the sinking. Greenpeace simultaneously released to the press the written pronouncement by a prominent scientist that the disposal of Brent Spar could bring about local damage to marine life. That afternoon, British Prime Minister John Major addressed the House of Commons: ' I understand that many people seem deeply upset about the decision to dispose of Brent Spar in deep water,' he said. 'I believe that it is the right way to dispose of it. ... Shell has my full support to dispose of it in deep water.' The Conservative government was firmly convinced that it was legally and scientifically on solid ground.

To Major's dismay and embarrassment, within a few hours, Shell issued a terse press release rescinding its decision and began towing Brent Spar back towards the UK. Under siege, experiencing a public relations nightmare, and with eroding support from European governments, Shell believed it had no choice. The embarrassed UK government accepted this course of action and helped Shell obtain a licence from Norwegian authorities that allowed Spar to be anchored in the deep waters of Erfjord pending re-evaluation of all options. The UK government, perhaps as a display of pique, would not pay an increase in the subsidy of 75 per cent of the original decommissioning costs, as it had promised. Greenpeace claimed total victory.

The controversy

Greenpeace's decision to elevate its moral stance over scientific claims gave it an initial tactical advantage in the court of public opinion. The news media found the controversy difficult to manage. It did not yield to the customary technique of instant verification used in news journalism, where complex conflicts are frequently reduced to two opposing views with the 'right answer' arrived at by finding an 'independent expert'. During much of the crisis, large segments of the media presented the controversy as a moral saga with 'white hat' Greenpeace environmentalists (forces of caution) fighting 'black hat' Shell (new icon of multinational corporate expediency) which was being secretly aided by Britain's Conservative-led government (symbol of governmental complicity). Shell's appeal to science and 'rationality' contrasted with Greenpeace's ethical arguments and the belief by many environmentalists that Shell had tried to engineer the most financially advantageous, not the most environmentally responsible disposal option.

That simplistic ethical paradigm held sway so long as the public believed Greenpeace's analysis of the toxic potential of the sludge still on the rig. Greenpeace had dismissed Shell's commissioned study which indicated that some 53 tonnes of oil remained onboard. It publicized tests from samples drawn by its guerrilla-occupiers that claimed there was more than one hundred times as much – 5,550 tonnes. According to newspaper accounts and Greenpeace press releases, it was further claimed that the rig contained '14,500 tonnes of toxic rubbish' and 'over 100 tonnes of toxic sludge'. Shell officials continued to insist that their figures were accurate, which sparked widespread and well-publicized ridicule by activists.

But within a month of Shell's surrender, public perceptions turned abruptly when it became clear that Greenpeace had wildly exaggerated or at least distorted (deliberately or innocently is still at issue) the potential hazards of Shell's disposal plans. The press first uncovered that Greenpeace's claim that marine life was threatened referred to a disposal option in shallow waters which Shell had explicitly rejected. In the most damaging disclosure, several independent companies coordinated by Det Norske Veritas undertook a new inventory examination. This comprehensive study indicated that between 74 and 103 tonnes of oil remained on the buoy, most of which could now be easily removed. That was very close to the Shell estimate and far less than Greenpeace's assertion that the buoy contained 5,000 tonnes. Only 30 tonnes was low-level radioactive waste, a level not considered dangerous and less than occurred naturally in areas where there are granite rocks. The radioactivity originated in the stored oil that was absorbed into the internal pipework. (Note: Another irony is that bringing this radioactive lining ashore, as Greenpeace proposed, would have been a violation of the UN convention against transferring contamination from one environment to another.)

By late August, interviews with scientists and evidence uncovered during the independent inspection revealed that the scuttling of the platform was far less environmentally problematic than Greenpeace had intimated. It turned out that Greenpeace took its sludge samples through the top of the vent pipes on the uppermost deck, and not from the storage tanks proper. These samples would have been predominantly oil that had floated to the top of these pipes.

The media turned, particularly the more conservative press. 'Minor Mistake Which Tipped The Balance', headlined the *Daily Mail* (6 September 1995). The *Express* ran a story entitled 'Dark side of Greenpeace do-gooders' under the heading 'DAILY EXPRESS – Asking The Straight Questions' (6 September 1995). Even the *Guardian*, which positioned itself as an ally of Greenpeace throughout the controversy, noted almost apologetically that

> almost all independent experts contacted by reporters regarded the proposed burial at sea as the best – or least bad – solution for the Brent Spar. It was not going to be sunk in shallow water but towed 150 miles out to West of the Hebrides. There, according to the majority of marine experts, the floating tank could be sunk without anything like the damage which would be caused by dismantling the structure disposed of on land.
>
> (*Guardian*, 7 September 1995)

In a dramatic turnaround, and just a few days before the results of an independent inventory assessment would have made their error public, Greenpeace officials issued a public apology to Shell. Greenpeace, which had been aware of the embarrassing findings for weeks, asserted it had mistakenly, yet innocently, exaggerated oil levels and toxic dangers. A few liberal stalwarts praised Greenpeace for its confession, but the damage was done. Some critics (including some environmentalists and former

Greenpeace officers) emerged to argue that Greenpeace's tactics had less to do with protecting the environment and more to do with invigorating financial support and reversing membership declines. According to detractors, Greenpeace and its supporters were casting around for a cause célèbre when the Brent Spar issue came to a head and Shell provided a near-perfect target. In response to these stories, the BBC publicly flagellated itself for being manipulated. The *New York Times* and *Wall Street Journal*, among others, raised questions as to whether Greenpeace officials might have massaged the story for less than honourable reasons.

With the political landscape now dramatically altered, an international consensus began to emerge, as most member countries at the Oslo and Paris Commission meeting in 1995 agreed to a moratorium on the seabed disposal of decommissioned offshore installations, pending further development of international standards. In the uncertain political climate that prevailed, no European government and few natural resource corporations would be willing to risk the kind of negative publicity that had swamped Shell over Brent Spar. Although Shell's pre-incident analysis was largely reconfirmed by post-crisis scientific studies, and Greenpeace suffered damage to its reputation, it was widely perceived that Greenpeace had 'won' the battle over Brent Spar.

In the two years following the incident, Shell sought and publicized input from a variety of sources it considered stakeholders: investors, governmental agencies, environmental experts from industry and academia and a range of environmental groups, including vocal critics such as Greenpeace. It embarked on a costly 'public involvement' campaign, which was initially designed to recover some of its reputation while repairing its relations with British ministers under the Major government. Subsequently, this campaign took on something of a life of its own with everything from an Internet web site established by Shell specifically for this purpose, to CDs for schools and journalists, to dialogue sessions for environmentalists around Europe. It is not clear whether this represented a philosophical shift in company perspective or a tactical change reflecting the new political reality. Greenpeace maintained its own site during the process, frequently disagreeing with Shell's interpretation of the ongoing dialogue.

Shell gradually winnowed the list of options, eventually announcing their choice of solutions in January 1998: a 'one-off' re-use as a Norwegian Ro/Ro ferry quay. The UK government announced its approval in August and the decommissioning was completed by the following summer. Cut and cleaned ring sections of the buoy's hull were placed on the seabed at Mekjarvik, near Stavanger, to form the base of a new quay. Taking into account expenditures related to the initial aborted deep-sea disposal of Spar, the costs totalled close to $96 million.

Scientific and ethical issues

Each side used science and appeals to rational prudence to justify its position. Shell also injected financial considerations into the debate while Greenpeace positioned itself as a steward for the environment. Ultimately, the conflict between two sets of scientific authorities eclipsed the issue over which disposal method was preferable and precipitated a fierce debate about the nature of scientific fact.

The scientific conflict itself appeared relatively straightforward. The Spar contained four main types of contaminants: heavy metals, traces of hydrocarbons, synthetic organic compounds and enhanced levels of radioactivity concentrated in the internal piping. There were two main schools of thought about the potential environmental impact: (1) Greenpeace and the Norwegian government voiced the belief that ocean disposal posed an unacceptable pollution hazard and therefore under no circumstance should any remnants of these structures be left at sea (Pearce 1995a), and; (2) Those who argued that Shell 'was right' (Rice 1996b) because deep-sea disposal is an environmentally reasonable option and the huge costs of removal were 'out of all proportion to the risks' (Gray, cited in Pearce 1995a). There was little debate over the environmental consequences to inshore and terrestrial environments that would have ensued if the Spar had been towed ashore for dismantling. Greenpeace and its supporters invoked a mystical belief, rather than citing scientific evidence, that the risks from land disposal were acceptable and the pristine sea should not be despoiled.

Shell, its consultants, and the British government concluded that such disposal would have had 'a negligible impact on living resources, human health, marine activities, amenity value and water quality'. Greenpeace argued that introducing these contaminants would reduce water quality and biodiversity, the greatest danger arising from the contaminants entering the food chain. Greenpeace argued that landfill must be the preferred option because only there could the impact be monitored and controlled. Although Greenpeace said at first that land disposal was the safer choice over a deep-sea burial on strictly environmental grounds, it mostly argued the 'slippery slope' theory: allowing the Brent Spar to be sunk risked opening the door to future disposals whose collective damage could turn the ocean into a pollution sink hole.

So, what impact might the contaminants in the Spar have had in the North Atlantic as compared to decommissioning on land? Each side attempted to frame its position as the most scientifically responsible. Greenpeace had successfully closed off dumping for radioactive waste at sea and for industrial wastes (campaigns started in 1978 and 1980 respectively, with both ending in 1993). These campaigns resulted in some types of dumping being banned worldwide. With the Brent Spar, Greenpeace was trying to avoid opening up an ocean dumping route for other types of waste as the older oilfields became progressively redundant, claiming that the potential hazards were too risky. To bolster its position, it consistently invoked the 'precautionary principle' (*i.e. one should avoid actions that involve significant unknown risk*), which focuses on the possibility that technologies or policies could pose unique, extreme or unmanageable risks. In this instance, however, appeals to a precautionary principle offered no guidance, for no matter what option was chosen there would be some unpredictable deleterious effects.

Some scientists disputed Greenpeace's short- and long-term projections of likely disaster. It was widely believed that monitoring of the deep ocean is perfectly feasible technically. Dr Angel (1995) noted that deep-sea monitoring is also, in practice, easier than in shallow seas where instruments deployed long-term *in situ* are constantly being trawled. Fear arises partly from the mistaken belief that the oceans are pristine and that we lack enough understanding about how they function to take such a risk. 'It is a question of choosing the lesser evil', Angel wrote, echoing scientists on both sides of the issue (see Appendix 2).

Most scientists (many independent of Shell) expressed their belief that the natural resource company and the British government had chosen the Best Practicable Environmental Option for disposal. Among other experts siding with Shell's perspective:

- Sir John Vane, winner of a Nobel Prize for medicine, wrote 'in the clamour (made by Greenpeace) ... the quiet, logical voice of science, and of common sense ... drowned. Reason said that the Brent Spar should be buried. Emotion and irrationality have dictated otherwise' (*Daily Mail*, 22 June 1995);
- University of London professors Euan Nisbet and Mary Fowler suggested, 'The environmental damage from the disposal of the Brent Spar in (the Atlantic) would probably be minimal. ... By concentrating on and sensationalising relatively small problems, we risk making poor judgments and neglecting more serious issues facing the environment' (*Nature*, June 1995);
- Emeritus Professor Jack Pridham, also of the University of London, claimed that the 'toxic contents of this platform would have been a biological pin-prick in this immense volume of water' (letter to *The Times*, 23 June 1995);
- Dr Martin Angel noted, 'Every day more metal is pumped into the oceans from volcanic vents of the seabed than is produced from mines on land. The sea copes with this quite effectively. Brent Spar would not have changed a thing' (letter to the *Observer*, 2 June 1995);
- Aberdeen University professor, Alastair McIntyre, who was privy to the AURIS research promoted by Greenpeace, opined that Greenpeace had mistakenly claimed that onshore disposal was the preferable

> option noting, 'Once ashore the many operations involved in dismantling could produce a diversity of pollution problems – terrestrial, aquatic and atmospheric. The risk to the workforce from all these operations would be considerably greater than that posed by the more straightforward deep-sea disposal' (letter to *The Times*, 26 May 1995).

Greenpeace published its own scientific study, the conclusions of which contradicted those of some of the scientists who had previously given advice to Shell. The Scottish Association for Marine Science (SAMS), which had been studying the proposed disposal area for the Brent Spar, the Rockall Trough, contested claims that fishing grounds would not be adversely impacted by a deep-sea burial. SAMS also dismissed the belief that seabed currents were not strong enough to disperse any radioactive wastes that might be released at that depth. Citing this study, Greenpeace claimed that disposing of Brent Spar in the North Atlantic would precipitate long-term damage to the marine environment and ultimately affect the food chain, chiefly from leakage of the toxic sludge that remained within the structure. As a matter of perspective, it is worth noting that a single floundering vessel (of which there are dozens each year) puts as much if not more contaminants into the ocean than sinking the Brent Spar.

Greenpeace also cited the UK Offshore Operators Association (UKOOA) study, 'Options for Oil and Gas Structures in the North Sea', commissioned by the Aberdeen University group AURIS. UKOOA is the representative organization for the UK offshore oil and gas industry whose 35 company members are licensed by the government to explore for and produce oil and gas in UK waters. Their report concluded that, on balance, the on-land disposal and recycling of oil rigs is preferable to sea dumping on environmental grounds.

The study would not have influenced the handling of Brent Spar, however, since it reaffirmed that the decommissioning of large structures, such as the Spar, were still to be assessed on an individual basis. These views were incorporated in the international convention known as OSPAR, drawn up in 1992, which came into force in March 1998. After the Brent Spar affair, a moratorium was issued on all disposals at sea of offshore structures (although not signed-up to by the UK and Norway).

Perhaps recognizing a minority of scientists held its scientific position, Greenpeace framed much of its argument in symbolic rather than scientific terms. It argued that deep-sea disposal of oil rigs was wrong in principle, invoking broad ethical terms such as the stakeholder 'rights' of the natural environment. 'It is wrong in principle to dump oil installations at sea', Greenpeace argued on its web site.

> To dump structures, such as the Brent Spar, in areas of high marine biodiversity with poorly understood ecology infringes the precautionary principle and presents unknown environmental risks. To do so would set dangerous precedents for future dumping of wastes at sea. It ignores the impact of many similar decisions that would be taken in isolation without consideration of their cumulative effect. It amounts to a reversal of promises made when development of North Sea oil began.
>
> The availability of the 'quick and dirty' dumping option reduces the incentive to pursue innovative decommissioning and recycling options. Further, it flies in the face of growing international political and public consensus not to use the sea as a dump for wastes.

Although positioning itself as taking the ethical and scientific high road, Greenpeace never made a persuasive case. Greenpeace did not provide substantial risk–benefit analysis to support their view that land disposal was the environmentally superior choice. All actions, and even inaction, entail some degree of risk, some identifiable and some not. Greenpeace's campaign rested on a visceral belief that deep-sea disposal would disrupt 'nature' more than land decommissioning. By the time Shell officials had authorized the burial of the Spar, the risks were widely documented (and generally considered less severe than the land disposal option). It's clear that Shell did not flaunt the 'precautionary principle.'

Initial media reports were far more sympathetic to Greenpeace than to Shell. That may have reflected the lack of scientific sophistication of many reporters, a general disdain for risk–benefit analysis, and a suspicion of corporate greenwashing. Yet, in the months and years since the controversy, numerous independent reports have reaffirmed Shell's scientific analysis that deep-sea disposal was environmentally and economically the best disposal option. Greenpeace's original claims, on which they justified their guerrilla actions, appeared increasingly far-fetched. One of the most authoritative independent analyses, by the National Environmental Research Council (NERC 1996), was commissioned by the UK Department of Trade and Industry. It concluded that despite the presence of 'glaring errors' in Shell's original BPEO, the global impact of the deep-sea disposal of Spar would have been very small (Rice 1996a).

The NERC assessment stated, 'In reaching decisions about disposal options … factors including social, ethical, aesthetic, legal and economic factors must be considered in addition to the scientific evidence.' It examined a range of disposal options and their potential effects, negative and positive, on the environment:

Deep-sea disposal

- Destruction of organisms through physical impact of the structure and associated smothering by disturbed bottom sediments; and

through poisoning by the toxic materials contained within the structure or metals released as the frame itself degrades.
- Risk of toxins entering food chains, and even reaching humans, as deep-sea fishing of depths down to 1,800 metres increases (Pearce 1995b).
- Threat to safety of navigation.
- Sunken structures may act as artificial reefs, 'creating or improving the habitat and, therefore, increasing productivity and harvests of desirable species' (Bombace 1989). Most artificial reefs are deployed in shallow water (depth < 30 m), but they may also be beneficial in the deep sea (Picken and McIntyre 1989).
- Risk of conflict of use would be far less in the deep sea than in shallower water.
- The high dispersal rates of the toxic materials in deep sea would pose less threat to the environment than disposal on land.
- Deep-sea disposal would not add to the problem of diminishing space for waste disposal sites on land.

Alternative decommissioning options included:

- Disposal to landfill and disposal in shallower seas.
- Recycling: The structures could be brought ashore and the broken up scrap could be recycled. This would remove the bulk of the demand for land disposal space, but the installations would need to be thoroughly cleaned first which would produce waste. The demand in energy used in transporting the installations and in the recycling processes must also be taken into account.
- Re-use: The structures, or parts of them, could be reused for production elsewhere or for new uses such as artificial reefs, lighthouses, harbour walls, marine research centres, or even offshore casinos.

The NERC concluded that each disposal option resulted in deleterious effects and competing 'principles'. It noted that there might be cases where deep-sea disposal (to well-researched sites, chosen for their low physical disturbance and relatively low abundance of life) is the best environmental option. If there is no potential to reuse the installation, and the implications of the high-energy requirements needed to transport the structure to its recycling site outweigh the disadvantages of deep-sea disposal, then the latter would seem to be acceptable. In this case, only a small localized area would be affected and the estimated recovery period would be between two and ten years. NERC endorsed the scientific consensus that even for cases like the Spar with significantly higher content of hazardous materials than most offshore structures, 'the global impact of deep-sea disposal of large structures such as the Brent Spar would be very small' (Rice 1996a).

Conclusions/lessons

Nobody came out of the Brent Spar battle well. By any measure, Shell sought an objective assessment of the various Brent Spar disposal options. Yet it sought to keep its original scuttle plans secret. That can be seen as a display of arrogance or a prudent decision, considering the absolute opposition by Greenpeace and (initially) sections of the media to the option that the scientists suggested was scientifically and financially most responsible.

Greenpeace consistently made its moral opposition to deep-sea dumping loud and clear. Yet it compromised its appeal to the moral high ground by exaggerating the dangers posed by the ocean disposal of Brent Spar. Moreover, it grounded its campaign on a radical interpretation of the precautionary principle, which allowed it to justify a scientifically questionable claim of imminent danger.

Neither side had clean hands, which is usually the case when ethical principles are so ambiguous. Greenpeace saw its reputation for integrity eroded among the international press corps, although the UK government and Shell faired worse with the general public. In 1996, Bob Worcester, chairman of the polling firm MORI (Market & Opinion Research International), in a paper 'Business and the environment: in the aftermath of Brent Spar and BSE' concluded that 'Greenpeace won the battle by ten to one in the eyes of the British public' but its 'scientific methods were flawed'. The UK government lost credibility and its 'confidence [hubris?] in its own infallibility' was 'unshared by the public', while 'Shell lost some of its most precious asset, its reputation'. It was, Worcester concluded, 'a turning point in British attitudes to companies, to government and to environmental groups'.

As a consequence of the backlash, British officials became far more cautious in dealing with the decommissioning issue as they recalculated trade-offs between industry and government and assessed the political fallout. However, a major shift in policy did not occur until May 1997 when Britain elected a new Labour government, which declared in autumn 1997 that it would operate a presumption against ocean disposal.

Brent Spar was also a wake-up call to the press, which has traditionally assumed as its default predilection that corporations lie and activists' groups tell the truth. It underscores the reality that the media are never impartial, although they can strive for reasonable disclosure of their own biases and for basic fairness. They must become more vigilant and sceptical when it comes to choosing sources. Greenpeace had long boasted in its publications of its skill in manipulating the media. At the Edinburgh International Television Festival in August 1995, the BBC, ITN and Channel 4 led reflections on the way the media had portrayed a one-sided view of the Brent Spar debacle. As it turned out, Greenpeace had spent more than $(US)500,000 for TV equipment to beam back the deep-sea battle scene. David Lloyd of Channel 4 acknowledged that his news organization had relied too much on Greenpeace news releases. 'Greenpeace was pulling us by the nose', added an embarrassed Richard Sambrook, head of newsgathering at the BBC. During the public brouhaha, the BBC had let its enthusiasm for good pictures trump its responsibility for integrity by willingly airing whatever exciting video beamed its way. In referring to Greenpeace, Sambrook noted, 'This particular David was not armed with a slingshot so much as an AK-47' (6 September 1995).

With the passage of time, certain journalists have engaged in what can only be called historical revisionism. In one prominent example, *New Scientist* gave Greenpeace UK executive director Peter Melchett two pages of free advertising in the guise of an annual update to make the case that Brent Spar was actually a 'defining (positive) moment for the environmental movement'. While admitting that 'Greenpeace made mistakes too', Melchett excused its actions with the claim that this was only because 'we allowed ourselves to follow the agenda set by the [Department of Trade and Industry], Shell and the media – too often getting into arguments about the potential toxicity of the Spar' (*New Scientist*, 23 December 1995). In other words, Greenpeace erred in so far as it let the issue turn on the particulars of this case rather than on the slippery slope argument that this dumping would open the way to massive dumping and irreparable pollution.

Greenpeace's actions during and since Brent Spar have emboldened those who assert that pressure groups need to be held more accountable and that exaggerating environmental hazards weakens the credibility of the entire environmental movement. 'Deep-sea disposal seemed the least harmful option', concluded Robert Sangeorge, a spokesman for the Switzerland-based Worldwide Fund for Nature. Brent Spar 'was a circus and sideshow that distracted from the big environmental issues affecting the world' (*Wall Street Journal*, 7 July 1995). One overriding lesson of Brent Spar is usually lost on both sides: beware of all spin-doctors, in suits and even those dressed in green. Although government agencies and corporations have long charged that environmental activists exaggerate hazards, engage in scare tactics and stoke media controversies through the use of out-of-context anecdotes, rarely have the stakes been so high. In this media-driven age, clever 'green' and 'progressive' companies and 'public interest' groups sometimes act like the old hard-line corporations they ridicule.

According to the common wisdom, Brent Spar radically altered corporate environmental management strategy. 'Shell did everything by the book', wrote the environment-business magazine *Tomorrow*, 'It's just that the Brent Spar changed the book.' Shell postponed its annual Better Britain environmental awards due to the 'inappropriate' atmosphere. The high-profile Greenpeace campaign also had an effect on other major companies who were struggling to balance increased financial demands from investors with the public's newly inflamed environmental concerns. In an effort to help this process, the UK oil and gas industry recently set up the North Sea

Decommissioning Group (NSDG). The group brings together representatives from the oil industry, government, marine contracting companies, and Norwegian groups. The main aims of the new group are to encourage the development of new technologies, create a mood for co-operation, identify areas of synergy between the operators and contractors, and to promote good communication between all parties.

A number of commentators have argued that the primary lesson is the value of 'dialogue'. In what became a familiar refrain, offered without empirical support, one analyst wrote that 'Failure to engage in an ethical dialogue led to damaged reputations for both Shell-UK and Greenpeace because they failed to build effective relationships with their stakeholders' (Wood 1996). According to John Elkington, chairman of the British consultancy SustainAbility Ltd, this incident has introduced three new factors into corporate decision-making: (1) 'Producer responsibility: Life Cycle Analysis is clearly going to be essential in future large scale industrial undertakings. No structure the size of an oil platform or with a similar function should ever be designed without built-in disassembly plans'; (2) 'Stakeholder responsibility: permission from regulators is obviously no longer sufficient'; and (3) 'Shared responsibility' – two frequently hostile factions, radical environmentalists and multinational corporations, would now have to actively dialogue, if not agree. The post-Brent Spar discussion, wrote Elkington, has opened the way for Shell and other multinationals that must 'succeed in laying the ghost of Brent Spar ... signal[ling] the beginning of a new era of stakeholder capitalism' (Elkington 1997).

During and since the Brent Spar affair, environmental activists invoked a 'new era of stakeholder capitalism', which they claim requires protection of the 'natural environment'. This view reflects the tenets of a new generation of eco-economists and corporate social responsibility academicians who have expanded the notion of stakeholder responsibility to include relationships with customers, employees, franchisees, trading partners, the local community and even society at large (Freeman and Reed 1983; Jennings and Entine 1998). These views contrast with the narrow conception of corporate responsibility enumerated by conservative economists such as Milton Friedman who wrote:

> The only entities who can have responsibilities are individuals ... A business cannot have responsibilities. So the question is, do corporate executives, provided they stay within the law, have responsibilities in their business activities other than to make as much money for their stockholders as possible? And my answer to that is, no, they do not.
>
> (Friedman 1984)

Friedman concluded that businesses that act in the best interest of shareholders maximize the benefits to all stakeholders. 'There is one and only one social responsibility of business – to use its resources and engage in activities designed to increase its profits so long as it stays within the rules of the game, which is to say, engages in open and free competition, without deception or fraud' (*ibid.*).

By traditional standards, Shell's decision to commission risk/benefit analysis of the various disposal options demonstrated that it took its social responsibilities seriously. Shell officials believed they were carefully weighing investor expectations and their stewardship responsibilities for the environment. The key problem, according to more liberal stakeholder theory, is that these ethical calculations were made by Shell officials alone and only included other potential stakeholder perspectives at Shell's behest. Although the company sought input from a variety of sources that it considered stakeholders, it acted with little public consultation and certainly against the wishes of some environmental groups that, rightly or wrongly, believed that they better represented the interests of the natural environment.

The issue over who deserves a place at the negotiating table as legitimate stakeholder (or stakeholder representatives, as Greenpeace saw itself) haunted the Brent Spar controversy throughout. Dialogue can only work when the participants are perceived as legitimate.

Publicly, Shell appeared to embrace the broader conception of stakeholder responsibility, asserting that it would make 'openness' the watchword for the future (BBC 1996). Heinz Rothermund, managing director of Shell Exploration UK said the Spar had set a precedent in how Shell treated the public. 'Brent Spar will enter history as the symbol of our failure to establish our position and connect in a meaningful way with a wider audience' (*Scotsman*, 16 April 1997). However, it is reasonable to suspect that Shell's post-crisis confessions of myopia and calls for dialogue were more reactive and tactical than defining. Most corporations, Shell included, have long recognized that they operate at a disadvantage in the court of public opinion because of deep concerns about their motives, which Greenpeace exploited. This incident made them more sensitive to public opinion, which Shell believed was not always rational. 'We hadn't taken into account hearts and emotions, you know, where people are coming from, which is in part today's debate', noted Chris Fay, chairman of Shell UK (BBC 1995).

In retrospect, the lessons appear ambiguous and contradictory. Dr Angel, for one, has expressed his 'enormous frustration' at the lack of sophistication displayed by all sides over the scientific issues, even by Shell and the British government. Dr Angel writes:

> One example of this was when we were trying to put some information about biodiversity in the public domain. There had been a[n erroneous] comment made in the media that disposal of the Spar off Rosemary Bank would result in the extinction of several species. We argued that while dumping the Spar would undoubtedly kill one or two million worms, similar numbers would be killed by dumping the waste in landfill. The problem was that Tim Eggar proceeded to put out a statement in which he left out the 'million' [he wrote: 'one or two worms'] and proceeded to argue that the deep-sea is a low diversity environment. We [Angel's research group] were then pilloried for this obvious untruth. Greenpeace showed a remarkable facility for selective deafness.
>
> (Angel 2001)

Greenpeace consistently ridiculed any option other than land decommissioning, frequently accusing independent scientists of being tools of Shell or corporate spokespersons, charges repeated endlessly and sometimes uncritically in the media. Without any scientific evidence, Greenpeace placed a far higher value on marine environments than on terrestrial or even atmospheric environments. They refused to consider the impact of their favoured solution, insisting they were taking the most 'ethical' position. Such righteousness nonetheless took a toll on Shell and the government's position. MORI' s data from before and after the incident (1993, 1995 and 1996) indicate that confidence in 'scientists working in industry' and 'scientists working for government' was significantly lower than those 'working for environmental groups'. Another MORI survey commissioned by the industry itself showed that the public's approval rating of the offshore oil and gas industry slipped from 72 per cent in the 1970s to 32 per cent by 1996 (Elkington 1997).

However, predictions by activist groups that Shell would replace Exxon as a corporate symbol of the absence of corporate responsibility have not materialized. The scientific situation was far more ambiguous in this incident when compared to Valdez; and Shell's moral culpability was never fully established, partly as a result of missteps by Greenpeace. In fact, according to the MORI surveys, Greenpeace suffered a severe blow to its image that persists to this day. The incident underscores the plasticity of public opinion when it comes to hot button issues with complex, if not murky, scientific issues at stake.

Is there a process which could have resulted in scientific consensus and a possible Greenpeace–Shell rapprochement? Despite public embraces by both sides of the need for stakeholder dialogue, intractable practical realities confound an easy solution. As a consequence, the Brent Spar incident has triggered many prickly ethical questions:

- Was dialogue ever really possible considering Greenpeace's absolute opposition to risk–benefit analysis based on its invocation of a distorted 'precautionary principle'?
- Is classic risk–benefit analysis, which weighs both environmental and financial factors, appropriate, considering Greenpeace's insistence that the environment stands as the premier stakeholder, eclipsing the rights of investors, workers, vendors and the broad public who consumes Shell's products?
- What changes if Greenpeace's assessment of what is most environmentally appropriate is superficially attractive but scientifically flawed, as Shell claimed?
- Once the conflict erupted, could Shell or Greenpeace have handled their respective situations differently to attain a goal that both publicly embraced: the most environmentally sensitive solution to a complex and expensive project?

Faced with the level of disingenuity displayed by Greenpeace, Shell may never have overcome the hearsay and misinformation that marked this incident. It is also far from certain that Greenpeace could have got a hearing on its perspective without the use of extreme tactics. Considering the circumstances of this case, the suggestion that more dialogue or openness could have short-circuited this confrontation is simplistic, for it assumes that the dispute was rational.

As the decommissioner at Shell-UK noted, in the search for publicly acceptable, but environmentally questionable, solutions, scientific and engineering logic and rigour might be cast aside completely (BBC 1996). Capitulation, not negotiation, was always Greenpeace's stated goal. It was wedded to an *a priori* conviction that even minimal pollution from Shell's decommissioned oil rig was environmentally unacceptable. Therefore, dumping under any circumstances crossed an ethical line. Asked what would happen if Shell did not abandon its plans, Jochen Vorfelder, the Greenpeace spokesman in Germany, stated that the protests would continue and escalate. 'If you call that blackmail, that's okay with me', he said (BBC 1995).

Only in the aftermath of the blow to its reputation has Greenpeace pledged, at least for public consumption, its willingness to engage in dialogue. 'Industry is now the main player in society', noted Thilo Bode, manager of Greenpeace Germany, who took over as the executive director of Greenpeace International in the wake of the Spar incident. 'That's why we need to talk to them.' Bode added that Greenpeace itself needs to open itself and repair its image for being 'bureaucratic, secretive, even untrustworthy' (*Financial Times*, 10 January 1996). Bode told *Time* that Greenpeace might even abandon its long-time reliance on guerilla tactics. 'The campaign against Shell's plans to dump the Brent Spar oil rig at sea started what we call 'the post-Brent Spar effect,' he commented that same summer. 'Now we're seeing that as soon as we announce a campaign, companies back down. This happened most recently with Unilever. The company said it would stop using products obtained by industrial fishing in the North Sea before we could even launch our campaign actions. But perhaps the most important lesson was the realization of what we can do with market forces. It wasn't Greenpeace's strength that made Shell back down; it was the consumer boycotts' (*Time International*, 10 June 1996).

It is not clear whether dialogue would benefit the causes Greenpeace has historically supported. As Paul Horsman, the Greenpeace leader of the Brent Spar campaign said, 'With the environmental movement, there's a sleeping giant that can be awakened very, very easily and very, very quickly' with such tactics (*Wall Street Journal*, 7 July 1995). It is arguable that in the face of enormous corporate resources (Shell), and a less than receptive government (UK Conservative Party), anything short of a shrill, high-profile campaign in which violence was a threat would have resulted in public debate. In other words, the anti-rational, emotive campaigns that Greenpeace now claim they may eschew may yet remain its most effective tactic considering the natural imbalance of power when public interest groups square off against multinational corporations or conservative governments.

Incident-driven development of international standards in a politically charged atmosphere raises complicated business and ethical concerns. In retrospect, managing public perception, rather than the need for more dialogue and scientific rigour are the most important lessons from Brent Spar. Brent Spar reaffirms that the simplistic distinction between 'progressive' activist groups that purportedly fight for the little guy and so-called 'evil' corporations is a caricature that disguises a more textured reality.

Does this conclusion suggest that future conflicts are inevitable? Not necessarily. There are encouraging, though limited, signs that dialogue outside of the crisis framework that prevailed in Brent Spar might offer some relief. As *The Economist* noted, the incident encouraged a 'growing universe' of corporate behaviour to which 'standards of correctness are being applied', so that 'good firms will have to listen hard and explain even harder' (10 May 1997). Shell, like many companies during the nineties that faced challenges about their environmental practices, established a Social Accountability Team to review corporate practices.

Is this a sincere effort or strategic corporate greenwashing designed to inoculate Shell against protests that are more virulent? Undoubtedly, it's a little of both. In the short term, Shell is determined to resuscitate its public image. More than two years after the affair, in April 1998, Shell issued a social accountability report, 'Profits and Principles – Does There Have to be a Choice?' At Shell's invitation, John Elkington prepared a 'triple bottom line' analysis that was incorporated in the report assessing economic, environmental and social bottom line impacts of Shell's international operations. 'The sustainable development community ... must develop its toolkit for triple bottom line accountability and management', Elkington wrote in explaining his decision to collaborate with Shell.

> If sustainable development is to become a global reality rather than remain a seductive mirage, governments, communities, companies and individuals must work together to improve their 'triple bottom line' (economic, social and environmental) performance. To this end, we not only need new forms of accountability but also new forms of accounting.
>
> This does not mean that every aspect of a company's performance can – or should – be reduced to a 'common currency' of money values. But if we are to manage a given company's performance effectively we also need to be able to measure it. We must find accurate, useful and credible indicators of progress in terms of economic prosperity, environmental quality and social justice.

Of most significance, Elkington broke from the Greenpeace model of perpetual confrontation, which rendered dialogue impossible. 'Companies exist to create wealth', he wrote, 'so the most direct contribution they can make to sustainable development is to create long-term value on an economically, socially and environmentally sustainable basis. A key twenty-first century challenge, in short, will be "sustainable value. ... Happily, the evidence suggests no fundamental conflict between sustainable value creation and long-term shareholder value added".'

Empirical research provides only ambiguous support for Elkington's 'happy' belief that there is 'no fundamental conflict between sustainable value creation and long-term shareholder value added.' Although it is intuitively likely that proactive environmental corporate policies, including expensive outlays for new technology, could lead to some efficiencies and reduced exposure to regulation or negative publicity, thus yielding a net gain for the corporation, empirical evidence to support this intuition is very sparse. While several studies have shown that better pollution performance improved profitability (Bragdon and Marlin 1972) and reduced risks (Spicer 1978), others have shown no significant link between measures of environmental performance and profitability (Fogler and Nutt 1975; Rockness, Schlachter and Rockness 1986). Historically, in a world with varying regulatory standards, multinational corporations are in a position to externalize and therefore bury environmental mistakes. Consequently, many corporations rationally expect to avoid paying a price (e.g. lost efficiencies, negative publicity, regulatory compliance costs), for environmental cost cutting. As a result, corporations face frequent temptations to place shareholder financial interests over 'sustainable value creation'.

As controversies in the early 1990s that damaged the reputation and profitability of the Body Shop and Ben & Jerry's have demonstrated, firms whose environmental practices do not meet industry standards or a corporation's marketing persona can experience significant damage when stakeholders believe they have been betrayed (Entine 1994, 1995).

It is far too early in this experiment to determine if a commitment to greater dialogue will prove attractive to either environmentalists or corporations after the initial honeymoon ends and conflicts arise. A major problem is that the theoretical appeal to the value of dialogue, which underpins this working agreement, presupposes that it is clear who is entitled to participate and be listened to. Key members of the environmental activist community, Greenpeace in particular, do not embrace the Sustainability–Shell co-operative model, which is based on the notion that 'companies exist to create wealth'. As it now stands, Greenpeace, which provoked the Brent Spar affair, is a guest at its own wedding. Another factor is that dialogue only works when common interests overlap. 'The difficulty of dialogue is that the two sides must be in communication – i.e. listening to each other – and should be looking for practical solutions', notes Dr Angel. 'There also have to be agreed criteria on how to make the final decisions. The Greenpeace attitude that any solution involving marine disposal was out was a bit like Henry Ford's comment that "you can have a car of any color you want so long as it is black"' (Angel 2001).

This central paradox of Brent Spar – a confusion of the identity and legitimacy of stakeholders – suggests that dialogue may prove an illusive goal when grounds for compromise do not exist. The privileged dialogue model now encouraged by Sustainability and Shell, which leaves the most vocal activists as sideline observers, remains a problematic tool for resolving fractious environmental disputes in which sharply coloured ideology, rather than risk assessment, is the basis for discussion.

References

Angel, Martin V. (1995) 'Brent Spar: no hiding place', *Biologist* 42(4): 192.

—— (2001) E-mail exchange with author (May).

Bahree, Bhushan, Pope, Kyle and Sullivan, Allana, 'Giant outsmarted: How Greenpeace sank Shell's plan to dump big oil rig in Atlantic', *The Wall Street Journal*, 7 July 1995, p. A1.

BBC (1995) 'The Battle for Brent Spar', *BBC Public Eye*, transmitted 2 September 1995.

BBC (1996) 'Will Green Warriors Get a Say in the Boardroom?', *The Money Programme*, 24 March.

Bombace, G. (1989) 'Artificial reefs in the Mediterranean Sea', *Bulletin of Marine Science*, 44(2): 1023–32.

Bragdon, J.H. and Marlin, J.A.T. (1972) 'Is pollution profitable?', *Risk Management*, 19(4): 9–18.
The Economist, 'Shell man says sorry', 10 May 1997.
—— 'The non-governmental order: will NGOs democratise, or merely disrupt, global governance?', 11–17 December 1999: 18–19.
Elkington, J. (1997) 'Laying the ghost of Brent Spar', *Resurgence*, 3 September 1997.
Entine, Jon, (1994) 'Shattered image: is the Body Shop too good to be true?', *Business Ethics* 8(5): 23–8.
—— (1995) 'Rain-forest chic', *Toronto Globe & Mail Report on Business* 12(4): 40–52.
Financial Times, 'Greenpeace's new head outlines the organisation's strategy for working with business', 10 January 1996.
Fogler, H.R. and Nutt, F. (1975) 'A note on social responsibility and stock valuation', *Academy of Management Journal* 18: 155–60.
Freeman, Edward and Reed, David L. (1983) 'Stockholders and stakeholders: a new perspective on corporate governance', *California Management Review* 25(3): 88–106.
Friedman, Milton (1984) 'Milton Friedman responds', interview in *Business and Society* 84(5).
Greenpeace Web Site: *http://www.gre.ac.uk*.
Guardian, 'A Flotilla of Questions, 7 September 1995.
Jennings, Marianne and Entine, Jon (1998) 'Business with a soul: a re-examination of what counts in business ethics', *Hamline Journal of Public Law and Policy* 20(1): 1–88.
Melchett, Peter (2001) 'Green for danger', *New Scientist* 148 (2009): 50–1.
National Environmental Research Council (1996) 'Scientific Group on the Decommissioning of Offshore Structures: First Report', April 1996, Swindon: NERC (*www.nerc.ac.uk*).
Pearce, F. (1995a) 'Breaking up is hard to do,' *New Scientist* 146(1983): 14–15.
—— (1995b) 'Storm warning over Brent Spar,' *New Scientist*, 147(1992): 4.
Picken, G.B and McIntyre, A.D. (1989) 'Rigs to reefs in the North Sea,' *Bulletin of Marine Science* 44(2): 782–8.
Rice, A. (1996a) 'The beached buoy', *The Times*, 31 May 1996: iv.
—— (1996b) 'The lessons of Brent Spar,' *Endeavour*, 20: 47–9.
Rockness, J., Schlachter, P. and Rockness, H.O. (1986) 'Hazardous waste disposal, corporate disclosure, and financial performance in the chemical industry', in M. Neimark (ed.) *Advances in Public Interest Accounting*, vol. 1, Greenwich, CT: JAI Press, pp. 167–91.
Scotsman, 'Brent Spar a gaffe says Shell chief', 16 April 1997.
Spicer, B.H. (1978) 'Market risk, accounting data, and companies' pollution control records,' *Journal of Business, Finance, and Accounting* 5: 67–83.
Time International (1996) 'The man who keeps the Echo Warriors in control', 10 June: 147(24).
United Kingdom Oil and Gas Industry Association: *http://www.ukooa.co.uk*.
Wood, Graham (1996) 'Guarding the corporate reputation: learning the ethical lessons from 'Brent Spar', August 1996.

Suggestions for further reading

Abbott, Alison (1996) 'Brent Spar: when science is not to blame', *Nature* 380(6569) March: 13–14.

Angel, M.V. (1996) 'The deep ocean: a sustainable option for waste disposal?', in B. Earll (ed.) *Marine Environmental Management: Review of Events in 1995 and Future Trends*, Proceedings of a meeting 24–5 January 1996, Glos. pp. 107–12.

Bebbington, K.J. and Gray, R.H. (1993) 'Corporate accountability and the physical environment: social responsibility and accounting beyond profit', *Business Strategy and the Environment* 2(2): 1–11.

Craig-Smith, N. (1990) *Morality and the Market: Consumer Pressure for Corporate Accountability*, London: Routledge.

Dickson, Lisa and McCulloch, Alistair (1996) 'Shell, the Brent Spar and Greenpeace: a doomed tryst', *Environmental Politics* 5.

Dowling, Grahame R. (1995) 'Corporate reputations: the company's super brand', *Journal of Brand Management* 2(6): 377–85.

Gray, R.H., Bebbington, K.J. and Walters, D. (1993) *Accounting for the Environment*, London: Paul Chapman.

Groth, Lucreesha (1996) 'Risk assessment and the disposal proposal', *Oceanography* (Spring 1996) 9(1): 403–503.

Hart, S. and Ahuja, G. (1994) 'Does it Pay to Be Green? An Empirical Examination of the Relationship between Pollution Prevention and Firm Performance', working paper, University of Michigan, Ann Arbor.

Lofstedt, R.E. and Renn, O. (1997) 'The Brent Spar controversy: an example of risk communication gone wrong', *Risk Analysis* 17(2): 131–6.

Macilwain, Colin (1996) 'Risk: a suitable case for analysis?', *Nature* 380(6569) March: 10–11.

McGowan, Richard A. and Mahon, John F. (1995) 'The ends justify the means: the ethical reasoning of environmental public interest groups and their actions', *International Journal of Value-Based Management* 8(2): 135–47.

Phillips, Robert A. (1997) 'Stakeholder theory and a principle of fairness', *Business Ethics Quarterly* 7(1): 51–66.

Piasecki, B.W. (1995) *Corporate Environmental Strategy*, New York: Wiley.

'Playing the Trump Card of Uncertainty', *Nature* 380(6569), March, 1996.

Power, M. (1991) 'Auditing and environmentalism expertise: between protest and professionalism', *Accounting, Auditing and Accountability Journal* 4: 30–42.

Russo, Michael and Fouts, Paul A. (1997) 'A resource-based perspective on corporate environmental performance and profitability', *Academy of Management Journal* 40(3): 534–59.

Shrivastava, P. (1995) 'Environmental technologies and competitive advantage', *Strategic Management Journal* 16(Summer): 183–200.

Starik, M. and Rands, G.P. (1995) 'Weaving an integrated web: multilevel and multisystem perspectives of ecologically sustainable organizations', *Academy of Management Review* 20: 908–35.

'Stakeholder Capitalism,' *The Economist*, 10 February 1996: 23–5.

'Stakeholder Management in a Situation of Crisis: Shell's Problems with "Brent Spar"', in L. G. Brusati (ed.) *Business, Government and Society*, proceedings of 2nd AIDEA Giovani International Conference, Bocconi University, 6–8 June 1996.

Appendix I

Extracts from selected Greenpeace news releases

Greenpeace occupies scrapped North Sea oil platform before it's dumped at sea (30 April 1995)

Greenpeace today scaled and took up residence on an old North Sea oil platform to stop its owner, Shell, from dumping the rusting hulk and its highly toxic contents to the sea bed.

Four climbers used ropes and winches to scale the Brent Spar, which is the first of 400 North Sea oil platforms to be dumped at sea. The climbers have food and supplies for what is expected to be a long occupation. The Moby Dick is standing by as a safety vessel. The activists first climbed the steel ladders on the installation, then scaled the outer part of the rig, 28 metres high above the waterline.

After Moby Dick captain Pelle Pettersson notified the five other rig support vessels in the area, stating that Greenpeace was protesting the dumping of the Brent Spar, a Shell standby vessel then sailed very close to the Moby Dick and the inflatables, harassing them.

The Brent Spar contains over 100 tonnes of toxic sludge – including oil, arsenic, cadmium, PCBs and lead – including more than 30 tonnes of radioactive waste ...

A Greenpeace report released today, 'No Grounds for Dumping: The decommissioning and abandonment of off-shore oil and gas platforms' ... concludes that total removal is not only the best environmental option but also the most cost-effective, feasible and job-saving.

Dumping oil platforms 'should be stopped' says EU Commissioner for the Environment (13 May 1995)

International support for Greenpeace action to prevent the sea dumping of toxic laden North Sea oil platforms continues to grow.

Quotes translated from Danish TV:

> *Actually, I think most countries in the EU think this is dirty and that it should be stopped ... [I]t is good that Greenpeace is around to ensure these things do not go on secretly.*
>
> *Ritt Bjerregaard, EU Commissioner for the Environment*

> *There are many problems in the North Sea. Many of the platforms out there are about to reach the time when they will have to be scrapped. This has to be done in a safe manner and the only way this can be done is on land.*
>
> *Svend Auken, Danish Minister for Environment and Energy*

It is quite simply a catastrophe. For the environment, for the fishermen, for all of us ... if a permit is given now, what is to be expected for the 400+ other installations out there.

Peter Sand Mortensen, Chair of Fishermen's Sector, International Transport Federation (ITF)

Greenpeace welcomes important decisions at North Sea conference (9 June 1995)

[M]ost North Sea States have agreed that it is totally unacceptable to dump offshore installations at sea and recommend the decommissioning of rigs on land. The only objections to this recommendation came from the UK, France and Norway.

Greenpeace response to the UK Government proposal that dumping the Brent Spar remains an option (20 July 1995)

The opposition to dumping the Brent Spar was based on the following facts:

(i) There has been no formal inventory of the Brent Spar's contents, so the environmental impacts could not possibly be properly assessed.
(ii) There is a lack of understanding of the deep sea environment, and it is currently impossible to predict the effects of the proposed dumping on deep sea ecosystems.
(iii) The documents which supported Shell's licence application are highly conjectural in nature. They contain numerous unsubstantiated assumptions, minimal data and extrapolations from unnamed studies.
(iv) Dumping the Brent Spar would create a precedent for dumping other contaminated structures in the sea and would undermine current international agreements. The environmental effects of further dumping would be cumulative.
(v) Dismantling of the Brent Spar is technically feasible and offshore engineering firms believe they can do it safely and effectively. The necessary facilities are already routinely in use and decommissioning of many other oil installations has already been carried out elsewhere in the world.
(vi) To protect the environment, the principle of minimising the generation of wastes should be upheld and harmful materials always recycled, treated or contained.

Greenpeace believes Shell UK were right in not dumping the Brent Spar. This view is supported by most governments in Europe and a vast majority of the public. There will always be scientific debate, but in the arena of this debate the principle of precautionary action is applied and the benefit of the doubt given to the environment.

Letter to Shell UK (from Peter Melchett, Executive Director, Greenpeace UK, to Dr Christopher Fay, Chairman and Chief Executive, Shell UK Ltd, dated 4 September 1995)

As you know, we were concerned that no full analysis had been done of the contents of the Brent Spar prior to your decision to dump it. Greenpeace therefore took some samples from a storage tank on the Brent Spar during our occupation ... We thought samples had been successfully taken from storage tank 1, but we have realised in the last few days that when the samples were taken the sampling device was still in the pipe leading to the storage tanks, rather than in the tank itself.

In many references to our sampling, we stressed that the results were not definitive, but I'm afraid that in writing to you and your colleagues on the Shell UK Board on 19 June, I said that our sampling showed a particular quantity of oil on the Brent Spar. That was wrong, and I apologise to you and your colleagues for this.

As I've said, our main concern was that there should be a full and independent inventory of the contents of the Brent Spar, and Greenpeace is delighted that, following your decision not to dump the Brent Spar at sea, such an inventory is being compiled by the independent analysts DNV.

As you also know from my letter to you of 16 August, since your decision not to dump the Brent Spar, scientists have now made it clear that there were fundamental flaws in the scientific arguments that Shell UK put forward to the public and to UK Government Ministers, justifying your decision to dump, in particular, concerning the ecology of the area where you proposed to dump the Brent Spar. I hope that is something, now you have the evidence for this, that Shell UK will be prepared to admit publicly.

In any event, as you know, the basic argument between Greenpeace and the European governments that supported our position on the one hand, and Shell UK and the UK Government on the other, was not about the contents of the Brent Spar, nor the physical characteristics of the proposed dump site. The argument was about whether it was right to dump industrial waste of any sort in the deep oceans, whether dumping the Brent Spar would be a precedent for dumping other oil installations, and indeed other waste in the oceans, and, fundamentally, over whether we should dump wastes into any part of the environment, as opposed to reducing waste, and recycling, treating or containing harmful materials. Our view remains that the division between us on the Brent Spar depends on how deeply we value our environment, and what damage and precedents we find unacceptable.

Brent Spar meeting between Greenpeace and Shell (8 September 1995)

Shell UK are now studying 200 different options for onshore disposal or re-use of the Brent Spar. Greenpeace welcomes this following a constructive meeting with the Chairman of Shell UK.

North Sea oilfields must be dismantled on land: Greenpeace (5 February 1996)

Greenpeace today called on the UK Government to rule out dumping at sea for all oil installations and abandon the so-called 'case-by-case' approach.

'The issue at stake here is whether we live in a throwaway society' says Greenpeace Campaign Director Chris Rose. 'The public knows it is wrong to dump old cars in the village pond – and it's wrong for the Government to let the oil industry treat the sea as its rubbish dump. The UK Government must rule out dumping at sea and abandon the so-called case-by-case approach.

Greenpeace also pointed out that in December 1995 a report for the oil industry group UKOOA (UK Offshore Operators Association) noted that the 'best environmental option' for decommissioned steel installations is to bring them ashore.

Greenpeace welcomes scientists' report on Brent Spar (22 May 1996)

Greenpeace today welcomed the report by international scientists brought together by UK Energy Minister Tim Eggar.

Working under the auspices of the Natural Environment Research Council (NERC) and chaired by Professor John Shepherd of Southampton Oceanography Centre, the scientists concluded:

- *The UK Government should not assess each installation purely on a 'case by case' basis. It should also take into account the cumulative impact of all disposals of waste at sea.*
- *The decision making process before licensing the dumping of the Brent Spar should have included factors such as the need to conserve energy and resources by reducing, re-using and recycling waste. Other factors such as public acceptability should also be taken into account in future.*
- *Any problems with disposing of the Brent Spar on shore are no more difficult than have already been overcome with other installations.*

'This report clearly shows that scientific opinion does not back Government policy', said Dr Helen Wallace of Greenpeace UK. Energy Minister Mr Tim Eggar 'should stop using science as an excuse to ignore public concern about the environment'.

Greenpeace said today's report gave a strong backing to the decision made by the Oslo Paris Commission last year to agree a moratorium on the disposal at sea of decommissioned offshore installations. The UK and Norwegian governments have expressed reservations to the moratorium.

Appendix 2

Martin V. Angel (1995) 'Brent Spar: no hiding place', *Biologist* 42(4): 192

Mass media coverage and a vigorous campaign by Greenpeace, waged mainly at the petrol pumps in Germany, caused Shell to cancel plans to sink the Brent Spar. But was this decision the correct one?

The Brent Spar disposal issue has opened a Pandora's Box, bringing into focus some of the gargantuan problems of waste management that will face mankind as its population doubles in the next 50 years or so. Lifestyles in industrially developed countries are very wasteful. But even if the amount of waste we produce can be reduced, it can never be completely eliminated. More should be recycled, but recycling demands energy and often has its own inherent environmental problems. In Britain, our customary solution has been to bury it in land-fill, but this also causes problems. So why not use the oceans deeper than 2000 m, which cover 65% of the earth's surface, for waste disposal?

The Greenpeace view is that any such use of the deep oceans is unethical – end of argument. But why is the contamination of land or atmosphere not just as unethical? This attitude arises partly from the mistaken belief that the oceans are pristine and that we lack enough understanding about how they function to take such a risk. Arguments about ethics and stewardship are very important but need to be discussed coolly, free from the passions roused during a fevered campaign. Leaving the question of ethics aside, what were the main arguments produced by Greenpeace against the deep ocean disposal?

The Spar contains four main types of contaminants: heavy metals, traces of hydrocarbons, synthetic organic compounds and enhanced levels of radioactivity concentrated in the drilling fluids. Shell, in being granted a licence for disposal in the deep ocean through the International Maritime Organization, must have demonstrated to the satisfaction of the Department of Trade and Industry (admittedly not the most environmentally aware branch of Government!) that such disposal would have had 'a negligible impact on living resources, human health, marine activities, amenity value and water quality'. Greenpeace argued that introducing these contaminants would reduce water quality and biodiversity, the greatest danger arising from the contaminants entering the food chain and becoming bio-accumulated. Land-fill must be the preferred option, Greenpeace argued misleadingly, because only there could the impact be monitored and controlled. Monitoring of the deep ocean is perfectly feasible technically, and also, in practice, easier than in shallow seas where instruments deployed long-term *in situ* are constantly being trawled. So what impact might the contaminants in the Spar have had in the North

Atlantic? The first point to make is that *no matter what option is chosen there will be deleterious effects*. It is a question of choosing the lesser evil.

The quantity of heavy metals now left in Brent Spar after decommissioning is probably less than that in any large ship. Since hydrothermal vents expel heavy metals into the deep ocean in quantities that rival the output of the world's mining industry, many deep ocean inhabitants are well adapted to cope with a metal-rich environment. The site chosen was in 2000 m of water in a hollow, southwest of Rosemary Bank, through which swirls one of the outflows of cold Norwegian Sea water. This swirling flow would have rapidly dispersed any contaminants leaking from the rig. This deep dense water takes at least 250 years to return back to the surface, by which time the relatively small amounts of heavy metal would have been stripped out by the sedimentary rain of material from the surface and redeposited onto the bottom, and gradually incorporated into the geological record.

It is most improbable that bio-accumulation within the food-web would have been a problem. At depths of 2000 m the standing crop of organisms is less than a fiftieth of those in shallow water. Consequently, there are no potential living resources at such depths, and there are very few biological pathways along which contaminants might move back up to the surface.

Similarly, the residual hydrocarbons pose no serious environmental threat – hydrocarbons occur naturally in the deep ocean. Where there are natural seeps, large communities of animals use them as a source of organic material. Nor would the enhanced radioactivity in the stored drill cuttings pose much of a risk. The radioactivity is at such a low level that even on land it would pose no more radiological threat than living in a granite building in Aberdeen.

There is less certainty about the persistent synthetic organic compounds; we know so little about how they might move in deep ocean communities. However, since the ultimate fate of all such materials is to become incorporated into deep ocean sediments, discharging them at the bottom of the deep ocean is likely to be a short-cut.

Questions of biodiversity are complex. The sediment faunas of macro- and meio-benthos at 2000 m in the deep ocean appear to be as species rich as some of the most diverse terrestrial habitats. We know that larger species inhabiting the sea-floor have enormous geographical ranges, and it seems reasonable to assume that the smaller organisms will be similarly widely distributed. One habitat type that is in short supply in the deep ocean is provided by hard surfaces, so in that sense the rig would have enhanced the diversity of habitat.

The aspect that Shell was most concerned about was whether the rig would trigger a mass wasting event when it landed on the bottom, and this was one reason for their having selected a hollow in the sea-bed. In the North Atlantic, the geological record contains evidence of repeated underwater landslides involving hundreds of cubic kilometres of sediment which have slipped from the continental slopes into deep water. However, compared with the millions of square kilometres of the world's deep-ocean floor, the few thousand square metres impacted by the Spar would have been insignificant.

'by him all things were created' – *Colossians 1.16*

Ever since mankind started to cross the oceans in ships, the ocean bed has been littered with his debris, ranging from sunken wrecks to clinker and other rubbish. During the last World War, millions of tonnes of shipping were sunk, each wreck representing a source of contamination comparable to the Spar. Are the impacts of these tragedies yet another environmental time-bomb ticking away, or are they serendipitous experiments that we can use to evaluate the safety of deep ocean disposal? The deep ocean is potentially a safe repository for many types of waste, so long as it is properly managed, monitored and controlled. However, there is a general distrust in the ability and willingness of Industry and Government adequately to manage such disposal, and this will sway many into supporting the Greenpeace view. Yet we cannot afford to discard the option of using the deep ocean without full and proper environmental audit of the costs entailed. Was this a victory for the environment? Personally, I doubt it, but now that Pandora's Box is open, how are we to close it?

Appendix 3

Brent Spar Timeline

June 1976

Brent Spar installed in Brent Field, a unique design for oil storage and tanker loading. Two of six tanks later damaged in operation. Structure also later found to have been stressed during installation making major difficulties in reversing procedure to raise from water.

September 1991

Brent Spar ceases operating.

1991–1993

Detailed decommissioning studies carried out by Shell and independent external organizations and contractors to assess options. Two compared in detail – horizontal onshore dismantling and deep-sea disposal with deep sea emerging with six times lower safety risks, four times less cost and minimal environmental impact.

1994

February
Independent Aberdeen University study (AURIS) endorses choice of deep-sea disposal. Formal consultations with conservation bodies and fishing interests. Draft Abandonment Plan submitted.
December
Shell submits final Abandonment Plan to UK Government Department of Trade and Industry and receives approval.

1995

February
UK Government announces approval for deep-sea disposal and notifies 13 other contracting parties (12 nations and EC), signatories to the Oslo Convention covering protection of the marine environment. No objections raised within normal time limit. Shell announces deep-sea disposal plan.
30 April
Greenpeace activists occupy Spar, wrongly alleging Spar is 'a toxic time-bomb'; '14,500 tonnes of toxic rubbish'; or contains 'over 100 tonnes of toxic sludge'. Over next months they say Spar will be 'dumped in the North Sea' rather than disposed of at a carefully selected site in the deep Atlantic and suggest 'more than 400 oil rigs in the North Sea' might also be 'dumped'. They say Spar contains 5,550 tonnes of oil.

5 May
UK Government grants disposal licence to Shell UK.
9 May
German Ministry of the Environment protests against disposal plan.
13 May
Independent UK scientists begin stating support for deep-sea disposal for Brent Spar.
23 May
Activists removed from Spar. Greenpeace calls for Shell boycott in continental Europe.
8–9 June
Fourth North Sea Conference at Esbjerg, Denmark. Several European countries now call for onshore disposal for all oil installations. UK and Norway, the countries with the largest, heaviest, and most difficult deep-water structures, argue for 'case-by-case'.
11 June
Shell UK begins to tow Spar to deep Atlantic disposal site.
15–17 June
Public opinion in continental northern Europe strongly opposed. Chancellor Kohl protests to UK Prime Minister John Major at G7 summit.
14–20 June
Protesters in Germany threaten to damage 200 Shell service stations. 50 are subsequently damaged, two fire-bombed and one raked with bullets.
20 June
Several continental northern European governments now indicate opposition. Shell UK decides to halt disposal plan in view of untenable position caused by European political shifts, increased safety risks from violence and need for more reasoned discussion.
Late June
UK scientific debate intensifies, with growing support for Shell approach to environmental decision-making based on reason and sound science.
26–30 June
Eleven states call for a moratorium on sea disposal of decommissioned offshore installations at meeting of Oslo and Paris Commissions. Opposed by Britain and Norway.
7 July
Norway grants permission to moor Spar in Erfjord while Shell reconsiders options.
12 July
Shell UK commissions independent Norwegian foundation Det Norske Veritas (DNV) to conduct another audit of Spar's contents and investigate Greenpeace allegations.

12–18 July
UK Government makes clear that any new plan for which Shell UK seeks approval, must be at least as good or better than deep-sea disposal on the Best Practicable Environmental Option criteria.
26 August
UK television executives admit to lack of objectivity and balance in coverage of the Spar story, and to using dramatic film footage from Greenpeace which eclipsed the facts.
5 September
Greenpeace admits inaccurate claims that Spar contains 5,550 tonnes of oil and apologises to Shell.
8 September
After a meeting between Dr Chris Fay, Chairman and Chief Executive of Shell UK and Peter Melchett, Executive Director of Greenpeace UK, Greenpeace says it recognizes that Shell UK must work within the legal framework of UK Government policy and the BPEO.
11 September
UK scientists reiterate support for rational, science-based environmental decisions at British Association for the Advancement of Science.
June–October
Shell receives more than 200 proposals for onshore disposal or re-use of Spar.
11 October
Shell Expro outlines new 'Way Forward' to find a solution for Spar disposal or re-use. Notice placed in the Official Journal of the European Communities inviting expressions of interest from major contractors. Their submissions, with the 200 unsolicited proposals, to be analysed to produce a 'Long List' of 20 to 30 organizations then to be asked to meet pre-qualification criteria.
18 October
Det Norske Veritas (DNV) presents results of its independent audit, endorsing the thoroughness and professional competence with which Shell and its consultants prepared the original Spar inventory. DNV confirms that the amount of oil claimed by Greenpeace to be in the Spar was 'grossly overestimated'.
30 November
DNV further report no PCBs (polychlorinated biphenyls) on Brent Spar.

1996

22 March
Shell Expro launch original Brent Spar web site.

22 May
'Scientific Group on Decommissioning Offshore Structures' report published by the Natural Environment Research Council confirming earlier Shell studies that environmental effects of deep-sea disposal of Spar would have been very small and localized.
3 July
Shell announces 'Long List' – 21 leading contractors from eight nations on the challenge to find the BPEO for Brent Spar. Competitors given four weeks to develop outline concepts.

New structural analysis confirms that reversing Spar's original installation procedure to raise it out of the sea for dismantling would be far from straightforward.

Shell outlines how the new Spar Dialogue will help Shell identify a solution by gathering a wide range of views and values.
31 July
Thirty outline proposals for Brent Spar disposal submitted by Long List contractors.
15 August
Shell publishes Long List outline proposals.
1 November
First Brent Spar Dialogue Seminar in London – organised for Shell by the Environment Council, an independent charity which helps different interest groups work together to find common ground.

1997

13 January
Shell announces 'Short List' – six leading international contractors and consortia to develop in detail 11 different ideas for re-using or scrapping Spar.

Short List contractors given four months to complete studies and make detailed commercial bids.
20 February
DNV commissioned to carry out independent evaluation of proposals to ensure technical, safety and environmental aspects of each bid can be compared on a like-for-like basis.
11 March
Brent Spar Dialogue Seminar in Denmark.
9 April
Short List contractors' deadline extended by a month to beginning June.
14–18 April
Brent Spar and the Way Forward a major feature of the British Pavilion at the Hanover Fair in Germany.

30 May
Brent Spar Dialogue Seminar in Rotterdam.
2 June
Six Short List contractors submit nine detailed proposals.
17 June
Shell publishes CD-Rom of proposals with computer animation, interactive maps and video sequences.
13 October
Shell announces Way Forward final stages and DNV publishes independent findings together with contractors' bid prices.
15–28 October
More Brent Spar Dialogue seminars in London, Copenhagen, Rotterdam and Hamburg.
November–January 1998
Shell carries out its final BPEO evaluation.

1998

29 January
Shell announces its choice of solution for Spar – a 'one-off' re-use as a Norwegian Ro/Ro ferry quay.
Decommissioning Plan submitted to UK Government – the first step in gaining approval.
26 August
UK Government announces its approval of Shell Exploration and Production's choice of solution.
25 November
Spar topsides are successfully removed.

1999

10 July
The project is effectively completed when cut and cleaned ring sections of Spar's hull are placed on the seabed at Mekjarvik to form the base of a new quay. Taking into account expenditures related to the initial aborted deep-sea disposal of the spar, the costs total close to $96 million.
1 September
Shell Expro hosts a feedback seminar in London for interested parties and stakeholders providing details of Spar's decommissioning.

Chapter 4

Whistleblowing

The new perspective

Gordon Borrie and Guy Dehn[1]

Whistleblowing – [a] Bringing an activity to a sharp conclusion as if by the blast of a whistle (*Oxford English Dictionary*); [b] Raising a concern about malpractice within an organization or through an independent structure associated with it (*UK Committee on Standards in Public Life*); [c] Giving information (usually to the authorities) about illegal or underhand practices (*Chambers Dictionary*); [d] Exposing to the press a malpractice or cover-up in a business or government office (*US, Brewer's Dictionary*); [e] (*origins*) Police officer summoning public help to apprehend a criminal; referee stopping play after a foul in football.

Introduction

Whistleblowing is relevant to all organizations and all people, not just those few who are corrupt or criminal. This is because every business and every public body faces the risk of things going wrong or of unknowingly harbouring a corrupt individual. Where such a risk arises, usually the first people to realize or suspect the wrongdoing will be those who work in or with the organization. Yet these people, who are best placed to sound the alarm or blow the whistle, often fear they have most to lose if they do.

Unless culture, practice and the law indicate that it is safe and accepted for them to raise a genuine concern about corruption or illegality, workers will assume that they risk victimization, losing their job or damaging their career. Firms and companies aware that a bribe has been solicited will fear not only that they will lose the contract if they do not pay, but that if they blow the whistle their future economic interests will be damaged and their staff will be harassed.

In considering this issue, it may be helpful to bear in mind the approach taken with a criminal who decides to testify in criminal proceedings against his or her former accomplices or colleagues. The authorities in all nation states value such collaborators and will often offer them protection and rewards. This is explained by their role in providing the necessary evidence that helps the police and authorities to secure convictions. However, where a responsible worker or a law-abiding firm blows the whistle on corruption, the best they can hope for seems to be isolation and disapproval. The effect (albeit unintentional) is that someone who informs on corruption which he has participated in will receive more protection and help from the authorities than an innocent colleague or competitor who blows the whistle on the wrongdoing.

In the context of bribery this situation has particular relevance. Unless people are enabled and encouraged to blow the whistle, when a bribe is solicited from them, it is not clear how far the fight against corruption can succeed. Without information from firms about the solicitation of bribes or from workers about corrupt colleagues, the authorities will have to rely on evidence from either the bribe-payer or the bribe-recipient. As these two people will have effectively conspired against the public good, it may be rather optimistic to rely on one of them to 'see the light' and to provide the evidence which will allow the law to be enforced.

The consequence of this culture is that it discourages the great majority of normal, decent people from raising concerns about serious wrongdoing. It also encourages unscrupulous people to use the information for their own advantage and at a time of their own choosing. In this way this culture actually increases the risk of abuse. Malicious workers and aggrieved competitors do already make damaging disclosures. Put simply, they are able to exploit the absence of clear signals about how to blow the whistle properly. Because there is neither a safe procedure nor an accepted way to blow the whistle, they may also maintain that they are justified in communicating false information to the authorities or the media anonymously. With nothing more than anonymous but interesting allegations to go on, the authorities may start investigations and the media are likely to report damaging rumours.

The dilemma

In practical terms, if someone is concerned about corruption or serious wrongdoing in or by an organization, they have three options. These are

- to stay silent;
- to blow the whistle internally or with the responsible person;
- to blow the whistle outside to the authorities or the media;

Silence

Silence is the option of least risk both for the individual worker and for a responsible firm which comes across corruption. It will be attractive for many reasons. The whistleblower will realize that his or her facts could be mistaken or that there may be an innocent explanation. Where colleagues or competitors are also aware of the suspect conduct but stay silent, the whistleblower will wonder why he or she should speak out. In organizations where labour relations are adversarial, and in cultures where corruption is common, the whistleblower is likely to assume that he or she will be expected to prove that the corrupt practice is occurring, rather than see those in authority investigate and deal with the matter. Even though he or she has no control over it, the whistleblower may feel responsibility for any action that may be taken against the wrongdoer. Finally, unless the whistleblower believes there is a good chance that something will be done to address the wrongdoing, it is almost inevitable that he or she will stay silent.

Even if he or she thinks the alarm should be sounded, the whistleblower will want to consider his or her private interests before taking action. Without reassurance to the contrary, the whistleblower will fear reprisals – be it harassment or dismissal. The whistleblower may also suspect (rightly or wrongly) that the corruption involves, implicates or is condoned by more senior people in or outside the organization, in which case he or she will fear the matter will be covered up. Even where these obstacles are overcome or reduced, the whistleblower will fear that he or she will be labelled as disloyal by the generality of colleagues whose respect and trust the whistleblower may want or need in future.

The results of this culture of silence are that:

- responsible employers are denied the opportunity to protect their interests;
- unscrupulous competitors, managers or workers are given reason to believe that 'anything goes';
- society focuses more on compensation and punishment than on prevention and deterrence.

Blowing the whistle internally

Addressing the effects of this culture in the public sector, the UK Committee on Standards in Public Life commented:

> Placing staff in a position where they feel driven to approach the media to ventilate concerns is unsatisfactory both for the staff member and the organization. We observed in our first report that it was far better for systems to be put in place which encouraged staff to raise worries within the organization, yet allowed recourse to the parent

department where necessary. An effective internal system for the raising of concerns should include:

- a clear statement that malpractice is taken seriously in the organization and an indication of the sorts of matters regarded as malpractice;
- respect for the confidentiality of staff raising concerns if they wish, and an opportunity to raise concerns outside the line management structure;
- penalties for making false and malicious allegations;
- an indication of the proper way in which concerns may be raised outside the organization if necessary.[2]

In formulating these recommendations, the committee took account of good practice in the private sector where there has been considerable experience (particularly in the finance industry and in food retail) of providing failsafe reporting channels to senior management. These initiatives started in more competitive markets where there was little doubt that the early reporting of suspected wrongdoing was in the organization's self-interest. The following analogy may be drawn here. Competitive sectors were also the first to gather information from their consumers about how a product or service operates in use. This practice has now been adopted through much of the public sector.

However, the approach many organizations now take to information from workers is similar to the attitude taken towards consumers thirty years ago (that they were troublesome, untrustworthy complainants). This is a mistake since, not only is information from the workforce readily accessible and free to collect, but it enables the organization to put a potential problem right before it causes any real damage to it, its reputation or its stakeholders. The self-interest of the organization in whistleblowing is now being recognized and, recently, a few large firms have begun to use outside advice lines to encourage and reassure staff to raise concerns about wrongdoing. These developments have been given added impetus – particularly in the USA – by legal requirements to demonstrate due diligence, where safety, competition, finance and certain criminal laws have been breached.

Organizations are now beginning to realize the importance of providing an alternative to (but not a substitute for) line management since, without it their managers will have a monopolistic control over the information which goes to those higher up. As with any monopoly, one weak link – be it a corrupt, lazy, sick or incompetent person – will break the communication chain and stop those in charge receiving information which could be critical to the organization.

Blowing the whistle outside

If, however, it is not safe and accepted for people to blow the whistle internally, then we need to turn to the options which exist for those people who consider some action is warranted when they come across corruption. Without a safe internal route, the only option is for them to disclose the matter outside – be it to the authorities or more widely. This is an increasingly important matter since the opportunities for such wider disclosure particularly to the media and public interest groups are likely to be increased with new technology. A relevant example to consider in the context of any anti-corruption measure is where a worker or an audit firm discovers, or reasonably believes, that account books or entries may conceal bribes. If they feel unwilling or unable to blow the whistle internally, the only options they will have are to blow the whistle outside, or to stay silent.

Such outside disclosures raise ethical and legal issues of confidentiality and business secrecy. They also influence the balance of relationships between business, the state and the media. An outside disclosure will involve at the least some regulatory intervention and inconvenience and, at worst, unjustified adverse publicity. This will cause unnecessary damage and disruption to a responsible organization which would have dealt with the matter properly had it been aware of it. As shown above, a culture where – in the absence of safe alternatives – it can be argued that media disclosures are a legitimate first port of call is an open invitation to an aggrieved or malicious person to cause damage, rather than raise the issue responsibly.

In most legal systems, there is no protection for a worker who makes an outside disclosure – even if it is in good faith, justified and reasonable. Accordingly, such disclosures are often made anonymously. This raises a number of issues. Anonymity will be the cloak preferred by a malicious person. It also makes the concern difficult to investigate and even impossible to remedy. Finally, in any event, anonymity is no guarantee that the source of the information will not be deduced. Where the person is identified, the fact that they acted anonymously will often be seen as a sign of bad faith, jeopardizing their position. In the worst cases, such people forfeit their careers. Their plight then attracts media attention, which can only discourage others from sounding the alarm.

The near certainty that an outside disclosure will lead to serious reprisals means that often the matter is not raised until the worker is leaving the organization or the firm has lost the contract. By then the problem may be much worse (indeed the disaster may have happened), the evidence will be old, and the motives of the whistleblower may allow the wrongdoer to distract attention from the corruption. In some cases this delay may also allow the information to be used to damage or even blackmail the organization.

The consequences of the current culture

The implications of the current culture of silence can be far-reaching:

- The failure of officials in the European Commission to respond to the internal whistleblowing of an auditor caused him to disclose his concerns of financial misconduct to the European Parliament. This led to the resignation of the College of Commissioners, and a crisis in confidence in the European Unions.
- The Bingham Inquiry into the corruption at the Bank of Credit and Commerce International found that there was an autocratic environment where neither workers nor firms were willing to voice concerns. This led to new rules in the UK on the duties of auditors and other firms to report suspected irregularities;
- The victims of HIV-contaminated blood products in France complained that the ministers and officials had known of the problem but had said nothing and done nothing. This led to criminal prosecutions against ministers and the resulting public scepticism about attitudes to safety influenced the position the French Government took on the dispute about UK beef imports;
- Two years before Robert Maxwell stole almost $1 billion pension funds, he sacked a union official who had challenged what he was doing with the pension money at a Scottish newspaper. Maxwell, a powerful businessman, was able to ensure that the man could not get another job in the industry, so destroying his career;
- A major leak at the nuclear power station near Tokyo happened because no one questioned poor safety practices based on an unauthorized manual drawn up by a key contractor.[3]

Time and again similar messages come out of official inquiries into major scandals and disasters. They reveal that people who worked in or with the organization had seen the problem but had either been too scared to sound the alarm or had raised the matter in the wrong way or with the wrong person. Quite apart from the tragic human costs and enormous financial damage caused in these cases, they undermine public confidence not only in the organization concerned but also in business and governments more generally. These wider implications are serious. In a changing competitive world, the very success of business, public bodies and new technologies relies on public confidence in their openness and probity.

Whenever there is a scandal or major disaster that could have been averted, there is pressure for new regulatory controls. Although these are aimed at the reckless, they often impose burdens on responsible organizations in the sector, thereby damaging competition. Each disaster also calls into question the mechanisms by which law and society oversee the conduct of private and public bodies. And each successive scandal renews mistrust and scepticism about the role and work of governments and business. The resignation of the European Commission in March 1999 is a case in point. The Committee of Independent Experts remarked that the facts demonstrated 'the value of officials whose conscience persuades them of the need to expose wrongdoings encountered in the course of their duties. They also show how the reaction of superiors failed to live up to legitimate expectations.'[4]

The aims of a whistleblowing culture

The primary aim of a whistleblowing culture is that concerns about corruption and wrongdoing should be properly raised and addressed in the workplace or with the person responsible. Crucially, it sees the whistleblower as a witness, not as a complainant. Where communication channels in organizations are designed for grievances and complaints, that is how they are used by the workforce. In the context of concerns about abuse, it is important to bear in mind that malicious and aggrieved people do already make damaging disclosures when there is no recognized whistleblowing scheme. Recognizing this, a whistleblowing culture should be concerned with the silent majority who think it is not in their interests to blow the whistle on corruption or serious wrongdoing. Drawing on the theory of efficient markets (that competitive forces begin to operate once one-quarter of consumers will consider switching suppliers), a whistleblowing scheme will help organizations and societies deter corruption and wrongdoing where a significant minority of those who now stay silent can be encouraged to see internal whistleblowing as a viable, safe and accepted option.

The main beneficiaries of a culture which disapproves of, and penalizes, people who blow the whistle in good faith are those few corrupt firms and individuals. Knowing that the alarm will not be sounded, they are confident that their wrongdoing (especially if it is corruption or bribery) will go undetected and unpunished. (In any case, when the successful investigation and prosecution of criminal activity outside of the workplace depends overwhelmingly on the information the police receive, it is not clear why the communication of information about wrongdoing in organizations is generally assumed to be undesirable.) Quite apart from people with a predisposed criminal intent, the current culture adversely affects the conduct of the great majority of people. For them the strongest deterrent is the fear of being caught and the shame and embarrassment that goes with it. Where a culture of secrecy and silence exists, some people may be tempted to engage in malpractice because they believe that they will not be caught. Equally, if such a culture exists in a society, then otherwise responsible organizations may feel that they will be at a competitive disadvantage if they do not also pay bribes or engage in illegal practices.

The essentials of a whistleblowing culture

A whistleblowing culture cannot succeed without a strong and clear signal from the very top of the organization that it is against corruption and is resolved to go about its business lawfully. Such a culture will provide assurances against reprisals for whistleblowing on wrongdoing. These will apply even where the whistleblower is mistaken, provided he or she acted honestly and reasonably. In terms of disclosures, such a culture will direct the worker toward seeking impartial advice (be it from unions, lawyers, professional bodies or a designated ethics service) and/or to blowing the whistle internally or with the person responsible. This will help ensure that even if the whistleblower is mistaken, no unwarranted damage is done to the organization or to individuals within it. Critically, it provides a safe and viable alternative to silence.

To be effective, such a system will also provide that where there is good evidence to support the concern, whistleblowing to a designated authority will be protected. This will greatly encourage the organization to reassure the whistleblower that the matter can safely be raised internally. One recent example demonstrates the value of such a provision. When an international bank 'road-tested' a new compliance culture, employees in all cultures said that they did not believe the assurances that they would be protected. The bank then introduced new whistleblowing mechanisms and declared that it would rather concerns were raised with regulators than left unreported.

Such a clear provision will also encourage managers to be receptive to concerns about corruption and to deal with them properly. As importantly, it will reassure those in charge that managers will address the matter properly. It will give a clear indication to the authorities that the organization is seeking to operate responsibly and this will influence the conduct of any investigation that may prove necessary (whether prompted by a whistleblower or not). It will also enable the authorities to readily distinguish reputable organizations from reckless ones. The practical consequences of this provision will be that an organization with a whistleblowing culture will be able to demonstrate that it is fit to regulate itself. Furthermore, it will itself be well placed to notify the authorities of any proven wrongdoing a whistleblower has raised with it.

If such a culture is to maintain the confidence of the wider community, any scheme must also address the particular circumstances in which a wider disclosure may be justified. Essentially this should be an option of last resort and, where reasonable, may include a disclosure to the media. An example of such circumstances would be a flagrant cover-up or the failure by the authorities to deal effectively with a serious issue such as the sexual abuse of children in a care home or the payment of bribes to a senior official or politician. One way forward is to introduce a carefully weighted four-step structure: (1) impartial advice; (2) internal whistleblowing; (3) whistleblowing to the authorities; (4) wider whistleblowing (where appropriate, to the police, victims, shareholders, politicians or the media). Such a structure should also influence the actions of a malicious person as he or she will for the first time have reason not to go direct to the media. If he or she does, society will have good reason to expect the media to look into his or her motives.

Winds of change

For all the above reasons there is growing acceptance of the case for a new approach to whistleblowing. With the changing nature of employment, globalization and the increased flow of information, there is also a recognition that the traditional approach of trust and confidentiality in the workplace cannot be relied upon to operate as it did through the twentieth century. While trust and confidence is of critical importance in any community or organization, to be effective it cannot be blind or unquestioning. Whistleblowing cultures which emphasize internal reporting are a means by which the abuse of trust and confidence can be checked and by which asymmetrical accountabilities of those within the workplace can be understood and developed. If the organization is prepared to promote and implement such a culture, any risk of it being hijacked by petty vendettas will be minimized, if not removed.

This approach sees whistleblowing as a means to deter wrongdoing, promote transparency and good governance, underpin self-regulation and maintain public confidence. It is the approach which has been put on a legislative footing in the UK and in South Africa in recent years.[5] These laws differ somewhat from the protection offered in the USA, which has had whistleblowing legislation for over a century offering substantial rewards to employees. While other provisions in the USA are rooted in the concepts of freedom of expression, and those in Australia and New Zealand are concerned with ethics in the public sector, these recent developments in the UK and South Africa address the issue of accountability across all institutions.

Essentially, the new approach sees whistleblowing as a means to deliver good management, to maintain public confidence and to promote organizational accountability. These help everyone identify who is accountable for what and to whom. While this has secured strong support from business, unions and professional interests, it would be misleading to suggest that the underlying principles are anything new. Based on ethical provisions recognized by many religions, the principles were adopted and developed into a balanced and practical approach in jurisprudence. Such judge-made laws recognize both the public interest in maintaining confidences and the particular circumstances where whistleblowing disclosures outside can be justified. Like race and sex discrimination laws, the pre-eminent aim of the UK initiatives has been to declare a change in culture. The resulting legislation was commended by one of the most senior UK judges for 'so skilfully achieving the essential but delicate balance between the public interest and the interest of employers'.[6] It seeks to embed a system where, in the words of independent experts called in by the European Union, 'the duty of loyalty and discretion should not become an empty concept, but neither must it be used to install a conspiracy of silence'.[7] This UK approach has also been commended by both management and labour interests at the OECD, who have recommended that it is fed into the forthcoming revisions to the Anti-Bribery Convention.[8]

Notes

1 Gordon (now Lord) Borrie and Guy Dehn were, respectively, the founding chairman and director of Public Concern at Work, an independent UK charity which addresses ethics, accountability and whistleblowing. More information about the charity's activities (including details of the UK legislation and *Third Report*, July 1997, p. 49) are available on its website at *www.pcaw.co.uk*.
2 UK Committee on Standards in Public Life, *Second Report*, May 1996, p. 22.
3 *Asia Week*, 19 November 1999, commented that Japanese culture deprecates whistleblowing yet seems to condone the resignation or even suicide of top executives when unchecked wrongdoing leads to major disaster.
4 The Committee of Independent Experts, *Second Report*, para. 7.6.9.
5 The Public Interest Disclosure Act, 1998, provides protection against reprisals for good faith whistleblowing on wrongdoing. It directs the worker toward seeking confidential advice and to blowing the whistle internally or with the person responsible. Provided there is good evidence to support the concern, it also protects (a) whistleblowing to designated authorities and (b) wider whistleblowing where both the circumstances justify it (cover-up, victimization or failure to address the matter) and the particular disclosure is reasonable (having regard to the recipient of the disclosure, seriousness, risk, obligations of confidence and the employer's whistleblowing culture). The Protected Disclosures Act, 2000, creates a similar regime in South Africa.
6 Lord Nolan, who had also chaired the Committee on Standards in Public Life.
7 See note 8, para 7.6.10. The European Commission's proposals were published in Feb 2000.
8 See OECD Labour/Management Programme – PAC/AFF/LMP(2000)1. This chapter is a revised version of the discussion paper set out in that report, originally published under the title 'Whistleblowing to combat corruption', PAC/AFF/LMP (2000)1, copyright OECD, 2000.
It can also be found at *www.whistleblower.org/www/oecdreport.htm*.

Chapter 5

The Rick and Bianca case history[1]

Rick and Bianca work in a regional accounts office of a major company, which supplies services to businesses throughout the UK. A year ago Bianca noticed what she considered to be a flaw in the calculation and billing process. She checked this with Rick, a colleague, who agreed that customers were being routinely overcharged.

Once they had collected the data they met with the regional manager, David. He did not seem too concerned, though he said he would look at the evidence. He knew that Rick had a long history of complaining about everything and that few of his colleagues liked working with him. He couldn't understand why the company had not got rid of him.

Rick and Bianca left the meeting disheartened and annoyed. They were not confident that the issue would be taken seriously and Rick said that they couldn't trust David because, if the overcharging was corrected, he and the other senior managers would lose their performance-related bonuses.

Whilst the matter was being looked into, Rick and Bianca were suddenly transferred to two different offices. Bianca accepted the move. Rick was livid. He made an appointment with the Chief Executive of the company, Adrian, who reacted swiftly to the allegation and asked the Head of Internal Audit to make an investigation. Within a week his report showed that the problem existed nationally and urgent plans were made to develop a new billing system.

When Rick and Bianca learned of the changes from the Chief Executive, Rick demanded that they should be returned to their previous post and rewarded, and that David should be disciplined. The company responded, saying that Jan, Head of Personnel, would review their posting, that they did not give rewards and that, if they took any disciplinary action against David, it was a private matter and did not concern Rick and Bianca.

During Jan's review of their postings, Rick commented that if the company did not do right by him it wouldn't be the last they heard about the matter. However, Jan decided that Rick and Bianca should stay where they were – she knew it would be a disaster if they went back to work with

David. She gave assurances that they would not be victimized and that their careers would not suffer in any way. Bianca was unhappy with the company's responses, but she didn't want to take things further. However, Rick thought their attitude was unacceptable. He then wrote to Adrian asking if the company would refund all of its customers who had been overcharged. Adrian's reply simply said that the company had taken appropriate action and that it did not have to answer to Rick. Rick, who estimates that the company has wrongly profited by about £1 million, has told Bianca that they should warn the company that unless things are sorted out they will go to the press.

Notes

1 This case history has been contributed by Public Concern at Work.

Chapter 6

Challenger Flight 51-L

A case history in whistleblowing

Simon Robinson

> For a successful technology, reality must take precedence over public relations, for nature cannot be fooled.
>
> (R.P. Feynman, member of the Presidential Commission on the *Challenger* Disaster)

Challenger flight 51-L was the tenth launch of the *Challenger* series, the first launch from Cape Kennedy Launch Complex 39-B. Though this case history focuses on the *Challenger* flight which ended tragically some 73 seconds into its flight on 28 January 1986, it is more to do with the whole National Space Transportation System – the 24 launches prior to this one and the ones scheduled after it. The *Challenger* was simply part of a programme that summed up the technological capacity of the United States. The programme as a whole was built on a series of myths, social, technical and managerial, which sustained the national and political interest and made management as well as politicians believe that over-ambitious targets were feasible. In fact the whole programme remained essentially experimental, with many threats to safety involved. Hence, safety should have been at a premium. The safety programme, however, was gradually eroded in the face of the many economic and political pressures, and the management structure did not encourage managers or engineers to state or press their concerns about safety. At various points these concerns were expressed, but their implications were not taken seriously by the management, and the critical issues were never addressed.

This case history will first outline the facts of the case. Then it will examine the various points at which the whistle might have been blown, drawing out the different perspectives of the people involved and also the implications for the practice of whistleblowing. Finally, it will note the conclusions of the Presidential Commission, with recommendations for a more transparent management system which would encourage whistle-blowing.

The space shuttle: National Space Transport System

On 9 August 1972 authority was given to proceed with the orbiter space shuttle project. The delta wing space shuttles *Columbia*, *Challenger* and *Discovery* had originally been given a sleek design. This was replaced to accommodate a huge payload bay for the needs of the US Air Force, which had been ordered to use the shuttle, instead of its own expendable rockets, for launching satellites.

In 1972 Morton-Thiokol Industries (MTI) were awarded the contract to build the solid rocket boosters for the shuttle, and in 1974 NASA accepted their design, a larger version of the successful Titan missile. The solid rocket booster (SRB) provided the thrust that was critical to taking the shuttle out of the earth's gravitational pull. Solid fuel of this kind produces more thrust per pound than liquid counterparts. The drawback of such power, however, is that, once engaged, it cannot be turned off or even controlled, hence the need for careful design.

One booster was attached to each side of the external fuel tank. They were 149 feet long and 12 feet in diameter. Each weighed two million pounds before lift-off. The rocket fuel was cast into separate segments of the SRB at the MTI plant in Utah and transported to Kennedy Space Center where the complete SRB was assembled. The joints where the different segments were brought together were known as field joints and these were critical to the safety of the booster. They consisted of two elements, the tang and the clevis. These were held together by clevis pins and each was sealed by two rubber O-rings, the primary (bottom) and the secondary (top). A second O-ring was a modification from the Titan missiles design because humans would be going into orbit in the shuttle. The point of O-rings was to prevent the escape of hot combustion gases from the rocket. To secure this, a heat-resistant putty was applied to the inner section of the joint. To ensure that the gap between tang and clevis was minimized, and thus to ensure compression on the O-ring, shims were inserted between the outer part of the clevis and tang.

Engineering design problems

The size of any gap in the field joint was determined by many possible things including:

- the ambient temperature;
- the diameter of the O-rings;
- the thickness of the shims;
- loads on the segment.

When the SRB was ignited the zinc chromate putty, which was above the O-rings, was displaced. This had the effect of compressing the air between the putty and the primary O-ring. The O-ring was then forced by the air into the gap between tang and clevis. However, it was discovered that the pressure then caused the walls of the cylinder to bulge slightly, which caused a gap to open, increasing the risk of the gases escaping at the joint. This was known as joint rotation.

In discussion with NASA, MTI set about altering the design so as to increase the O-ring compression and thus decrease the joint rotation effect. This led to three things: tightening the metal joints; increasing the O-ring diameter and tightening its tolerance; and the use of shims, as noted above.

After the flight of the second *Challenger* mission (November 1981) a further problem occurred. The O-rings were eroding during the flight, due to the hot gases escaping past the putty. The solution was found in providing different kinds of putty.

Of greater concern was a third problem, found in the shuttle flight 51-C (24 January 1985). This flight was launched in extreme cold. Examination of the SRB joints after this flight showed black soot and grease on the outside of the casing, caused by the gas blowing through. This led to the development of the Seal Erosion Task Team to study the compression and reliability of the O-ring in low temperatures. In July of that year a new design for the joint was being developed, and MTI ordered new steel billets which would be used in the redesigning. The process of making these billets was a long one and by 26 January 1986, the launch of the *Challenger* 51-L, they were not ready.

Launch delays to *Challenger* 51-L

There were several initial delays to the *Challenger* 51-L mission. The first three arose because of the possibility of rain and low temperatures. The US Vice President was also expected at one launch attempt and it was determined that he should not be invited unnecessarily, not least because he was an important ally for the project and NASA were concerned to maintain goodwill.

A further launch attempt was delayed because of a defective microswitch in the hatch locking mechanism and difficulties in using the hatch handle. Once that problem was solved, winds had become too high, and record low temperatures were expected in the Florida area.

The social context of the *Challenger* launch

The delays in the launch had made NASA all the more keen to launch the *Challenger* as soon as possible. There were other pressing and significant reasons:

1 NASA had experienced unexpected competition from the European Space Agency. This meant that the Space Transportation System's commercial viability and cost effectiveness needed to be firmly established. NASA's response was to schedule a record number of missions for 1986 to make a case for the project's budget.
2 NASA needed a speedy launch so that they could refurbish the launch pad for their next mission, a probe to examine Halley's comet. If this was launched on time then it would have gathered data before a similar Russian attempt.
3 There may also have been pressure to ensure that the *Challenger* was in orbit when President Reagan gave his State of the Union speech. One of the major topics was to be education and he was going to mention the first civilian in space, teacher Christa McAuliffe, who was one of the *Challenger*'s crew. McAuliffe had become a significant celebrity, with Americans able to identify with the first 'ordinary hero in space'.

As we shall see, other factors emerged in the discussion before the launch.

The night before launch: the teleconference

The temperature for the rescheduled launch date was forecast as the low 20s°F. This led Alan McDonald, the management representative of MTI at Kennedy Space Center, to direct his engineers to make a presentation on the effects of low temperature on the performance of the SRB. A teleconference was arranged to discuss this. It was held between management and engineers from the Kennedy Space Center, the Marshall Space Flight Center in Alabama (responsible for the propulsion system) and MTI in Utah.

Roger Boisjoly and Arnie Thompson, two of the engineers at MTI who had been involved in the Seal Erosion Task Team, had only a short time to prepare their presentation but saw this as an opportunity to put across their concerns about the SRB O-rings. In their hour-long presentation, they concluded that the expected low temperatures would aggravate the problems of joint rotation and the O-rings. The lowest temperature previously experienced by the O-rings had been 53°F in the January 1985 flight. The predicted ambient temperature was 26°F, placing the estimated temperature of the O-rings at 29°F.

The Engineering Vice President of MTI (Utah), Bob Lund, then summed up the conclusions and recommendations. He stressed that there was no empirical evidence about the effect of temperatures below 53°F. They could not prove that it was unsafe to launch the *Challenger* at lower temperatures. However, given that the predicted temperature was outside their database, he recommended a delay of the launch until the ambient temperature had risen to 53°F.

The presentation and recommendations confused NASA managers and engineers. They believed that the design specifications allowed for operation of the SRB in temperatures as low as 31°F (as will be seen, it was later to emerge that MTI believed that the 31°F limit was for storage and not operation).

Larry Mulloy, Marshall's Solid Rocket Booster Project Manager, then challenged the engineers' reasoning, arguing that the data was not conclusive. After several minutes of heated debate, Mulloy turned to Joe Kilminster, MTI Vice President for booster rockets. Mulloy said that he was looking for a management decision, without specifying what this meant. Kilminster stood by his engineers' recommendations. Several of the managers at Marshall expressed their doubts. At this point Kilminster called for a meeting with his MTI colleagues, away from the teleconference, to review the data.

At this separate meeting, Boisjoly and Thompson argued that they should stick with their original recommendations. Jerald Mason, a senior executive of MTI, argued that a management decision was required. The managers concluded from the given data that the O-rings could be eroded by up to a third of their diameter and still operate. Mason finally turned to Lund and said, 'take your engineering hat off and put on your management hat'.[1]

The result was that a new recommendation was then presented to the reconvened teleconference. This stated that the cold was still a concern for safety, but that they had found the original evidence to be inconclusive and that their 'engineering assessment' was that the launch should go ahead. This recommendation was presented even though the engineers had no part in rewriting it and refused to sign it. Surprised at this *volte-face,* Alan McDonald, the MTI representative at NASA in this conference, appealed to the NASA management not to launch. However, they decided to approve the SRBs for launch, even though the predicted temperature was below even their original operational specifications.

The launch

That night temperatures were even lower than forecast, at 8°F. To keep the water pipes on the launch pad from freezing, safety showers and fire hoses were turned on. Some of this water accumulated, forming ice over the platform. The ice inspection team feared that this might break away from the platform and damage the heat-resistant tiles of the shuttle. A further worrying and uncertain factor was the possibility of ice forming in the O-ring grooves. The *Challenger*, the SRBs and the external fuel tank had all been on the launch pad for 38 days, and, up to the freeze, seven inches of rain had fallen. Nonetheless, the launch director decided to go ahead. Key personnel, who did not know about the teleconference or the fears of the MTI engineers, waived safety limitations on low temperatures.

When the launch came, the impact of ignition caused a shower of ice from the platform. Some of this made contact with the left-hand SRB and some was sucked into its nozzle. Shortly before lift-off, 0.678 seconds into the flight, photographs clearly show a burst of grey smoke emerging from the area of the aft field joint on the SRB, the area which faced the external fuel tank. This already showed that there was 'not complete sealing action within the joint'.[2] The putty which protected the O-rings had collapsed. The cold had made it too stiff, allowing gases from the ignited solid fuel, with temperatures of over 5,000°F, to blow past both O-rings. Between 0.836 and 2.500 seconds into the flight there were eight more distinctive bursts of smoke. The black colour and dense composition of the smoke seemed to confirm that the grease joint insulation and O-rings were being burned. Soon after the tower had been cleared the smoke stopped, indicating that the oxides produced by the propellant had temporarily sealed the field-joint gap before flames could escape.

At 37 seconds the *Challenger* was hit by the first of several high altitude wind shears (winds of different speeds and directions close together which lead to severe stress on aircraft). The steering mechanisms responded to the buffeting, leading eventually to an increase in the SRB thrust. The first small flame at the field joint was shown at 58.788 seconds, indicating a breakdown of the temporary seal. At 59 seconds the most violent wind shear of any shuttle mission was experienced. At 59.26 the small flame grew into well-defined plumes and the breakdown of the seal was confirmed when telemetry showed a pressure differential between chamber pressures in the right- and left-hand SRBs. As the flame increased in size it was deflected directly on to the external fuel tank. At 64.660 seconds the colour and shape of the flame changed markedly, indicating that it was mixing with hydrogen leaking from the tank.

Within 45 milliseconds a bright glow developed on the underside of the *Challenger* itself. At 72.20 seconds the lower strut which linked the *Challenger*'s SRB and the external fuel tank gave way and the right SRB began to rotate around the upper strut. At 73.126 seconds, the after-dome of the fuel tank gave way, releasing huge amounts of liquid hydrogen. The subsequent forward thrust pushed the tank up into the lower part of the liquid oxygen tank, leading to 'structural failure'. At 73.137 there was an explosive burn of hydrogen and oxygen that enveloped the *Challenger*.

The effect on the American nation was profound and the President immediately ordered a commission, chaired by Senator Rogers, to investigate the technical and other contributing causes of the accident, and to make recommendations.

Analysis

Different managers and engineers at different points were presented with key moments when the safety programme of the shuttle might have been challenged:

- at the very beginning of the programme, when priorities were being established;
- during the work of the Seal Erosion Task Team;
- during the teleconference on the eve of the launch;
- after the teleconference and before the launch.

The safety programme

The shuttle's field joints were one of 700 items on board of criticality 1. This means that there was no back-up for them, and thus that any failure could lead to loss of life. The project was by definition experimental. NASA historian Alex Roland sums this up well:

> The American taxpayer bet about $14 billion dollars on the shuttle. NASA bet its reputation. The Air Force bet its reconnaissance capability. The astronauts bet their lives. We all took a chance. When John Young and Robert Crippen climbed aboard the orbiter *Columbia* on April 12, 1981 for the first shuttle launches, they took a bigger chance than any astronaut before them. Never had Americans been asked to go on a launch vehicle's maiden voyage. Never had astronauts ridden solid propellant rockets. Never had Americans depended on an engine untested in flight.[3]

Hence, safety had to be a paramount concern for the project. However, from the word go, safety was not seen as the highest priority. Initial work on the shuttle itself, for instance, had involved consideration of the possibility of an escape mechanism for the astronauts should the mission be aborted soon after take-off, the time of greatest risk. It was decided against this because the payload of the shuttle needed to be maximized. How should engineers or managers have responded to this early statement of priorities?

The low priority of safety was also reflected in the lack of an independent safety system and procedures which could be appealed to in the face of the drive to launch. There had been an extensive safety programme for the lunar project, but this had been downgraded, leading to reductions in safety and quality assurance work in Marshall and NASA headquarters. Indeed safety work was placed under the supervision of the very organizations that had to be checked. Requirements for reporting problems were not clear or concise and failed to get critical information to the appropriate levels of management at NASA.

In this specific case, the weather-related problems, such as the ice formation before the *Challenger* launch, were increasingly ignored, and protocols about constraints to launch, or waivers of such constraints, were not taken seriously. Whilst the ice on the platform was not thought to contribute to the 51-L disaster itself, it could have compromised safety, not least if the launch had been aborted before take-off, requiring the astronauts to escape via the platform.

Once the problems with the O-rings emerged, the response was not well documented or worked through. For instance, no significant trend analysis was performed on the O-ring erosion and other joint problems. Five weeks after the 51-L accident itself, the issues to do with the field joint were still not properly documented in the reporting system at Marshall.

In fact, no one spoke out about the lack of attention to safety or the erosion of the safety standards that were in place. The overriding pressure to keep up with the shuttle programme dominated management thinking. Another reason why there was no clear whistleblowing at this early stage was the lack of transparency in management. As we shall see, no person or group in the project was able to see the whole safety picture, even at the top of management. A further reason, perhaps, was simply that no crises had occurred, thus lulling the management into a sense of false safety. The 51-L disaster was the first real setback.

The Seal Erosion Task Team

Faced with some clear problems, not least the fact that eight out of ten of the *Challenger* SRBs had suffered a problem with their O-rings, Boisjoly and his engineering colleagues were the first to raise the issue of safety in a significant way. In 1985 Boisjoly had written in one memo that the result of neglecting this problem 'would be a catastrophe of the highest order – loss of human life' (memo to Vice President, Engineering, 31 July 1985).[4] The memo had a limited distribution. Nonetheless, it resulted in NASA asking for a breakdown of the problems and in the setting up of the Seal Erosion Task Team, headed up by Boisjoly and another MTI engineer, Bob Ebeling.

The team, however, did not work well. Far from providing a speedy resolution to the problem, it led to further delays. Ebeling wrote in one memo 'HELP! The seal task force is constantly being delayed by every possible means ... This is a red flag.'[5] Boisjoly wrote of the team experiencing 'business as usual from the supporting organizations'.[6] By this he meant that management as a whole did not understand the importance of the task team's project, and that bureaucracy was leading to constant delays. At one point, requests for spare parts had to go through eight different offices. The last report sent by Boisjoly, highlighting the delays, received no reply from management.

Boisjoly did many of the things recommended to whistleblowers. He kept good records of his interaction with management, and was clear about the possible consequences of ignoring the O-ring problem. He ensured that all memos were circulated to his direct superiors. However, he and his colleagues were not ready for the less than positive response from management. When there was no feedback towards the end of the team's work they did not press the point or seek to clarify if their managers or NASA had understood. This may have reflected a concern for their own careers or a belief that the ultimate responsibility for dealing with the erosion problem was not theirs but their superiors.

Underlying the work of the Seal Erosion Task Team and the problems about delays was the more fundamental issue that the team was dealing with a design fault and that such a fault should have led to the recommendation that the shuttle programme be suspended until it was dealt with. NASA engineers realized that there was a problem and for a time worked with the task team. However, the problem was still defined in terms of the need to speed up the delivery of the new design rather than as an essential matter of safety. One of the difficulties was that the response of the NASA engineers seemed to indicate that NASA had heard Boisjoly's complaints. In fact, the presence of the NASA engineers did not mean that the issues were being communicated to NASA managers. Indeed, the essential matter of safety remained unacknowledged by NASA management, who even claimed to the Presidential Commission that they were not aware of the problems.

In all of this the MTI engineers remained firmly within their own system relying on their managers to communicate any problems to NASA. This in itself may have led to unclear communication. At no point were they encouraged by their organization either to go beyond their line managers within MTI or to go outside to key personnel in NASA. Equally, they had nowhere that they could go to discuss the implications of the problem, or to discuss the engineering data and consider what other evidence might be needed. For their part, there was no attempt by NASA to see matters globally, or to check out thoroughly the nature of the complaints that were emerging from the MTI engineers.

What more could the MTI engineers have done at this point? How might the MTI management have best handled the material coming from them? How could NASA have best kept itself better informed about this aspect of the project safety?

The problem in the flow of information meant that the case which the engineers had to make was never fully communicated, indeed was never fully made, something which came to the fore in the teleconference itself.

The teleconference

All involved in the shuttle programme were aware of its high profile and the consequent pressure to achieve targets. There was also economic pressure, with some in the Reagan administration suggesting that turning the operation over to an airline would make it more efficient. NASA had to ensure that the programme was successful and also that it could pay for itself. In turn, this put pressure on Rockwell (the firm responsible for the development and maintenance of the shuttle itself) and on MTI. The result was a strong incentive for managers to think and plan unrealistically. As far back as 1982 NASA had begun a planned acceleration of the launch schedule. An early plan looked to an eventual launch rate of one per week. In 1985 this had been reduced to a projected annual rate of 24 by 1990. Even this modified goal was over-ambitious, leading to difficulties, including:

- a critical shortage of spare parts;
- a strain on the IT production system which meant that it would not have been able to deliver crew training software for scheduled flights by due date. This in turn would have meant inadequate time for crew training;
- no enforcement of cargo manifest policies, leading to numerous payload changes at the last minute.

The Presidential Commission underlined how this had affected attention to safety:

> When flights come in rapid succession, current requirements do not ensure that critical anomalies occurring in one flight are identified and addressed appropriately before the next flight.[7]

It was precisely this tension which came to a head in the teleconference. Up to that point the engineers had communicated largely through internal memos to their direct superiors. However, the reality of the design fault and the need, as the Presidential Commission noted, to stop the shuttle programme until the safety factors had been resolved, were not really heard or believed at any level of management. MTI did not accept the implication of early tests that noted 'a serious and unanticipated design flaw'.[8] NASA did not accept the view of its engineers that the design was unacceptable. NASA minimized the field-joint problems in their briefings and reports. MTI's position was that ' the condition is not desirable but is acceptable'.[9]

The result was, in the words of Commission member Feynman, a 'kind of Russian roulette' in which standards of safety were gradually lowered.

The shuttle flies with O-ring erosion and nothing happens, 'Then it is suggested that the risk is no longer so high for the next flights.'[10]

None of this was based on thoroughly researched evidence. On the contrary, as the Presidential Commission found, prior to the accident neither NASA, MTI managers nor engineers fully understood the mechanism by which the field joint was sealed. The Commission also discovered a massive discrepancy between the engineers' and management's view of safety margins. Engineers estimated a shuttle failure rate of 1 in 100 launches. NASA management had figures of 1 in 100,000. When the NASA figures were questioned by the Commission, the response of their chief engineer was 'We did not use them as a management tool. We knew that the possibility of failure was always sitting there.'[11] This leaves the unanswered question as to how their figure was arrived at. As to the use of such figures, it seems that they were submitted in response to a risk analysis for the Department of Energy, the aim of which was to calculate the safety of the use of small atomic reactors as power sources for deep-space probes, which the shuttle could carry into space. The next mission of the *Challenger* was scheduled to carry the *Galileo* probe, with 47.6 pounds of plutonium-238.

The NASA figures were, in Feynman's words, exaggerated 'to the point of fantasy', and were part of a dynamic which led to a reversal of the usual view of safety. NASA management even argued that the fact that a third of the O-rings had been eroded and yet the shuttle had still flown, demonstrated a 'safety factor of three'. No one involved in the Commission could understand what this phrase meant, given that erosion of a seal indicates a diminution of safety by a third, not a safety margin of three.

This confusion was carried through into the teleconference. Though there was a correlation between O-ring damage and low temperature neither NASA nor MTI had carried out extensive tests in temperatures below 53°F. The engineers had not had the time or resources to prove conclusively that it would be unsafe to fly the shuttle precisely because this would have needed the shuttle programme to be suspended. Hence, NASA and MTI were not fully prepared to evaluate the risks of the launch in conditions more severe than they had experienced before. Boisjoly, Thompson and McDonald could all have argued strongly, on the basis of the initial correlation, that the flight should be delayed. But they did not have a case tested at all temperatures.

The response of the NASA and Marshall managers and engineers to Boisjoly's presentation was fourfold. First, there was hostility, doubtless because of a series of delays, and because of the pressure they were experiencing, not least in virtue of the State of the Union speech planned for that day. Second, they questioned the engineers' figures. NASA engineers questioned the temperature figures, believing that the original design specification was for temperatures as low as 31°F. The extent of confusion was to emerge later when MTI argued that the temperature of 31°F was the limit for storage and not operation. Either way the actual temperature at the time of launch was below this. Third, along the same lines, the NASA managers focused on the lack of absolute evidence over safety, and on the fact that previous O-rings had already been eroded by a third, without compromising safety. Finally, it was later argued that the MTI engineers were not unanimous in their findings.

Thus the MTI engineers found themselves suddenly having to prove that the *Challenger* was unsafe to fly at low temperatures. As Lund in his testimony to the Commission noted:

> We have dealt with Marshall for a long time and have always been in the position of defending our position to make sure that we were ready to fly, and I guess I did not realize until after that meeting and after several days that we had absolutely changed our position ... And so we got ourselves into the thought process, we were trying to find some way to prove to them it wouldn't work, and we were unable to do that.[12]

So the MTI engineers had been sucked into a situation in which the discussion was focusing purely on the feasibility of the launch and not upon the issue of safety procedures *per se*. This meant that they had to defend their judgement in a limited area with inadequate data, rather than approaching management with a concern which would then have had to be investigated and tested. Hence, there was no one to stand out for the principle of 'safety first', something all the more remarkable given that the American Board for Engineering and Technology Code states that the 'safety, health, and welfare of the public shall be paramount'.[13]

This raises major questions about responsibility, which in turn point to differences in the roles of engineers and management. Lund was both an engineer and manager and when the manager Mason invited him to wear his 'management hat' this implied very different responsibilities. Harris *et al.* suggest that engineers are more traditionally concerned with risk–benefit analysis and management with cost–benefit analysis.[14] Mason appears to have taken this further when he invited Lund to discount the questions of risk raised by the MTI engineers, and to think primarily of cost–benefit.

From the management perspective, another consideration might have been the fact that MTI's contract with NASA was up for renewal. The Presidential Commission was more direct, concluding that MTI had altered its original decision 'to accommodate a major customer'.[15]

Whatever the final judgement on that point, it is clear that managers and engineers had come to a critical point in decision-making without reaching any agreement, not only on safety procedures but also on the criteria of standards for safety in the first place. By being drawn into the particular issue of the launch, the engineers allowed themselves to be deflected from a defence of the key principle – above all do no harm. Without a clear focus on that fundamental issue any attempt to blow the whistle could have had little success.

Once this responsibility divide was crossed, the decision was taken away from the engineers. Whose responsibility then was it to maintain safety? What could the MTI engineers have done at the point where they and MTI management were discussing the matter away from the teleconference? Was their disagreement fully communicated to NASA? Is it morally acceptable for an engineer or another employee to make a case about safety and then pass the responsibility for outcome to the management involved?

Before the launch

The impression given in this case is that once the teleconference had ended the die was cast. However, this was far from the case. Both managers and engineers could have blown the whistle up to the point of the final minutes of countdown. Initially, this might have involved going to the MTI board. But a simpler route would have been to communicate directly with Arnold Aldrich of NASA, who had ultimate responsibility for deciding to launch. He expressly encouraged any key personnel to contact him at any time before the launch.

So what more could the MTI engineers in Utah and the MTI management representatives at NASA have done to communicate their unease? The basic problem appears to have been that the management system worked against such open communication. The decision-making process was very complex and fragmented, with different sites and different levels of decision-making. Lawrence Mulloy, for instance, represented Marshall Space Flight Center at the Kennedy Space Center. He therefore acted as the conduit for information about the SRBs to NASA launch staff. However, he did not tell Arnold Aldrich about the details of the teleconference because he was at level III and Aldrich at level II of decision-making.

This system encouraged those at level III to solve problems and make decisions, without sharing the full discussion behind their reasoning with those at levels II and I. Hence, the Presidential Commission was troubled 'by what appears to be a propensity of management at Marshall to contain potentially serious problems and to attempt to resolve them internally rather than communicate them forward'.[16] This propensity was 'altogether at odds with the need for Marshall to function as part of a system working towards successful flights missions, interfacing and communicating with the other parts of that system which work to that end'.[17] In effect, the management system encouraged both narrow thinking, concentrating purely on a limited area of responsibility and not seeing the broader connections, and also secretive thinking, not sharing difficulties which might cause problems, or require major work, for the next level of management. This, in turn, led to a lack of transparency, and with it to lack of concern about critical safety procedures which higher management were not kept abreast of. Hence, for instance, there was no system that ensured that launch constraints and waivers of launch constraints should be considered at all levels of management. As noted earlier, this led to six launch constraints (including adverse weather) being waived before the launch of 51-L, with no record being held of either the constraints or the waivers.

Not only did the system of management for the *Challenger* clearly discourage whistleblowing, but it was also at the root of most of the problems. The system encouraged unrealistic planning, and with that the growth of myths about what was possible and yet consistent with safety being maintained. Greater transparency, with proper checks and balances, would have tested these views.

The case history also raises the issue of perceptions of responsibility. The fragmentation of decision-making led to different parts of the organization focusing purely on their areas of responsibility, and thus not feeling responsible for safety as a whole. The Presidential Commission, and subsequent reports, stressed that all levels of management should feel responsibility for safety, and not simply leave it to one designated group. At the same time, they argued for a change in system and ethos that would ensure transparency and encourage whistleblowing. The Commission concluded that safety would have to have greater priority and that this required that an independent safety group be set up. This would deal with safety organization and hazard analysis. The Commission also recommended greater oversight from the project manager, with all parts of the project accountable to him and not simply to particular centre managers. In addition there is now an anonymous reporting scheme for employees on the NASA project.

What this case history draws attention to is the irony that, in a situation that was under so much scrutiny from the public, scrutiny actually undermined safety. This was because the management structure in the key organizations was fragmented and divisive, leading to crucial safety data not being collected or properly appreciated. That, in turn, underlines the critical importance of seeing the question of whistleblowing as not simply a matter to be addressed in terms of individual dilemmas. The question of whistleblowing is something that organizations as a whole should take responsibility for.

Notes

1 Cited in C. Harris, M. Pritchard and M. Rabins (1995) *Engineering Ethics: Concepts and Cases*, New York: Wadsworth, p. 72.
2 *Report of the Presidential Commission on the Space Shuttle Challenger Accident* (PCP) (1986), Washington, DC: US Government Printing Office, p. 3.
3 Cited in Martin, M. and Schinzinger, R. (1989) *Ethics in Engineering*, New York: McGraw–Hill, p. 79.
4 Boisjoly, R. *The Challenger Disaster* (wysiwwyg://41/http://onlineethics.org/moral/boisjoly/RB-intro.html).
5 Cited in Martin and Shinzinger (1989), *op cit.*, p. 86.
6 Internal report 4 October 1985.
7 PCP, 14.
8 *Ibid.*
9 Cited in PCP, 12.
10 PCP, Appendix E 3.
11 Cited in Martin and Schinzinger (1989), *op. cit.*, p. 83.
12 Cited in Harris *et al.* (1995), *op. cit.*, pp. 285–6.
13 Robinson, S. and Dixon, R. (1997) 'The professional engineer: virtues and learning', *Science and Engineering Ethics* 3(3): 340.
14 Harris *et al.* (1995), *op. cit.*, pp. 274 ff.
15 PCP, 11.
16 *Ibid.*
17 *Ibid.*

Chapter 7

Pain and partnership

John Edmonds

Human beings have an amazing ability, which is sometimes admirable and sometimes depressing, to focus on a single objective to the exclusion of all other thoughts and feelings. A group of volunteers were recruited to take part in a research project apparently to establish how people react to electric shocks. Behind a screen were the victims, who jumped as the volunteers administered each successive shock. The volunteers were told that the voltage levels should be steadily increased during the course of the project.

In fact, the 'victims' were not receiving electric shocks at all. The real aim of the experiment was to establish the point at which volunteers would say, 'I have had enough. I do not believe that I should be causing this pain.' In the event, the volunteers continued with their task in committed fashion. Whatever the apparent level of suffering, the volunteers followed their instructions and kept throwing the switches.[1]

I was interested in this experiment because there are many parallels with what is going on throughout British industry. Perfectly ordinary people, acting as managers, are able to suspend the operation of their consciences to administer policies which are extremely unpleasant. The difference is that in real life there is no pretence. The pain is real.

Global competition

In British industry, the received wisdom is that companies face intense global competition and that only the best will survive. To be the best, a company needs low costs; the ability to adapt very rapidly to change; and a workforce which is highly flexible. In this environment, the theory goes, high levels of job security are unthinkable and the labour market must be deregulated so that managers have the ability to make whatever changes are necessary to improve competitiveness. The disadvantage suffered by employees is regretted but is essentially irrelevant; improved performance within the terms of the system is the overriding objective.

Once the threat of global competition is accepted, low pay can be justified by reference to pressure from competitors in low-wage countries.

Redundancies can be justified on the same basis. People with bad sickness records must be eased out because companies cannot carry passengers. Extensive training arrangements impose an unacceptable cost which should be avoided. Equal opportunities cannot be taken too seriously because, at various times during their working life, women are allegedly more expensive to employ than men. And, of course, companies cannot waste time consulting the workforce for fear that the lead time for making a decision will lengthen to the point where the business will be paralysed.

The social consequences of these policies are undesirable. Britain has 4 million people being paid less than £5 an hour. Claims for unfair dismissal have increased year by year. A third of British workers have received no training whatsoever from their current employers. The gap between the pay of women and men has scarcely narrowed in the past ten years. Even the Labour government responds to this business agenda. Tony Blair tells us that we need a lightly regulated labour market and Labour ministers oppose the European Draft Directive guaranteeing information and consultation rights to British workers.

From time to time, the unpleasant effects of this agenda can cause managers some embarrassment. Then the hand-wringing begins. Redundancies are 'unfortunate'. Low pay is 'regrettable', but better than having no job at all. Consultation arrangements are always 'desirable', but should not be allowed to compromise management's right to manage.

What managers rarely wish to discuss is the precise nature of this global competition which is producing such unfortunate effects on fellow citizens. There is no doubt that many parts of the manufacturing industry face considerable competition from abroad. However, the manufacturing sector employs less than 5 million people out of a workforce of over 28 million people. Elsewhere, claims about the pressure of global competition seem spurious. Employees of water companies were surprised, after privatization, to be told that they were facing redundancies because of this global competition. There was still only one pipe supplying the water and only one set of reservoirs and only one sewerage system. When the arguments were unravelled, we found that global competition was being used as shorthand to describe the process whereby a company which does not produce a particular return on capital will find that its share price is pressed down to a level where the company will be taken over. Of course it is a matter of public policy whether we allow our water utilities to be taken over by other companies. Moreover, if a company is taken over, it is also a matter of public policy whether we allow the terms and conditions of workers in that utility to be worsened. The global competition argument has to be stretched very thin indeed before it reaches many companies in the United Kingdom.

Choice

Throughout parts of the public sector a new kind of employment competitiveness has actually been introduced by government decision. In the civil service, where there is no obvious market and certainly no global competition, the Conservative government introduced a system called market testing. In local authorities and the health service, the Conservatives introduced the process of compulsory competitive tendering by which public service work is packaged up and put out to tender. The Labour government has modified these procedures, but has maintained a similar pressure on the workforce. In place of compulsory competitive tendering, we now have the 'Best Value' initiative. In place of market testing, we have value-for-money examinations. In place of the Public Finance Initiative we have Public–Private Partnerships. These are entirely artificial devices. They are not introduced because competition is global. They are introduced because government has decided that competition in the public sector is desirable to improve efficiency. Stripped of the high-sounding rhetoric, these policies are based on the value judgement that employees need to feel a certain degree of insecurity if they are to perform at a level which is good for the economy.

So what about the trading sector? Is the pain inevitable there or do employers and governments have some discretion in the policies that they adopt? Certainly many continental countries think so. Throughout the European Union, workers have much greater protection than in Britain. In Holland, for example, it is really difficult to employ someone on a temporary contract. In Germany, it is more difficult to sack people than it is in Britain. In France, Germany and Italy, every worker has a much greater right to be consulted about changes in the company than is the case in the UK. Marks & Spencer reduce their workforce in Britain without great difficulty, but their attempt to close their major store in Paris gets the company into a legal tangle because the workforce has not been properly consulted.

Some business leaders have argued that continental countries have not faced up to the problems of global competition and that their economies are suffering as a result. The evidence for this is sparse. Throughout Northern Europe, production is significantly higher than in the UK and living standards are noticeably better. Sometimes these advantages are taken in terms of extra income and sometimes in extra leisure time. UK employees have to work about 40 per cent longer to achieve the same salary levels that are typically paid in France.

The British approach seems to be that commercial success can be achieved on the basis of low wage rates. The full implications of this nightmarish policy are rarely revealed. In Bangladesh, the average weekly wage of a textile worker is about £5 for 60 hours. In Haiti, the figure is about £7 for 50 hours. Comparisons are more difficult with the People's

Republic of China, but it appears that wage rates are less than 10 per cent of UK levels. So if we compete on wage levels with Bangladesh and Haiti and China, we have to contemplate a society in Britain where disposable income is reduced to a level which we have not seen for a hundred years.

In reality, the British response to global competition is neither inevitable nor even rational. Other countries with different political ideologies have taken different approaches. They have saved their workforce considerable pain and do not seem to have suffered significant economic disadvantage. So perhaps the best way of responding to global competition is not to say, 'The competition is so severe that we must cut pay and conditions'. Perhaps a more intelligent approach might be to say, 'We have to make the most of our advantages.' Certainly, Western countries seem to find it easier to compete if their people are highly skilled and if they use equipment which is modern and effective.

Aspirations

A good place to start in developing a new policy is to talk to managers and employees. When managers are asked what they want from their workforce, they will normally use two words: commitment and flexibility. However, if managers are asked what their employees want from management, the managers are often thrown into confusion. Unfortunately, British managers do not spend a great deal of time looking at things from the viewpoint of their employees. Nevertheless, the evidence is readily available.

Every three years, GMB uses MORI to survey people at work. MORI asks, 'What do you want from your employment?' To prompt an answer, a list of over twenty possible replies is given, including higher pay, a job to be proud of, better fringe benefits, managerial respect, and so on. MORI asks working people to pick out their top five aspirations in order of importance. The results are always the same. Since the early 1980s, the top two responses have been, 'a job which is satisfying and interesting' and 'job security'. Then there is a large gap until we get to the third aspiration, which is 'a feeling of accomplishing something worthwhile at work', and then the fourth, which is more predictable – better pay.

GMB also surveys new members to discuss whether the two topmost aspirations are being achieved. First, 'Do you strongly agree that your work is interesting and satisfying?' Only one person in four replies, 'Yes'. Second, 'Do you strongly believe that your job is secure?' Only one person in sixteen believes that their job *is* secure. The obvious conclusion is that there is a massive gap between what people say they want from work and what people are actually getting.

These results open up a productive line of thought. Perhaps the best way for managers to get the commitment and loyalty which they require is for managers to offer their employees the interesting work and job security which the employees say they want. Trade unionists always think in terms of negotiated agreements, but surely a deal by which managers and other employees secure their topmost objectives is a more worthwhile way forward than the pressure–pain model which we seem to operate at present.

A change of direction

Would this psychological deal lead to economic success? There are encouraging signs that it might. Some interesting research by Professor Michael West at Aston Business School has demonstrated that the best way to forecast whether a company will succeed or fail is to study how that company treats its workforce. In Britain, we tend to believe that heavy investment in new equipment, good design and effective marketing provides the key to success. According to Professor West, these important contributors are dwarfed by the importance of the people-treatment factor.[2] Of course, some of the indicators of good treatment also have direct economic benefits. Providing training will make the workforce feel valued and will also produce a direct improvement in productivity. Nevertheless, the results are an interesting corrective to the views expressed by British company directors and British ministers throughout the last twenty years.

Interestingly, a change of direction would resolve some of the tensions in the Labour government's industrial relations policy. Two examples stand out. First, the 'Fairness at Work' White Paper which led to the Employment Relations Act was said to be based on the principle of partnership. However, in the introduction to the White Paper, Tony Blair was keen to remind us all that the British labour market is the most lightly regulated in Europe. The fiasco at Rover, the neglectful behaviour of Coats Viyella and the arrogance of Corus have persuaded the Labour government to deplore the British managers' failure to consult their workers. Yet the government has drawn back from the obvious solution of giving British workers rights to information and consultation which are normal elsewhere. Second, the introduction of the National Minimum Wage was an obvious challenge to management's right to compete on the basis of wage rates, but the rhetoric of government ministers continues to suggest that a rapid increase in the National Minimum Wage would damage employment prospects in the UK. All governments want to ride a variety of ideological horses, but increasingly the difference between the pain approach and the partnership approach is requiring rhetorical skills which are even beyond the accomplishment of Tony Blair.

A change of direction must start with a lead from government. Government speeches should spend less time focusing on the flexibility of the labour market and more on the obligation of employers to provide work fit for the twenty-first century. An important symbol would be increased protection against unfair dismissal. In Britain, a person can be dismissed during the first year of employment for entirely unfair reasons and this is perfectly legal. Foreigners gasp at this anomaly. Government should also spend less time emphasizing the need for public service managers to imitate the behaviour of the private sector and more time celebrating the public service ethos which used to be such a strength of British society. Third, the government could end its opposition to the Information and Consultation Draft Directive of the European Union and give British workers the same rights to consultation as workers on the Continent.

Training

In many ways, Britain's attitude to training is the touchstone of industrial policy. Training can develop and sustain satisfying work. Training is a very good way of delivering the message to people that they are valued. And, of course, training can substantially improve economic performance. At present, Britain's training record is appalling. The government's Skills Task Force reported in April 2000 that we suffer considerable deficiencies in basic and generic skills, in craft training and particularly in mathematical skills. The examples of inadequate performance are extensive. Twenty-three per cent of the adult population in Britain have such serious literacy problems that they cannot find the section on plumbing in the Yellow Pages. Over a third of the British workforce are not qualified to NVQ Level 2. In particular, Britain seems to distinguish itself from other industrialized countries by the very large number of companies who provide no training of any sort.

In order to change the culture of British workplaces, we have to lay an obligation on employers to provide training for all employees. This obligation could be enforced by a training levy or by tax incentives and penalties or by simply giving every worker an entitlement to a particular level of training. In 1995, the CBI surveyed member companies to ask whether the voluntary system of employee training in Britain was actually working. Nearly half of CBI companies admitted that the voluntary system was not producing adequate results. Unfortunately, there has been no CBI survey in the last six years, but personal experience would suggest that the level of dissatisfaction has grown. Nevertheless, CBI leaders continue to insist that compulsory training is wrong and will only lead to bureaucracy and extra costs. Inadequate training means damaged economic prospects and blighted lives. A change of approach is urgently needed.

Most social issues in Britain seem to lead back to questions of class. The curious assumption in Britain that wisdom in an organization resides solely in senior management contrasts sharply with the outlook of managers in Scandinavia, where management is by consent and where problems are solved as far as possible on the basis of consensus. A company which structures itself so that management decides all of the strategic matters in isolation from the workforce is destined for conflict and failure. Research carried out for ACAS by Purcell and Kessler demonstrates that problems in a company are best resolved by bringing together a group of people from all levels with the task of finding a solution.[3] Not only does this problem-solving approach produce a solution to over 90 per cent of the problems, but the process also improves the trust between managers and employees.

Perceptions of failure

Finally, and most important of all, management should accept a change in their priorities. In most companies, to cut the dividend is an admission of failure. Indeed, it is so traumatic that it usually produces resignations amongst senior managers. By contrast, reaching for the P45 and making people redundant is often seen as an acceptable tactic to deflect criticism from the City of London. Employees are not stupid. They understand that within this value system they are less important than shareholders. If we saw a change of priorities so that redundancy was regarded as management failure, the commitment of people to their company could improve dramatically. This is not just theory. There have been many examples in Guinness, in Blue Circle Cement and elsewhere, of the way in which employment relations are transformed once a guarantee of employment security is put on the table. Flexibility becomes more possible because people know they can contribute their ideas without threatening the employment prospects for themselves and their colleagues. For managers to accept that employees are the most important stakeholders in a business will no doubt require a conversion of Pauline proportions, but it is the essential requirement of long-term economic success.

My conclusion is that Britain has been fundamentally wrong about the needs of a modern industrial economy. Many managers and politicians act as if a deregulated economy with low pay and low levels of job security is the only route to high economic performance. In fact, this approach is producing great pain and demoralization. The analysis is economically counter-productive because the pressure–pain model ensures that people will not deliver their talent and will not produce of their best. Success in a modern economy can only come by valuing people, motivating them and training them effectively. They will contribute more enthusiastically if they have a reasonable say in the development of their organization. The aim is to produce a synthesis between modern management and human dignity. Managers ought to take a more sensible view of the best interests of each enterprise. Failure is guaranteed when the workforce regards itself as disposable; success is a real possibility when every employee feels valued and informed.

Notes

1 Milgram, Stanley (1974) *Obedience to Authority: An Experimental View*, London: Tavistock.
2 West, Michael and Patterson, Malcolm (1999) 'The workforce and productivity', *New Economy* 6(March): 22–7.
3 Purcell, J. and Kessler, I. (1995) 'Joint problem solving: does it work? An Evaluation of ACAS Advisory Mediation', Occasional Paper no. 55, London: ACAS.

Chapter 8

John Lewis Partnership

A case history

Simon Robinson

> The Partnership's supreme purpose is to secure the fairest possible sharing by all its members of the advantages of ownership – gain, knowledge and power; that is to say their happiness in the broadest sense of the word so far as happiness depends on gainful occupation.
>
> (John Spedan Lewis)

John Edmonds, in his chapter, contrasts the world of global competition and the need for tight financial discipline with the needs of the workforce. He asks why the demands of global competition should be used as a reason for not attending to the needs of the workforce. He claims that not all businesses are subject to this competition and that where they are it does not provide grounds for ignoring these needs. Underlying this is a fundamental point about ethics and moral psychology, highlighted by the Milgram experiments, which purport to show how easy it is for the most reasonable of people to deny their responsibility to others.[1] Is it possible, though, to balance responsibility towards the workforce with the need to respond to the pressures of the free market? The John Lewis Partnership (JLP) is one of the most remarkable examples in Britain of awareness of, and attention to, the work community, embodying respect for the workforce and corporate integrity. At the same time it succeeds in the market place.

Case history

The first John Lewis shop, a drapers, was set up in Oxford Street, London, in 1864. In 1905 Lewis bought the Peter Jones store in Sloane Square, and by 1914 his son Spedan was made owner and manager. It was at this point that Spedan began to experiment with reform and the sharing of power. He had three guiding principles:

- The company should deal fairly with all stakeholders, principally customers, suppliers and employees. At the core of that was a simple

concern for the inequality which existed between the employees and the owners. When Lewis first joined the firm, the combined income of its 300 employees was equal to that of the three owners. In the vein of R.H. Tawney, he argued that too great an inequality was not only inequitable but also damaging both to the rich and the less well off.[2]
- Employees should feel that they own the company, participating as far as possible in decision-making.
- The company should be able to compete successfully in the market place and attract the best in the profession into management. It was clear to Lewis that this required two things. First, all employees should feel that they were responsible for the success of the business and that therefore any benefits which they accrued would be directly connected to the standard of service. Second, aware of the failures in previous co-operative approaches, he demanded tight commercial discipline.

This led to three initiatives: Committees for Communication, a house journal, and a staff bonus. The Committees for Communication were just that, aiming to ensure communication between management and workers, 'to bridge the gulf that in large scale businesses develops between, on the one side, the workers, ... the people who have no authority over others and, on the other side, the Principal Management, the people who have the ultimate authority, the real control of the whole business'.[3] The committees have survived to this day and are made up of 'rank-and-file' members, i.e. they involve no managers. The committees are not a system for formal representation but rather a means of airing and responding to grievances. Work here is characterized by speed of response and the appropriate director has to reply within three weeks.

The in-house journal, the *Gazette*, was first published in 1918. A weekly production, it ensures that all members are aware of the results of the previous week's trading in each branch, and in the business as a whole. Every operating unit, store or warehouse, also has its own journal, the *Chronicle*. These are also a means of communicating criticisms to the management, anonymously, through the correspondence columns. Like the Committees of Communication, the relevant manager has to respond within three weeks.

Both these initiatives were essentially about ensuring transparency and the free flow of knowledge in the company. For Lewis, the development of well-informed 'public opinion' was an important element in any business.

The third initiative, a staff bonus, was paid at Peter Jones in the form of managing directors' IOUs. These later became the cash bonuses paid out by the John Lewis Partnership.

The Partnership

John Lewis died in 1928 and in the following year Spedan formally moved the firm into partnership, at the same time joining the Oxford Street store with his Peter Jones enterprise. He sold his shares to the John Lewis Partnership Trust Ltd, which controls the Partnership's principal holding company, John Lewis Partnership plc. From this, Lewis developed a Constitution which was based on three elements: the Central Council; the Central Board; and the Chairman.

The Central Council is a representative body composed of elected rank-and-file and management appointees. The Chairman and other senior managers are obliged to give an account of their stewardship annually to the Council. The particular responsibility of the Council is for the non-commercial aspects of company life, from social activities through to charitable giving. Nonetheless, it also has a watchdog function and has the power to discuss 'any matter whatsoever'.

The Central Board is responsible for managing the commercial enterprise. It has twelve members: the Chairman and deputy Chairman, together with five directors appointed by the Chairman and five elected by the Central Council. Hence, there is a direct link into the community structure of the firm.

The Chairman is also the Chief Executive Officer and is responsible for maintaining profit and fulfilling the aims of the Constitution. The Chairman has great power and can even name his successor. However, ultimately the Central Council can dismiss the Chairman if he does not fulfil his role in the terms of the Constitution. He is thus ultimately subordinate to the Constitution.

Lewis was aware that over time, despite these checks and balances, designed to keep the company focused on its organizational values and principles, these principles could be eroded. Hence, he set down that two directors should have as their only function the protection of the integrity of the Partnership Principles. The first, the *Chief Registrar*, ensures that the principles and democratic system are maintained. The second, the *Partners' Counsellor* acts as an ombudsman, receiving any complaints and ensuring that the rights of Partners are fully respected. The Counsellor has the function of ensuring that the Partnership is 'influenced properly by considerations of humanity'. Lewis saw these as dealing with the 'critical side' of the firm as distinct from the executive. Each operational unit of the Partnership has its own Counsellor and Registrar.

Principles of the John Lewis Partnership

Purpose: The Partnership's ultimate purpose is the happiness of all its members, through their worthwhile and satisfying employment in a successful business. Because the Partnership is owned in trust for its members, they share the responsibilities of ownership as well as its rewards – profit, knowledge and power.

Power: Power in the Partnership is shared between three governing authorities, the Central Council, the Central Board and the Chairman.

Profit: The Partnership aims to make sufficient profit from its trading operations to sustain its commercial vitality, to finance its continued development and to distribute a share of the profits each year to its members, and to enable it to undertake other activities consistent with its ultimate purpose.

Members: The Partnership aims to employ people of ability and integrity who are committed to working together and supporting its Principles. Relationships are based on mutual respect and courtesy, with as much equality between its members as differences of responsibility permit. The Partnership aims to recognize their individual contributions and reward them fairly.

Customers: The Partnership aims to deal honestly with its customers and secure their loyalty and trust by providing outstanding choice, value and service.

Business relationships: The Partnership aims to conduct its business relationships with integrity and courtesy, and scrupulously to honour every business agreement.

The community: The Partnership aims to obey the spirit as well as the letter of the law and to contribute to the well-being of the communities where it operates.

Since 1928, the Partnership has continued to grow. Numbers of partners have increased from 1,500 to over 54,000. Up to 1955, the major increase in productivity had been via the acquisition of new companies, including Waitrose (1937) and Selfridges (1940). From this base, growth has been organic, leading to some 28 stores and 136 supermarkets by 2001. The Partnership is now moving into Internet trading through the acquisition, in February 2001, of buy.com (UK), the leading online retailer of technology, software and office products. Links with buy.com (USA) will be maintained.

Since 1971, employment has risen steadily and sales have grown at an annual average of 6 per cent. In 2000, the sales for department stores were over £1,997 million, and for supermarkets over £2,095 million, with a turnover of over £4 billion, up by 10 per cent on the previous year.

Analysis

Although the writings of John Spedan Lewis tend to be discursive, they reveal a passionate concern for both the well-being of his workforce and right relationships with suppliers, customers and community. An account of well-being can be summed up in the industrial psychology of R.H. Tawney, and in particular in the work of contemporary psychologist P. Warr. In what follows, I use Warr's analysis of work, and the needs it fulfils, to examine the JLP approach to its workforce.[4]

Warr argues from a psychological perspective that work is necessary for the well-being of persons. He argues that there are basic human needs fulfilled in work, and fulfilling these needs gives content to respect for the workforce. The majority of these needs are fulfilled by JLP:

- *Opportunity for control*: This includes control over the content, procedure and pacing of the individual's work as well as the opportunity to influence the policy of the company. In the case of JLP, policy can be influenced both through the Committees and the Council.
- *Opportunity for skill use*: This includes opportunity to use skills and to acquire new ones. In JLP this occurs in a variety of ways. Support is provided for those who want to enter continuing or higher education – for example, by taking courses through the Open University. Many of the stores have Learning Centres where the staff can take vocational or non-vocational courses. Those who have been there for 25 years have the opportunity for a six-month paid sabbatical, either to pursue learning or simply to take time out.
- *Environmental clarity*: This involves feedback from staff and management on practice and progress, and sharing information on aims, objectives and future developments. All this is achieved in JLP through the councils, journals and committees.
- *Physical security*: This includes both an acceptable physical environment and satisfactory arrangements for health and safety at work. JLP extends the basic provisions of this in several ways. There is a well-staffed occupational health service, and the provision of pension and life assurance schemes.
- *Financial security*: As Edmonds noted in the previous chapter, this is often not perceived by employees as the primary need. Nonetheless, it

is a critical need to fulfil if the employee is to feel valued and perform to their best. In addition to their salary, Partners share in the profits of JLP. Profit is dealt with prudently, taking into account the needs of the company. After that, the profits are shared equitably, with all members receiving the same percentage of their salary. The concern for financial security also extends to Partners who experience particular hardship, with the facility of a loan or grant available.

- *Opportunity for interpersonal contact*: This is provided not only by the various organs of democracy but also by the immense variety of opportunities that there are for leisure and for contact with groups outside work hours. This ranges from various country clubs, which can cater for holidays, to sporting and cultural activities. The Partnership has a strong musical side with work-based performing groups, and there is also encouragement to make use of general cultural opportunities through ticket subsidies.
- *Valued social position*: There is a basic need to feel that work involves a function which is valued in society. Often this has been confined to the professions. In JLP the very fact of being one of the Partners provides recognition of value. The Partnership does not, however, focus on value as status. Instead it focuses on value which is derived from being part of a larger enterprise, and also the values found in the practice of skills and the offering of service. Ultimately, though, Spedan Lewis saw value as attached to purpose:

> The Partnership was meant to enable people to feel that they might be making a contribution of real value to the ceaseless experimentation that is necessary to human progress. It was meant for people who need not only something to live by but also something to live for.[5]

At the heart of this approach to managing the business and personnel there is an emphasis on the need for a strong sense of responsibility amongst the managers. This is seen in a ‘commitment to the organization and a concern for the welfare of its members’. Whilst management style may differ between different branches, there is a ‘general awareness that decisions have to be defended on rational grounds’.[6] Freedom to criticize is maintained throughout the organization and thus keeps management attention focused on both the workforce, and the basis for any decision-making.

Equally, because each Partner is involved so deeply in the company, there is a sense in which every employee feels responsibility for the whole company. This leads to the reduction of psychological distance between the different parts of the organization, something reinforced by the communication of knowledge. That, in turn, tends to encourage the development of proactive responsibility, responsibility more in the sense of a civic virtue, as distinct from responsibility simply for a task.[7] Hence, Lewis stressed a sense of responsibility which should go 'beyond the letter of the law', which he summed up in the idea of good citizenship applied to the workplace.

As a whole this gives members a sense of identity and purpose. The scope of this purpose is not simply confined to the production and sale of goods, and maintaining the well-being of the workforce, but looks to the higher purpose of contributing to and maintaining the well-being of the wider community in a variety of ways. This is exemplified in a number of different relationships:

- *Suppliers*: The Partnership aims to do business with firms who share the same values. This extends to global trading. The company aims to support open and free world trade, which works to the benefit of all countries. At the same time Waitrose endeavours to maintain the option of dealing with smaller local suppliers.
- *Community*: Concern for the community is shown in the planning stages of new developments. The design of new buildings takes into account how they will enhance the local community and environment and what the wishes and concerns of the local community are. The Partnership also supports broader campaigns which affect the local community such as the Focus on Food campaign (Royal Society of Arts). This aims to increase awareness amongst parents, families and schools of the need for proper nutrition in early life. The Partnership is also concerned with need in the community, from educational to social. In 1999, for instance, £1.5 million was donated to several different causes. There is now a £5 million Charitable Trust Fund and several examples of operational centres supporting their own local projects. Importantly, all Partners are encouraged to get involved with such projects.
- *Environment*: There is also a concern for the environment, which is manifest at various points in the decision-making process. Waitrose, for instance, is at the forefront of organic food retail. This includes support for new organic farmers through the Waitrose Organic Assistance Scheme. They also guarantee a market for produce where a farmer is converting to organic produce. In John Lewis Furnishings, the wood used for furniture comes from renewable sources.

In these latter factors, issues arise of both responsibility and a sense of purpose which extends beyond the workplace. Both have a bearing on well-being in the workplace.

Conclusions and questions

There may be may be a point about corporate integrity at the centre of the John Lewis case study. As Robert Solomons notes, integrity is perhaps more a collection of virtues than a single virtue.[8] Integrity can be taken, first of all, to involve integration, unified thinking which explicitly brings together the principles and practice of the corporation. The whole system of JLP is designed to ensure that practice is measured against the founding principles. Close to this holistic approach is the idea of harmony, much beloved by Spedan Lewis. Richard Higginson notes the Jewish concept of *Shalom* – health, harmony, right relationships – as being a corporate form of integrity.[9] Second, integrity involves consistency of behaviour in different areas of operation, and different relationships. Flanders *et al.* note consistency and coherence as two key features of the Partnership.[10] Third, the development of such coherence and consistency is a function of long-term commitment, something critical to the growth of JLP. Finally, absolute integrity is an ideal, an aim which can never be fully achieved. Hence, central to its development has to be the capacity to learn, both for the individual and the organization. Again, written into the Partnership and its organization is the capacity to test out values and to learn. The Learning Centres provide individual learning. The system of Committees and Councils, along with the Registrar and Counsellor, provide a transparency which enables the organization to learn. Having two directors whose task is to stand apart from corporate decision-making, in order to provide an external perspective, is also an important part of the reflective process.

As Peter Hawkins notes, a learning organization does not simply focus on learning and developing skills and organizational process. It also demands that the purpose and meaning of the organization be reviewed.[11] Once again this is central to the Partnership. Moreover, JLP does not see itself as simply a retail company whose purpose is to make wealth. On the contrary, it sees the accumulation of wealth in the context of a higher purpose to do with contributing to the well-being of the community, including the workforce.

In the light of such a view of purpose, this case shows how a firm can operate a policy which makes concern for its employees the highest priority and still operate successfully in the free market. Evidence for success is that in the late 1980s and early 1990s JLP consistently outperformed much bigger companies such as Tesco, Sainsburys and Marks & Spencer.[12] Bernard Miller suggests that this success was due to confidence in the workforce that 'the enterprise is being operated in the interest of all who work in it'.[13] In turn, he argues that confidence gives to management 'the authority to manage subject to full accountability of the managed'.

Whilst all this reinforces the sense of good psychology being applied, many are still sceptical as to whether there are clear empirical connections between this and the success of the company. Robert Oakeshott suggests several pieces of evidence which do provide a connection. First, in the mid-1990s absenteeism was running at the low rate of 3.5 per cent. Second, the labour turnover is low – 7.1 per cent in 1984–5 compared to 30 per cent in the retail sector as a whole.[14] Third, there is anecdotal evidence that 'stock shrinkage', petty pilfering and so on, is low. These factors would indicate a settled workforce.

Nonetheless, there remain major questions regarding the effectiveness of the Partnership. As Flanders *et al.* note, the much-lauded industrial democracy is not as remarkable as some would argue. Decisions still rest with the CEO, who selects the deputy chairman as well as five other members of the Central Board. The Communications Committees rarely influence policy. Moreover, Flanders *et al.* argue that the strong stress on the basic principles, virtually unchanged since the Partnership began, smacks of paternalism.[15] Though acceptance of the underlying ideology is not a criterion for job selection, workers do have to work within this value system. Moreover, the company does not accept unions and may sound harsh at points. Regulation 186 of the Constitution, for instance, notes that if a Partner has been absent, for whatever reason, for three separate times in a period of six months the Registrar should refer this to the Staff Manager to determine if there is need for medical consultation, or 'consideration of his continued membership of the Partnership'. Is this paternalism or reasonable discipline born of mutual accountability?

The other questions are about how far this kind of system could be replicated outside the retail sector, and to what extent the success of this project is dependent on freedom from external investors. How far, also, is the system ultimately dependent upon the underlying principles and an acceptance of them? The Registrar and Counsellor, for instance, are not there simply as ethical consultants to help members work through ethical problems. Their task is driven by the ideology of the company and is to ensure that its principles are applied in the areas of human resources and decision-making.

This leads to a fundamental question championed by Friedman and Sternberg as to whether such principles should be imposed upon a company. They would not argue against the Lewis approach *per se* but rather that no such approach should be imposed on another company.

The JLP case, however, invites a more fundamental question about a business's awareness of the humanity of the workforce and the development of systems that will enable that awareness to remain in place. If this is fundamental, as Edmonds suggests, then how can it be applied in different contexts? How might the 'critical' and reflective side of a company be developed and the human needs of the workforce be attended to? How might the learning dimension be introduced and how might it relate to the success of the business?[16] As West and Patterson note, if the rallying call, 'People are our most important asset', is not to be just a management platitude then these issues have to be addressed in practice.[17]

Notes

1 Zygmunt Bauman develops this theme in *Modernity and the Holocaust* (1989), Polity: London, and *Postmodern Ethics* (1995) Oxford: Blackwell.
2 R.H. Tawney (1930) *Equality*, London: Allen & Unwin.
3 J. Lewis (1948) *Partnership for All*, London: Kerr-Cross.
4 P. Warr (1987) *Work, Unemployment and Mental Health*, Oxford: Oxford University Press.
5 J. S. Lewis (1948) *Partnership for All*, London: Kerr-Cross.
6 A. Flanders, R. Pomeranz and J. Woodward (1968) *Experiment in Industrial Democracy*, London: Faber & Faber.
7 C. Harris, M. Pritchard and M. Robins (1995) *Engineering Ethics: Concepts and Cases*, New York: Wadsworth.
8 R. Solomons (1992) *Ethics and Excellence*, Oxford: Oxford University Press.
9 R. Higginson (1996) *Transforming Leadership*, London: SPCK.
10 A. Flanders *et al.*, *op. cit.*, p. 184.
11 P. Hawkins (1991) 'The spiritual dimension of the learning organization', *Management Education and Development* 22(3): 172–87.
12 K. Bradley and S. Estrin (1986) '*The Success Story of the John Lewis Partnership: A Study of Comparative Performance*', London: Partnership Research.
13 R. Oakeshott (2000) *Jobs and Fairness*, Norwich: Michael Russell, p. 225.
14 Oakeshott, *op. cit.*, p. 226.
15 Flanders *et al.*, *op. cit.*, p. 193.
16 Unipart, for instance, have developed an in-house university which is integral to its business. Employees pass through this every day and courses apply directly to their work, increasing their efficiency and developing greater control and confidence. See J. Kinghorn (1999) 'U Turn at UNIPART', *Knowledge Directions*, Fall: 6–17.
17 M. West and M. Patterson (1999) 'The workforce and productivity', *New Economy* 6(March): 22–7.

Chapter 9

Nestlé baby milk substitute and international marketing

A case history

Simon Robinson

> *Can a product which requires clean water, good sanitation, adequate family income and a literate parent to follow printed instructions be properly and safely used in areas where water is contaminated, sewage runs in the streets, poverty is severe and illiteracy is high?'*
> (Senator Edward Kennedy, Senate Hearings on Infant Formula, 1978)

The so-called 'Nestlé Case' has been ongoing since the 1960s. The case focuses on the work of multinational corporations (MNCs), and in particular Nestlé, and how they market their products in the Third World. Key issues which emerge are:

- How far do MNCs influence cultures, governments and health organizations, through advertising and free gifts? This raises the question as to how far an MNC should adapt its approach to advertising, in the light of local needs.
- To what degree are MNCs responsible for the use made of their products not directed by them?
- Should MNCs be concerned about matters of justice? The attempt to market breast milk substitute is seen by many to be in itself unjust. On this view, not only is the MNC using those in poverty to try to further its own profits, but its marketing approach also leads to suffering and possibly the death of the babies involved. The plausibility of this view depends on the plausibility of competing views of justice, and this view questions the morality of simply operating in a free market orientation. Closely connected to this is the defensibility of a global view of child health. The medical judgement is that, where available, breastfeeding is best for the baby, whatever the nation.

This case history presents a heady mixture of issues: questionable marketing practices, injustice and poverty, as well as matters concerning health. Analysis of the case will raise these issues in the context of different ethical positions, specifically relating the issues to those positions outlined in the first two chapters.

The case also raises the issue of ethical dialogue and how different participants in a confrontation can begin to communicate, including how codes of practice can be interpreted.

The development of infant formula and its marketing

Whilst the case had come to the attention of the public in the 1970s, the history begins much earlier. Where mothers are unable to breastfeed there has always been the need for alternative nutrition. In 1867, Henri Nestlé developed a formula which aimed to be suitable for infants, 'fulfilling all the conditions sought for by physicians'.[1]

In the twentieth century, breast milk alternatives were increasingly commonly used and in the US in particular hit a sales peak in the 1950s. In the 1960s, there was a decline in the birth rate leading to a major fall in sales. Throughout this time, there was intense competition between five major companies: Mead Johnson, Ross Laboratories, Wyeth Laboratories, Nestlé and Borden. Mead Johnson and Ross Laboratories had cornered 90 per cent of the American market, but Nestlé were the world leaders with over 50 per cent of the global market.

The developing nations

With the birth rate in the developed countries beginning to decline, the companies began to search for markets elsewhere and focused on the developing countries where the birth rate was soaring. In moving into this market, the companies began to cross the divide between commercial and pharmaceutical industries that existed in the developed world. There, food companies tended to advertise directly to the consumer, while pharmaceutical companies promoted their goods primarily to the health professionals. The formula companies marketing in the developing nations targeted both health professionals and consumers. Marketing strategy included:

Babyfood booklets: All the companies produced booklets that gave advice for pre- and post-natal care. They used pictures to show correct feeding methods and made a variety of recommendations for 'mixed feeding', including the use of a bottle where there was insufficient or poor quality breast milk. All of this gave the impression of informed and careful advice, while at the same time managing to extol the quality of their own product. The booklets were careful not to denigrate breastfeeding, but some early versions did not actually mention it.

Advertising: Sustained radio advertising, posters, and information and pictures on cans again gave the impression of the importance of breast milk alternatives without initially mentioning breastfeeding.

Free samples and gifts: One widespread promotional technique was to offer potential users free samples of the formula. Free samples were also supplied to hospitals, a promotional technique known as 'dumping'.

Promotion through the medical profession: Given that consumers would be sensitive to the 'medical nature' of the product and have a desire to do the best for their baby, working through the health professional was a logical focus for the MNCs. The formula industry employed milk nurses to advise mothers on children's nutrition. These were mostly employed in hospitals but some did visit mothers in their homes.

Milk banks: In addition, milk banks were set up in some areas to sell formula at reduced prices to poor mothers, at a discount of between 33 per cent and 40 per cent.

Criticisms of these methods

First, not only did the initial advertising and booklets not mention breast-feeding, but they also gave the impression that the use of breast milk substitute would be the best option. The adverts implied that they would give the baby strength, energy and power, and pictures of plump, smiling babies on posters and cans reinforced this.

Second, the potential consumers were particularly sensitive to this kind of advertising. A new mother wants the very best for her baby and is open to being influenced at this time. The very best was, by implication, not simply a healthy baby, but also one who shared the prosperity of the West – the babies in the adverts were often white.

Third, promotion of formula was making use of threefold changes in the developing countries:

- increased urbanization. With increased urbanization the poorer mothers could see the wealthier families making use of the formula and would associate this with wealth and prosperity;
- a growth in medical services;
- an increase in live births in health centres and hospitals.

The coincidence of these factors enabled the companies to take advantage of social and economic change, and focus on limited areas to reach a wide and captive audience.

Fourth, the use of health professionals in the work of education led to what D.B. Jelliffe described as 'endorsement by association' and 'manipulation by assistance'.[2] In some cases, the health worker might be influenced by the promotion to accept the claims of bottle-feeding. In others, the simple fact that posters and cans were on display in the hospital gave the impression that the product was being endorsed by the medical staff. The use of milk nurses, in particular, was a controversial approach. The companies claimed that they were there for educational purposes, precisely to ensure the correct use of formula. They were, however, in a unique position to influence the mothers, especially if they were on commission for formula sales. At the very least, the practice raised a conflict of interest.

Fifth, promotional techniques ignored three critical factors in the Third World: poverty, hygiene and illiteracy. The mother left hospital with a limited amount of free formula and continued to use it, leading to her milk drying up. Those who were illiterate did not always mix the formula correctly, leading to use of unsterilized water and the baby suffering diarrhoea. The diarrhoea meant that the baby was unable to absorb the nutrients in the formula. The free sample, of course, began to run out and formula was thus thinned out to make it last, often with contaminated water, due to the lack of sanitation. This resulted in the death of the baby from malnutrition and dehydration. Finally, milk banks were not a solution to the problem, as the poor could not afford even these prices.

Criticisms such as these come together in the work of D.B. Jelliffe. He proposed the term *commerciogenic malnutrition* to sum up the effects of the marketing practice of infant formula companies in developing nations.[3] An expert in child nutrition, Jelliffe argued that the increase in infant mortality rate in the Third World and the decrease in breastfeeding were directly connected.

Jelliffe's testimony led the United Nations Protein Advisory Group to recommend that three major stakeholders take responsibility for ensuring that this situation was addressed. The formula industry was urged to encourage breastfeeding in new mothers; to avoid promotion in hospital; and to ensure that the directions for use on the cans were clear, not least about the need for hygiene.

Paediatricians were encouraged to stay in discussion with the formula industry, particularly about the needs of those on low income; and to keep up to date with developments in research on breastfeeding and the use of processed foods.

Governments, especially in the Third World, were encouraged to make use of the media for education on breastfeeding, and on the responsible use of formula products, and to consider financial help to the most vulnerable groups for infant and weaning foods.

The global debate

Up to this point the debate was confined to the health care professions. In March 1974, the debate became global through Mike Muller's pamphlet *The Baby Killer*. This was a broad restatement of an article which had appeared in the August 1973 edition of the *New Internationalist*. That article, by R. Hendricks and David Morely, focused on cases where bottle-feeding was not appropriate, accepting that there were cases where it was. Muller's article focused less on appropriate uses and a subsequent translation by a German group (ADW, Third World Working Group) put aside any qualifications and gave it the title *Nestlé Kills Babies*. Nestlé's response was to sue ADW, leading to a two-year court case, which they won. Nestlé, however, lost the publicity battle. They had given the impression of a global giant trying to stamp out the protests of ordinary decent people.

Instead of dampening down the global concern, there was increased collaboration between international health organizations and concerned groups, including the churches and NGOs, which led directly to a world-wide boycott of Nestlé goods in June 1977. In response to this, Nestlé was greatly concerned for its ethical integrity and reputation, and wanted to assert that to the public. This involved a fourfold approach.

First, in evidence to a US Senate hearing, Oswald Ballarin (head of Nestlé Brazil) characterized those responsible for the boycott as 'a world wide church organization with the stated purpose of undermining the free enterprise system'. These allegations of conspiracy were never withdrawn by Nestlé. Second, key professionals were targeted, including 300,000 clergy and community leaders, trying to refute the allegations directly.

Third, after a meeting between WHO, UNICEF and the formula companies, some initial guidelines on practice were developed with the declared intention of devising a full code of practice for marketing. Nestlé argued that they were already following these guidelines. This was a change in approach, urged by new PR consultants, aiming to avoid confrontation. Finally, Nestlé tried to align itself with, and fund, 'independent' research into child nutrition. At the same time, Nestlé worked with an industry council to try to develop self-regulation.

The WHO Code

The World Health Organization Code on marketing took until May 1981 to be ratified. Prior to this point, there were difficulties in communication between some governments represented at the World Health Assembly. Members of the formula industry themselves did not always see eye to eye and several companies, including Heinz, Kraft and Gerber, signalled that they would not be bound by the Code. Arguments still raged about basic data on formula use in the developing world. Several companies were adamant, for instance, that the Jelliffe thesis was focusing on a single issue without taking account of many other social and economic factors that accounted for the figures on morbidity and mortality.

Nonetheless the Code was passed, was accepted by Nestlé, and formed the basis of marketing practice. The Code directives included:

- All direct advertising and sampling to consumers should be stopped.
- Labels should carry the advice that breast is best, and there should be no text or picture that idealized the formula.
- Marketing should continue but only if it did not undermine breast-feeding.
- Health authorities in member states should educate health workers on the benefits of breastfeeding.
- Donations could be made to health care workers but not as sales inducements.
- Employment of milk nurses was to be stopped and industry personnel were not to receive any reward for the volume of formula sold.
- The responsibility of enforcing the code, and of passing whatever legislation resulted from it in any particular country, was to be left to individual governments.
- All those with an interest, especially the industry and non-governmental organizations, were encouraged to raise awareness of the Code and to report any infractions they saw.

End of the boycott

At this time Nestlé began to widen its non-adversarial approach. It entered into dialogue with the Methodist Task Force, which the American Methodist Church had charged to take a detailed look at this issue. It set up the *Nestlé Coordination Center for Nutrition* (NCCN), headed up by Rafael Pagan. This was intended to serve as an information centre for key issues in nutrition, and to act as receiver of information that might help Nestlé in meeting new demands and achieving organizational change in relation to the matter.

By May 1982, the continuing dialogue led to the development of the Nestlé Infant Formula Audit Commission, an independent monitoring agency chaired by Senator Edmund Muskie, former US Secretary of State. Nestlé's practice was seen as increasingly transparent and in line with the Code. Hence, support for the boycott of Nestlé products began to wane, with high-level commentators such as the editor of the *Washington Post*, and several activists, including Douglas Johnson (head of Infant Formula Action Coalition) accepting the company's response. The boycott was then officially suspended in October 1984.

The second front

On the face of it the issues had been sorted out through the Code and the various forums set up to develop dialogue. This led to the gradual scaling down of the NCCN, and eventually of the Muskie Commission. However, opposition still remained in certain quarters. The boycott, backed by the General Synod of the Church of England, had not yet been suspended in the UK.

Activists were now concerned that Nestlé was trying to find ways of getting round the Code. One key area was the supply of free formula to hospitals. This remained important for the companies, not least because where a mother had to use formula, and used a particular brand in hospital, she would tend to continue with that brand after her stay. Hence, competition was intense. In addition, bad practice was developing in some hospitals where, rather than bringing the baby to the mother for breastfeeding, the staff were using the free supplies of formula to feed the babies, purely for their own convenience.

Despite the fact that this practice of supplying free formula to the health centres was neither banned by the Code nor illegal, Nestlé remained committed to end all such supplies in developing countries, except for the limited number of babies who needed it. Nonetheless, conflict continued over the interpretation of the Code in several areas, including the matter of which language should be used for the packaging of formula. Despite this, the Church of England suspended its support of the boycott in 1994, though clearly signalling that if it became aware of any attempt to circumvent the Code then it would soon return to support of the boycott.

The early 1990s also saw important moves towards a goal of universal breastfeeding, driven by WHO and UNICEF, including the Baby Friendly Hospital Initiative. This led to further pressure on Nestlé, especially from UNICEF. In July 1993, UNICEF issued a document, *An End to Ambiguities*. This reflected a frustration with the difficulties in the interpretation of the Code. In an attempt to end those ambiguities, UNICEF expanded the Code without consulting either WHO or the industry. The first response from Nestlé was to argue that this went against the Code. Hence, far from resolving ambiguities, these changes led to further wrangles.

In May 1995, Carol Bellamy took over as the head of UNICEF and showed immediate concern about the formula industries. Initial requests for dialogue by Nestlé were turned down. In 1996 Bellamy suggested that UNICEF and the formula companies meet and that they all discuss their sales policy and practice, country by country. For Bellamy this was the only way in which transparency could be achieved and the ambiguities resolved. For the company lawyers there was the major constraint of US anti-trust laws. To reveal company policy and practice could lead to violation of those laws.

Meanwhile, a new activist coalition was formed, the Interagency Group on Breastfeeding Monitoring (IGBM). This claimed independence from the many different activist groups but had overlapping membership with many. Without fully consulting the formula industry, IGBM issued a sizeable document called *The Code Handbook*. This sought to provide the definitive approach to interpreting the Code and even provided a model law for countries to adopt. The pressure from this organization, supported by UNICEF, then led to a document called *Cracking the Code* (1997). The document aimed to present independent research into the controversy. In the event, Nestlé and the researchers could not agree over the methodology employed or conclusions. The report asserted that companies were systematically violating the Code and that the whole marketing policy should be altered. Nestlé responded with detailed questioning of methodology, and noted that, even if the methodology were accepted, the report included few details of Nestlé transgressing the code. Once more then, common understanding, even about data collection, proved to be elusive.

UNICEF continued with its policy of not talking with the formula industry, and even extended this to criticizing the International Paediatric Association for its discussions with the industry. In 1997, Carol Bellamy did meet with the new Nestlé CEO Peter Brabeck. Despite hope for a continued and open dialogue, Bellamy declined further contact.

The way ahead?

The way ahead for the Nestlé case is perhaps even less clear with the dawn of the twenty-first century. Attempts to resolve ambiguities become even more difficult with the spectre of AIDS in the developing countries. The proportion of mothers who had become HIV-positive in developing countries varied, according to different areas, between 30 and 70 per cent.[4] Though the research on this is continuing, the possibility of vertical transmission of AIDS through breast milk has become a real danger. In a conference in June 1998, organized by WHO and UNICEF, it was concluded that there needed to be a change in policy, with the UN issuing recommendations discouraging mothers who have AIDs from breastfeeding. This threatens to conflict directly with the global concern to encourage breastfeeding.

Nestlé, in the meantime, has continued to attempt to get its case across, especially in key areas such as universities, where many student unions continue to ban Nestlé products. In terms of presenting its case, the HE sector is important for two reasons. First, over 45 per cent of school leavers enter higher and further education each year in the UK, and these will be the opinion formers of the future. Second, academic support would lend credibility to Nestlé's arguments.

Even this approach has had its problems. Denied the chance to set out their case in the Oxford students' newspaper, Nestlé UK decided to place an advertisement in the local free paper. One of several claims in this was that 'even before the WHO International Code for Marketing Breast Milk Substitutes was introduced in 1981, Nestlé marketed infant formula ethically and responsibly, and has done ever since'. The response from Baby Milk Action was to take these claims to the Advertising Standards Authority. Here was an arbitrator who might be able to judge the case.

In the event the ASA ruled against the adverts on the basis that they contained implications that could not be easily substantiated. The response of Baby Milk Action was to claim that the ruling finally showed that Nestlé were unethical.[5]

Of course, the ASA was not saying that Nestlé was unethical. It was simply making a ruling on the narrow claims that were in the advertisement. The implication of the ruling was that if the advertisement had been reframed then it might have been permitted. Moreover, the ASA were clearly uneasy about having to make judgements on matters of ethics.

So the Nestlé case continues. At critical points it raises major questions as to how Nestlé might best have handled the issues, and beyond this further questions about the different ethical views that might be applied to the case.

Analysis

This case history illustrates the very different ethical positions which can be taken to marketing in the Third World. For Nestlé this has led to major changes in marketing strategies. With each major challenge to their ethical reputation, Nestlé developed a response which moved to a different ethical position. These positions are summed up by Sethi and Post in an analysis of a previous case which concerned the whole formula industry. They name the positions as follows: social obligation; social responsibility; and social responsiveness.[6] As each of these approaches is outlined in turn this will raise questions about what other options there might have been both for Nestlé and for others involved in the case.

Social obligation

The initial ethical standard of Nestlé in the Third World was one of social obligation, summed up as 'reasonable responsibility'. It determined first to operate within the law of the countries involved, and second, to ensure product safety. For Nestlé this included commitment to research both the need for breast milk substitute and the quality of the formula. It also accepted the need for truthful marketing: advertising should not make claims for a product which are inaccurate or misleading. Finally, it was concerned to identify and answer the consumers' needs.

In all this, Nestlé believed themselves to be perfectly ethical, precisely because they did not believe that they had any responsibility beyond the manufacture and proper marketing of the goods. As such they viewed the whole project from the perspective that the Third World is part of a global free market where there is great competition from other formula companies, and within which the company was only obliged to fulfil the legal and economic criteria governing its operation. This position is close to Sternberg's view noted in chapter 2.

The case, however, raises questions about that view when applied to corporate behaviour in the developing countries. First of all, this view led to myopia in the Nestlé approach involving:

- a lack of awareness of the broad issues of Third World poverty;
- a lack of critical awareness of the global/medical issues surrounding baby milk substitute.

Neither of these considerations was part of their decision-making process. These considerations make much broader demands than the simpler requirement to be aware of the legal and ethical norms in the different countries in which an MNC might operate. Moreover, the combination of these two further requirements is a potent one, regardless of any ethical judgement about Nestlé's practices *per se*. For these are the sort of considerations that can have an effect both on the company's standing in the world and upon their operations in general, as was shown by the subsequent boycott of Nestlé products.

Second, the social obligation position puts too much ethical weight on the concept of the free market, simply assuming its acceptability in the Third as well as the First World. However, even those who support the free market accept that the idea presupposes freedom and equality of choice, and a government that would provide a framework for this.[7] These are conditions that do not necessarily apply in developing countries.

Third, the *New Internationalist* and Muller articles introduced a very different ethical view, raising major issues of justice from a global perspective. They were concerned about inequality, and in particular the impact which the use of formula appeared to be having on the poor. The actions of the MNCs, they claimed, were exacerbating the already massive problems of Third World poverty and health inequity. They also raised the issue of how far Nestlé was creating need through its advertising campaigns, rather than responding to need. Developing nations would be susceptible to marketing campaigns that promised a Western view of well-being. Finally, this critique introduced the critical question of the power of the

MNCs and of their global interconnectedness. MNCs have more financial power than certain governments and are part of the global economic system that many believe has directly contributed to Third World poverty. Business in this context can influence politics. All these points lead to questions about the responsible use of great power.

At their most basic, these arguments support the need for practical wisdom and social and political awareness when entering a marketplace which is politically and culturally different from that of First World nations. Nestlé, however, was not ready for such a debate, and certainly not one which introduced different views of justice.[8] In answer to the activists' critique, they initially stuck firmly to the social obligation position. They simply asserted their view against an opposition whom they categorized as Marxist. The result was that a key moment of decision-making about how to handle the ethical debate was lost, and there built up a momentum which moved the discussion away from careful ethical argument to argument *ad hominem*, encouraging mutual demonization on the part of Nestlé and the NGOs.

Faced by the activist challenge, how might Nestlé have responded? How might Nestlé have ensured that it was better prepared? Alongside any social audit, could it also have set out an ethical audit, one which would look not simply at the effects of marketing but the values behind it, and the possibly conflicting values of those who considered themselves stakeholders, and who therefore might raise objections? How would such an audit have been carried out? Was Nestlé fully prepared to argue for its role as providing an important medical service, thus offering a very different ethical perspective? Is it possible to combine such a role with a free market approach? The answer may have been yes, providing supply was directly linked to medical need and did not involve attempts to persuade the consumer. How far does such an argument sit with Sternberg's view that business should stick to its purpose of increasing long-term owner value within the limits of justice and ordinary decency?

Social responsibility and the WHO Code

Though the debate has remained polarized to this day, Nestlé later tried to adopt a different ethical position, that of *social responsibility*. This ethical position argues that MNCs are responsible for the effects which they have on society and on different cultures. This therefore requires companies to raise their awareness of how they affect differing groups through, for instance, social audits, which assess the effect of marketing (for example) on a society, and seek to mitigate any bad effects.

For Nestlé this meant moving to a less aggressive marketing strategy, which not only avoided any misleading pictures or words but also made sure that the importance of breastfeeding was stressed. In all this it accepted that there might be second-order impacts from the sale of its goods. The impacts were on the babies who were not part of the company–consumer relationship, yet might in the end have died partly because of the sale of the formula. In accepting such a second-order impact the company was not accepting full responsibility for the death of the babies, but was accepting that it *shared* in responsibility for possible negative impact on the babies.

This concept of the shared or mutual responsibility of different stakeholders is what led to the WHO Code. In many respects, the WHO Code sums up a particular view of stakeholding in business ethics. The term stakeholder can mean anything from a group or person who has a financial stake in the business to the inclusive view of anyone who affects or is affected by the business in question.[9] The WHO Code embodies a view of stakeholding somewhere between the two. It was able to identify stakeholders who shared a particular concern for the well-being of newborn babies in the Third World. The stakeholders in this sense included: the formula industry; national governments; local health services; NGOs such as UNICEF and WHO. The shared concern was not focused on the business, but rather on the consumers and the wider effects of marketing. Moreover, this view of stakeholder theory was not about balancing competing interests so much as sharing responsibility. This meant determining together what the different responsibilities of the stakeholders were to the mothers and babies. Responsibility was roughly apportioned along these lines:

- The MNCs would be responsible for maintaining standards in marketing.
- The health services would be responsible for the distribution of the formula, according to need.
- The MNCs and NGOs would be responsible for monitoring practice.
- The national governments would be responsible for policing practice and ensuring that bad practice was effectively dealt with. They were encouraged to bring in specific laws to cover this.

The Code itself provided the criteria for good practice, and alongside this, acting as arbitrator, there was the Muskie Commission. For a time this provided the means whereby any allegations of Code-breaking could be discovered and dealt with. However, the Code had its problems:

- Like any code it could not be applied in an absolute way. It required interpretation.
- The fact that it was an international code meant that interpretation became ever more complex. Demands that the instructions on packs of

formula be written in the local language may be hard to fulfil if, for instance, it is not clear what the local language is.[10]

- The monitoring of the Code was down to the national government involved. This was difficult when some did not see this as a priority and others had significant but occasionally conflicting legislation. In India, for example, two different laws, brought into force in 1993, laid down different conditions about wording and language. Nestlé filed a petition to the High Court in October 1995, not to contest either law but to clarify the position. The complexity of the case made it difficult to determine the truth. Evidence from patients, health workers and health establishments, and local NGOs often conflicted. As a result, suspicions often re-emerged about the integrity of witnesses.
- The implementation of the Code had at its heart major ambiguities for the formula industry. The sales force on the ground was in danger of receiving ambiguous messages – the importance of increasing sales of the product, but also the importance of encouraging the potential consumer to use a different 'product'. It was not surprising that local sales forces might have found this hard to deal with.
- The Muskie Commission had its critics amongst the NGOs but did at least provide a mechanism for receiving allegations about the breaking of the Code and attempting to ensure that they were dealt with. Nestlé allowed this group to disband in the 1990s and did not attempt to replace it. In effect this produced a power vacuum with the return to polarization and both 'sides' insisting that they had the support of independent groups.

The Code then was important in providing a framework of meaning but was not sufficient. It required a system of arbitration which was accepted by all sides, and which could facilitate interpretation of the Code. The infant formula manufacturers had an ombudsman but such a post was no more objective than the various NGOs or IGBM. Could Nestlé have explored more carefully the possibilities of the different groups working together in monitoring? This was a second critical moment of decision-making for Nestlé. In fact, allowing the Muskie Commission to stand down altered the delicate balance of stakeholders, and the NGOs in particular began to take over responsibility for both data-gathering and judgement. Hence, the Baby Food Action Network in *Breaking the Rules 1994* bypassed an immediate referral to governments and the formula industry by collecting 455 allegations over the period of a year, and then releasing these to the public.[11] Similarly, UNICEF's document, *Cracking the Code*,[12] sought to review practice using criteria which had not been agreed on by the other stakeholders. Nestlé interpreted this as a further direct attack on its reputation. However, the problem here could equally be seen as arising from frustration with a system which no longer had a proper framework for arbitration.

In the light of this, was it sufficient for Nestlé simply to accept the demise of the Muskie Commission or of their own NCCN? What could they have done to develop an alternative? This stage of the case also raises questions about the stakeholder position in international marketing. Is it possible to sustain the collaboration of stakeholders without an agreed global code which is well policed? This would have to include agreement on criteria for the common good. In the first chapter, Cadbury suggests that not all stakeholder views should be given the same weight. In particular, he argues that single-issue groups outside companies do not have to take responsibility for solving problems. How far would this point apply to the NGOs in this case? As we have seen, they have often taken on too much responsibility and are not publicly accountable. It is not clear, however, that NGOs can be lightly dismissed. They would argue for a broader view of accountability, based on the claim that they fight for the rights and well-being of persons and groups who are powerless. Underlying this claim is once more a different view of justice. But to whom exactly does this make them accountable? They would also argue that they are prepared to share the responsibility for solving the problem.

How far does this move the ethical debate in this case away from simply the pros and cons of stakeholding theory towards the perspective of some form of virtue ethics, and the need to establish what is the higher purpose of business in this case and to develop collaboration to that end?

Social responsiveness

Faced by the most recent attacks of the NGOs, Nestlé began to change its ethical position from that of social obligation to one of social responsiveness. This involves a more proactive approach, which seeks to anticipate and prevent ethical problems from arising. Nestlé, for instance, proactively stopped the provision of free milk supplies in some forty countries, other than when it is provided under the direction of the local health services. It put more money into research on breastfeeding and offered to increase collaboration with the other stakeholders. Despite this, Nestlé's response has, at times, been ambiguous. It is clear that its practices have changed radically, particularly when compared to those of the 1960s. It is equally clear that its commitment to dialogue is genuine. However, in its dealings with the ASA, Nestlé appeared to be claiming that it had always worked according to the social responsibility model. This, in turn, was interpreted as an attempt to gain the moral high ground. In terms of tactics in the debate, this simply encouraged the return of the old polarized dynamic.

Attempts to increase dialogue and collaboration with UNICEF initially foundered because of UNICEF's suspicion of Nestlé's motives and because of the constraint of US anti-trust laws. Further attempts at dialogue would need to break through these. Cadbury has noted a different approach to codes which might have something to add to the debate. The Caux Round Table Principles were developed by a number of MNCs in 1997. At the root of these principles are the concepts of *kyosei* (harmony) and human dignity. These are then developed in a series of principles applied to different areas of work:

- Economic survival. The company has to prosper if the enterprise is to exist.
- Cooperating with labour. All parts of the company should recognize their mutual responsibility and so work together for the common good.
- Cooperating with external groups. Strikingly these were held to extend beyond suppliers and consumers to competitors and community groups.
- Attention to global concerns. In particular the principles note imbalances in wealth, trade and environment, and suggest ways in which MNCs can affect these.[13]

Such principles are important for several reasons. First, they suggest the possibility of pursuing at one and the same time several different purposes, including profit and concern for well-being and justice. Second, they set out a moral minimum in working in other countries.[14] Third, they provide a basis for trust.

In the light of such principles, the problems posed by AIDs may well cause the different parties in this case history to begin to explore very different ways of operating. Are there ways, for instance, of achieving co-operation with UNICEF without having to violate anti-trust laws? This would mean serious examination of how closer cooperation with the formula companies could be achieved.

Those who argue against stakeholder theory might suggest that no clear limit to stakeholders and their influence can be drawn. Thus this kind of approach threatens to lead to a significant diminution in the autonomy of companies and thence possibly to the complete transformation of the free market. However, this case might be taken to show that the capacity to make effective decisions in international business is dependent upon working with different groups with very different ethical views. The autonomy of the company can only be understood in that context.[15]

Conclusions

This case has highlighted a number of different ethical positions that can be held in relation to international marketing, ranging from social obligation to social responsiveness. Considering the case from these perspectives provides a way of testing basic theories about stakeholding and the social responsibility of business. At the same time, the case could be seen as showing the practical difficulties which emerge in attempting to resolve complex ethical issues and the need to work at communication and collaboration.

Underlying all this is the fundamental question as to whether Nestlé should have responded in the way it did. Should the company have taken the initial challenge from the NGOs so seriously? Should an MNC be responsible for the actions of its customers? Is it not more important to simply respect the autonomy of the customer, and not to pursue avenues that are the responsibility of local health services? It could be argued that the global campaign to ensure universal breastfeeding is more than simply a matter of providing information. It could be interpreted as aggressive and paternalistic in that it does not respect the autonomy of the consumer, the mother. Indeed it assumes that the mother is incapable of deciding for herself.[16] However, this is not an argument for avoiding the social responsiveness model. On the contrary, autonomy is a complex notion which depends in practice on the person developing the skills and virtues of decision-making. It is hard to develop these without dialogue and collaboration. The mother, for instance, needs to know the facts, options, constraints and underlying objectives of formula milk in order to make a choice about its use. The key question then is who should be enabling the mother to make that choice? This case might suggest that, in a situation where many of the stakeholders are powerless or are not convinced where their responsibility lies, such responsibility has to be shared. The work of the formula industry in research for, and in support of, health services, for instance, can enable those services to fulfil their responsibilities. The work of NGOs could enable national governments to fulfil their responsibilities in relation to the WHO Code. Would this view of stakeholding as collaboration fit into Sternberg's position or would it demand that there be recognition of shared purpose to begin with, so moving into more of a virtue ethics position? How might Nestlé begin to develop such a virtue ethics approach?

Finally, two further points might be suggested as worth considering in this case history. First, Nestlé cannot avoid the debate. Ethical reputation is of paramount importance to a multinational corporation. Second, without dialogue and collaboration the ground for ethical debate is lost: data are eroded; values and principles are distorted; and the range of possible options is diminished.

Notes

1 H. Nestlé, (1869) *Memorial on the Nutrition of Infants*, Vevey: Loertscher, p. 1.
2 D.B. Jelliffe (1971)'Commerciogenic Malnutrition? Time for a Dialogue', *Food Technology* 15: 55–6.
3 D.B. Jelliffe (1971) *op. cit.*
4 *New York Times*, 26 July 26 1998, cited in L. Newton case study (1999).
5 *Marketing Week*, 4 February 1999.
6 S. Sethi and J. Post (1989) 'Public consequences of private action: the marketing of infant formula in less developed countries', in P. Iannone (ed.) *Contemporary Moral Controversy in Business*, Oxford: Oxford University Press, pp. 474–87.
7 M. Novak (1993) 'Eight arguments about the morality of the marketplace', in J. Davies, *God and the Marketplace*, London: IEA.
8 De George notes that debates about justice are a key feature in international business ethics, see R. De George (1999) 'International business ethics', in R. Frederick (ed.) *A Companion to Business Ethics*, Oxford: Blackwell, pp. 233–42.
9 E. Sternberg (1970) 'Stakeholder theory: the defective state it's in', in W. Hutton, *Stakeholding and Its Critics*, London: IEA, pp. 70–85.
10 S. Robinson (1994) 'Modern business ethics and prophecy', *Crucible* Oct.–Dec.: 189–203.
11 Baby Food Action Network (1994) *Breaking the Rules 1994*, London: IBFAN.
12 UNICEF (1997) *Cracking the Code*, London: IGBM.
13 L. Newton (1999) 'Corporate codes from Borg Warner to the Caux Principles', in R. Frederick (ed.) *A Companion to Business Ethics*, Oxford: Blackwell, pp. 374–85.
14 T. Donaldson (1989) *The Ethics of International Business*, New York: Oxford University Press.
15 A quite separate area which could be explored within a complex case history of this sort is that of whistleblowing in MNCs. If it is part of the responsibility of the formula industry to monitor its own practice, how can it ensure that practice is sufficiently transparent to be monitored across so many fields of operation? Moreover, how can a positive climate for whistleblowing be developed when an increase in sales seems to be the highest priority?
16 L. Newton (1998) *The Controversy over the Marketing of Breast Milk Substitutes*, Columbus, OH: Council for Ethics and Economics 2(I): 7 (*www.i-case.com*).

Appendix I

Bibliographical and other resources

A great deal of material has been written about the Nestlé case over three decades, including three major books:

Dobbing, J. (ed.) (1988) *Infant Feeding: Anatomy of a Controversy 1973–1984*, London: Springer-Verlag.

Falkner, F. (1991) *Infant and Child Nutrition Worldwide: Issues and Perspectives*, Boca Raton: CRC Press.

Sethi, S. (1994) *Multinational Corporations and the Impact of Public Advocacy on Corporate Strategy: Nestlé and the Infant Formula Controversy*, Boston: Kluwer.

Much of this material focuses on the consequences of not taking seriously the challenges from NGOs. This case history is now distinguished by being one of the first to be found on the world wide web:

Newton, L.H. (1998) *The Infant Feeding Controversy*, Columbus, Ohio: Council for Ethics in Economics.

This is available online from *www.i-case.com* or as a CD-ROM.

This history attempts to provide a broader perspective on the case. It is interactive, offering both a history and analysis, and text and audio/visual resources. This radically develops the idea of the case history, encouraging students to move beyond the normal case boundaries and to develop their own views of the situation and of the ethical arguments, based on the many different source materials on offer. Ironically, when the study was being developed it became itself part of the case history, with Baby Milk Action suggesting that those involved in the writing of the case were strongly influenced by Nestlé and that the case was rewriting history (*Boycott News*, November 1995). However, whilst Newton's finished case has challenging things to say about NGOs, it also challenges Nestlé, and provides a comprehensive web link to all the major NGOs, including Baby Milk Action. Hence, it is an essential resource for those who wish to follow up the various strands of this case, and to explore further the uses of case histories discussed in the final chapter of this book.

Newton has also published an article, 'Truth is the daughter of time: the real story of the Nestlé Case' (1999) *Business and Society Review* 104(4): 367–95.

Part III

The role of case histories in business ethics

Chapter 10

The use of case histories in business ethics

Chris Megone

As was noted in chapter 2 of this book, a key question in ethics, and in applied ethics in particular, is 'what is the purpose of the study of ethics?'. Is the goal only to understand ethical questions more deeply, or should the study of ethics also be concerned with changing the students' behaviour,[1] developing their characters? In that same chapter it was argued that Aristotelian virtue theory explicitly addresses the question of character development. Aristotle's account emphasizes the importance of practice (or habituation) in the acquisition of virtue, but also gives a definition of virtue according to which virtuous acting is guided by rational principle. This suggests that the sort of reflection on ethics Aristotle engages in may also have a bearing on the acquisition of virtue as well as on practice. So what is the upshot of this regarding the goal of ethical study? Aristotle's account clearly gives advice as to how to acquire virtue, even if such acquisition may not occur in the lecture room. But is there any way in which study can directly affect behaviour? As has just been said, the relevance of rational principle to virtue may give study a direct input, but can any more be added?

In the present chapter the aim is to consider this question further by addressing the issue of the role of case histories in the study of business ethics. Three ways in which case histories might be used will be considered. But in particular it will be argued that case histories can play a role not merely in enabling students to achieve understanding of ethical issues, but in changing or developing their behaviour.

One way of using cases, it will be suggested, is indeed theoretical, namely, for the purpose of understanding different general approaches to business ethics. What is involved in using case histories for such understanding will be explained. It will then be argued that two other possible uses of case histories bear on the development of behaviour. In explaining these uses it will be shown that, in order to see these roles clearly, it is helpful to have in mind the account of virtue acquisition developed within the Aristotelian virtue ethics discussed in chapter 2.[2]

This discussion of the role of case histories will help to draw together the strands of the first two sections of the book. It will indicate the relation between the case histories presented in part II and the analyses offered both there and in the first part. And it will thereby point to a way of comparing analyses of key ethical issues arising in particular areas of business with the quite general theories outlined in the first part. As has just been indicated, it will also show the relation between a particular ethical theory and an understanding of the value of case histories.

Case histories and theories in business ethics

One approach to case histories would be to use them for the theoretical purpose of comparing both proposed ethical theories and the implications of those theories for ethical decision-making. What is going on here is a comparison of what ethical theories would mean, or come to, when applied. There are at least three aspects to such a comparison. They concern understanding the ethical theory, understanding the situations described in the case history, and assessing the theory. In practice, these three aspects need not come sharply apart. Thus assessment of the plausibility of a theory will clearly be affected by an understanding of what the theory really means and what it suggests should be done in the situations that case histories describe.

The first aspect of this use, then, concerns understanding an ethical theory. The suggestion here is that a proper understanding of an ethical theory cannot be achieved simply through a wholly abstract grasp of the principles of the theory. It requires appreciation of what these principles come to in concrete situations. This may be very clear if we consider the Aristotelian virtue of distributive justice, which is clearly a key virtue within the Aristotelian virtue theory outlined, and also has a role within Sternberg's theory of business ethics, though that is not explicitly a virtue theory overall. This virtue requires that distributions of goods be made in accordance with proportion. Aristotle does have a little more to say as to the relevant notions of proportion.[3] But the point here is that even then, when that theoretical amplification is understood, to appreciate fully what such distribution in proportion means, requires considering what it would demand in concrete situations. We understand the concept more fully by considering what it means in the case of the distribution of cake at a birthday party, or what it might suggest about profit-sharing within a particular business (though in the latter case a broader theory will probably be needed to make its concrete meaning determinate in that specific context). The virtue of justice may be a particularly complex abstract notion, but the claim would be that the understanding of even less complex concepts such as that of maximizing long-term owner value, or that of the stakeholder, for example, also requires appreciating the application of the concept to particular cases.

What is required here, therefore, is both an analysis of what principles from a given theory apply to the case history provided, and a grasp of what those principles then mean in the specific context given. This, then, will lead to a better understanding of the theory within which these principles operate, and thus a better basis for comparing that theory with rivals.

But a second feature of such a comparison will be to compare what the case history comes to from the point of view of distinct theoretical approaches. If the theoretical approaches are genuinely distinct they will identify distinct considerations as salient when it comes to considering what was ethically permissible or required at different stages in a case history. If a theory requires that a business agent maximize long-term owner value within the bounds of distributive justice and ordinary decency, then the analysis of any case history in those terms requires that at any particular stage in the case the agent consider the effects of possible actions on owner value. On the other hand if a theory requires that the agent be accountable to stakeholders, then any decision within a case understood from that perspective needs to be assessed solely in terms of obligations to relevant stakeholders.

One effect of reading a case history in the light of an ethical theory may be to indicate that the history lacks certain information which, from the point of view of the theory in question, is needed for appropriate decision-making. That need not undermine the value of the case, as an important skill in actual decision-making will be identifying whether the information already available is what is needed to make an appropriate decision. (Of course, time considerations may sometimes require the agent to proceed on the basis of what is known to be insufficient information.)

The third feature involved in using case studies for the comparison of theories is the assessment of the theories in terms both of what they pick out as salient, and in terms of the practical prescriptions that appear to follow from them. The factors identified as salient, and the practical prescriptions following from them according to the theory, will normally need to be assessed in relation to the case user's pre-theoretical convictions. (These are the beliefs (if any) that the case user holds about the case before attempting to examine it from any theoretical perspective.) For example, an application of stakeholder theory to a particular case history would identify which stakeholders an agent owed obligations to in specific circumstances. This then raises the question whether that approach to the notion of obligation coheres with pre-theoretical beliefs about obligations in that particular case, or indeed with the pre-existing notion of obligation itself. Is it plausible that the decision-maker really does owe obligations to all those apparently picked out by stakeholder theory? If not, then this may either tell against the theory or, if the theory seems to cohere with many ordinary beliefs but conflict with a few, this may lead the user to reconsider some of the pre-theoretical beliefs.

To take a second example, one might consider what a utilitarian theory would require agents to do in a case of possible whistleblowing, or in a case where the agent is offered an inducement. On a simple utilitarian theory the right thing to do would be that which maximized overall utility (however that is cashed out). Suppose, for the sake of argument, that whistleblowing would achieve most utility, or that accepting the inducement would be required by the theory in the second case. These prescriptions could then be compared with pre-theoretical beliefs. Once again, on the face of it, conflicts with pre-theoretical beliefs would tell against the theory, and thus inform an understanding of its plausibility. But, again, sometimes the theory can put some of the agent's pre-theoretical beliefs under pressure, if most of his beliefs are supported by the theory yet some are not.

As well as enabling a theory to be confronted directly with pre-theoretical beliefs, a case history may also provide a useful basis for reflecting on more theoretical objections to the theory. Thus, for example, Sternberg objects to stakeholder theory, among other reasons, because it gives rise to obligations of indeterminate force and gives no clear account of how to weigh them, thus making it quite unclear how conflicting obligations should be resolved into a final (all things considered) obligation. One way to assess stakeholder theory in the light of this is to consider what conflicting obligations it seems to demand attention to at any relevant point within a case, such as the Brent Spar case or the *Challenger* case, and whether it is at all clear how, from the point of view of some plausible version of this theory, such obligations are to be resolved.

Although it is possible to separate out in analysis at least these three aspects of the use of a case history in understanding a general theoretical approach to business ethics, it may well be that they are not sharply distinct. For example, it may be that part of fully understanding the meaning of the abstract principles of a theory is appreciating exactly what weight those principles have in contributing to a particular practical decision at a given point in a case. Nonetheless, the emphasis so far has been on understanding theories, not on affecting the user's behaviour. It is now appropriate to turn to this latter possibility.

Behavioural change and the use of case histories

In order to explain the remaining two possible uses of case histories, it will be helpful to recall aspects of the Aristotelian virtue theory outlined in the second chapter. As noted there, on the Aristotelian account of virtue, to be fully virtuous an agent must both be capable of judgements in accord with the principles that a practically wise person would use, and have appropriate desires and emotions. It was also a feature of this theory that the account of the nature of virtue was developed in conjunction with an account of the acquisition of virtue. Thus the acquisition of virtue involves the acquisition both of a disposition to make correct judgements, and of appropriate desires and emotions.

This overall picture has a number of implications. First of all, changes in behaviour may require changes either in the agent's judgements, or in his motivations, his desires and emotions, or in both. Thus a student of business ethics concerned with action may need to attend to both these influences on behaviour. Second, therefore, any account of the Aristotelian approach to these matters needs to attend both to the way in which correct judgement is acquired, and to how appropriate desires are formed. As was made clear in the second chapter, Aristotle lays some emphasis on the role of practice, or habituation, in the acquisition of virtue, and for present purposes this will be the focus of attention. For the aim now is to show how, against this background, case histories can have a role both in the acquisition of a capacity for correct judgement and in the formation of desires.

Case histories and the acquisition of *phronesis*

First, then, consider the role of case histories in the acquisition of good judgement. In order to appreciate this, it is necessary to understand Aristotle's account of good judgement. His view is that to do virtuous acts as the virtuous person does them requires *phronesis*, or practical wisdom, so as to act in accord with the relevant rational principles (those the practically wise person would act on). Thus his account of the decision procedure in the light of which correct judgements can be made appears to make essential reference to the *phronimos*, or practically wise person. A good judgement is the judgement that a *phronimos* would make.

But this leaves two worries. First, if there is no independently specifiable decision procedure and one must seek to do what a practically wise person (*phronimos*) would do, does this suggestion have any clear content? For it might seem that all one can do now is to identify a practically wise person as guide. But will it be possible to identify a practically wise agent without already knowing the sort of acts such a person will do (which have themselves been defined by reference to the practically wise person)? Second, if practically wise judgement is not a matter of following a definite decision procedure, how can one acquire it? On views of correct judgement in which there is a decision procedure, acquisition seems quite simple – it is simply a matter of understanding the decision procedure. That is all that is needed in order to learn how to use it. But if there is not such a procedure it is less obvious how the capacity for correct judgement can be acquired.

However, it is in just this context that case histories can be seen to have a role in its acquisition. If correct judgement were, by contrast, a matter of following a decision procedure, applying a utilitarian calculus for example, the sole practical use for the case history would be for practice in the use of the procedure. It would be a question of determining, by reference to the calculus, what agents should have done at various points in the story. In these circumstances the case history would have no role in the acquisition of the capacity for correct judgement, no role in this aspect of improving the agent's character. To understand its role in the acquisition of correct judgement, it is necessary to revisit the Aristotelian framework, and in particular Aristotle's account of *phronesis* (for he does have more to say about it and thus more to give aid in its acquisition).[4]

One place to begin is with some relatively obscure remarks that Aristotle makes in discussing *phronesis*, practical wisdom. The important point about this passage here is what it states about the relation between practical wisdom and intellectual perception.

> It is obvious that practical wisdom is not deductive scientific understanding. For it is of the ultimate and particular, as has been said – for the matter of action is like this. It is the analogue of theoretical insight: for *nous* is of the ultimately simple principles, for which there is no external justification; and practical wisdom is of the ultimate and particular of which there is no scientific understanding but a kind of perception – not I mean ordinary sense perception of the proper objects of each sense, but the sort of perception by which we grasp that a certain figure is composed in a certain way out of triangles.[5]

For present purposes, then, Aristotle's key point here is that practical wisdom about what to do in a particular circumstance requires some intellectual capacity (a perception distinct from sense-perception) to appreciate the nature of that particular situation.

These ideas can be further understood in connection with one of his remarks on the imprecision of ethics already alluded to:

> matters concerned with conduct and questions of what is good for us have no fixity, any more than matters of health. The general account being of this nature, the account of particular cases is yet more lacking in exactness; for they do not fall under any art or precept, but the agents themselves must in each case consider what is appropriate to the occasion, as happens also in the art of medicine or of navigation.[6]

Thus this capacity for intellectual perception, *nous*, is necessary because of the nature of particular cases. This is emphasized at the end of *NE* book II, when he is discussing the difficulty of hitting upon the mean, in other words the difficulty of doing what the principles of practical wisdom require.

> But up to what point and to what extent a man must deviate [from goodness] before he becomes blameworthy it is not easy to determine by reasoning, any more than anything else that is perceived by the senses; such things depend on particular facts, and the decision rests with perception.[7]

As Nussbaum suggests, Aristotle may have in mind three features of the particular encountered in action: first, that it has a lack of fixity in the sense of a capacity to present ever new situations; second, that there is a corresponding variety in those situations, and, third, an unrepeatability.[8] Features of circumstances we encounter, whether in business or in other aspects of life, may repeat many times. We may find people tell the truth, or lie on numerous occasions. But the overall combination of features that make up a complex situation may never repeat themselves. Given this variety, unrepeatability and lack of fixity, Aristotle argues, we need a capacity of intellectual perception (*nous*) to determine both what the relevant features of a new situation are, and to determine their relative importance in each specific circumstance. On Nussbaum's account, such an intellectual perception is 'the ability to recognise, acknowledge, respond to, pick out the salient features of a complex situation'.[9] It is this capacity (*nous*), then, that is required for correct ethical judgement in business.

Nussbaum then notes the next important point for present purposes, namely Aristotle's view of how such *nous* is acquired. It is gained only through experience.

> Young people can become mathematicians and geometers and wise in things of that sort; but they do not appear to become people of practical wisdom. The reason is that practical wisdom is of the particular, which becomes graspable through experience, but a young person is not experienced. For a quantity of time is required for experience.[10]

It may be helpful to summarize the position thus far. Ethical or virtuous behaviour requires, among other things, that the agent make correct judgements about what to do. In Aristotle's view the lack of fixity, the variety and the unrepeatability of particular actions means that in order to make such judgements on each occasion the agent must have a capacity of intellectual perception which will enable him to recognize, pick out and respond to the salient ethical features before him. This capacity is thus crucial if one is to make correct judgements. This is a capacity whose acquisition requires experience.

This last point may raise a worry. For if this capacity can only be acquired through experience, and if it is not inevitably acquired through experience, it seems that it will not be possible to avoid actual wrongdoing along the way to its acquisition. Clearly it would therefore be desirable if there were further resources for facilitating its acquisition other than real experience. Obviously actual experience will continue to play a role in the acquisition of the capacity, but such further resources would make it possible to achieve at least some of the development without moral wrongdoing. To explore this possibility it is necessary now to indicate how exactly experience does lead to the acquisition of such intellectual perception, perception of the sort that enables the agent to make correct ethical judgements

The role of experience here can be explained by reference to Aristotle's remarks on the role of habituation, or practice, in the acquisition of virtue, outlined in chapter 2. 'Men become builders by building ... so too we become just by doing just acts.'[11] As was explained, part of Aristotle's point is that habituation or practice has a cognitive role. At first a child will have to be guided towards just acts. It will do the right act because told to do so by a parent or teacher. At that point the child only believes that the act is just because told so by someone he trusts. This is purely 'external' knowledge. In time the child comes to see that the just act has a point, and then further to see that it has a point as just. At this further stage the child has some grasp of the concept of justice, and relates the point it sees in the action to this embryonic conception of justice. Then the child is internalizing the knowledge. This internalization can only be achieved through experience. This process is what is involved in the acquisition of *nous*, or intellectual perception.

To see that a just act, a certain sharing of a cake, for example, has a point the child must appreciate what features are relevant to that cake's being shared, who made it, to whom it belongs, who was invited to the party, and so on. In doing this, the child is recognizing salient features of the situation. But the child must also appreciate the relevance of these features, that these are features that need to be attended to in dividing up the cake. This is acknowledging these features. In doing these things the child is starting to acquire *nous*. And Aristotle's claim is that these achievements can only come through experience.

But why does Aristotle emphasize the need for long experience? Here the point about the particularity of action is relevant. A concept like justice is complex. A child has to internalize not just the relevance of these features in this cake situation, and in time that these are concerns of justice. The child also has to internalize that other similar considerations are also concerns of justice, though found in other situations. The child has to see that, say, the hard work and intelligence that are relevant to the appraisal of homework are comparable with the features of justice in the cake sharing, to see that this feature here is (comparable with) that feature there. Developing a capacity to perceive considerations of justice in all the variety of situations where it might arise requires long experience.

Furthermore, in addition to appreciating that a consideration is relevant, that it has a point, the child also has to internalize the relative weighting of different considerations. Again Aristotle might plausibly hold that such internalization requires experience of how different considerations weigh against one another in different circumstances. This requires both, again, comparing this situation with previous like circumstances, and appreciating the novelty of the new situation. Thus, too, determining the right thing to do in the light of this weighting, and perhaps also seeing that it is right, that it accords with some ill-formed conception of what is right overall, may also be aspects of intellectual perception that require experience.

Of necessity, then, this internalized knowledge is not something that can be acquired without actually being in relevant situations, having experience. Of necessity also, given the huge variety of circumstances that can be encountered, this is knowledge that can only be acquired with long experience.[12] The capacity for the intellectual perception to make judgements as to what virtue requires, comes with this knowledge. For it is a capacity which involves appreciating the considerations that are salient, in a particular situation, from the point of view of a relevant virtue, and weighing them appropriately. Its acquisition, therefore, requires long experience (a breadth and variety of relevant experiences).

Given this outline of the role of experience in the acquisition of *nous*, it is now possible to see that case histories may be able to make a contribution to that process, and thus, too, that actual experience may not be the only resource that can enable such an acquisition. One way to use a case history is as a presentation of experience to the student. In the business context, it can present the student with novel experiences, situations he has never in fact experienced. Furthermore, a case history such as the *Challenger*, or the Nestlé case, can present the reader with a variety of possible perspectives on the same situation, a range of ways of experiencing it.

Clearly, like any literature, a case history is a 'quasi-experience'. For the agent to have something like the experience of a real situation, he needs to be engaged in the situation. This may require imagination. But it is certainly possible for a case history to engage readers and to enable them to have the experience of appreciating the salient points of the situation, and weighing them; and also, as just noted, to differ from life in allowing the agent to internalize how the situation is experienced from a range of situations, not just his own. This allows the agent to appreciate that different features might seem salient from different perspectives, broadening his previous experience in still another way.

This use of case histories has a number of implications. First of all, as has been seen, the acquisition of *nous* is a long process and initially the process must be guided by someone external to the agent who already has it, or at least has a much more developed capacity, for example, a parent. Without such guidance the child cannot appreciate that a situation is to be thought of as a matter of justice (for example) at all. The child may also require guidance, at first, as to what it is about the situation that is a matter of justice ('it's her Easter egg too!'). Thus, in order to use a case history for the further development of *nous*, a student must already have gone beyond the initial stage in the development of *nous*, and no longer require such guidance, or at least not require it to the same extent. (This cannot be taken for granted, because it is not simply a matter of achieving a certain age; as Aristotle remarks, some remain childlike.[13]) The agent who can use case histories for the further development of *nous*, must already have, from past (guided) experience, sufficient grasp of salient features in relevant circumstances, and an embryonic conception of the concepts of the virtues to which they relate. These are prerequisites that will enable him to make intelligible comparisons with that past experience in appreciating the novel experiences he faces in the case history.

Second, case histories can vary considerably in length and depth. At one end of the spectrum are fairly short case histories like the Rick and Bianca case presented in this book. At the other is the Nestlé case history to be found here and in much more detail on CD-Rom and the Internet. There are reasons why the Nestlé case, as it stands, will be more suited to the kind of use currently being discussed. The case needs to be presented with considerable detail so that the student is in a position to discriminate what is salient. The case also needs to engage the student's imagination if it is to have the quasi-experiential character required for the student to internalize knowledge. Obviously apart from the depth and detail, the engagement of the reader can be affected by the quality of the writing. Some case histories are written in more engaging styles than others.

Even though it lacks the depth and detail of longer case histories, it might be suggested that a brief history like the Rick and Bianca case could be used as the basis for a role play in which students imaginatively develop the case. Just as the engagement of the imagination is important if longer case histories are to give students the necessary quasi-experience, so here, when successful, such creative imagination will help in the student's experiencing the situation from a participant's perspective. Used in that sort of way, therefore, such a case history could also contribute to the acquisition of *nous*.

All these factors, then, bear on the extent to which a case history actually serves to develop the student's *nous*. For the sorts of reasons just given, brief case histories like the Rick and Bianca case may need to be used in a particular way, or else they will be more suited to the theoretical uses that I outlined first. The main point here, however, is that case histories can, in principle, serve in the acquisition of *nous*, the intellectual perception that is crucial to *phronesis* or practical wisdom. Enormously developed and rich cases like those of Nestlé or Brent Spar or *Challenger* can clearly serve this purpose.

Furthermore, this role for case histories is extremely important since it provides a way in which the user can acquire the experience necessary to develop *nous* without having to have real experiences in which mistaken judgements can lead to wrong action. In using the case history the student can explain his perception of the salient factors to others and hope to learn from their responses as to whether or not he is or is not seeing all the salient factors in the situation, or weighing them correctly. Even if he is engaging in solitary study of the case history, he may develop *nous* simply through the process of reflection on what might seem salient from the different perspectives presented.

At that stage of reflection, the student might also bring to bear the way in which the case looks from the point of view of different ethical theories, the first way of using a case considered above. This may indicate how the development of *nous* may also be affected by such theoretical understanding; how there is a link between character formation and ethical understanding. If that were right, the possible role of case histories in character formation would be more central still.

Case histories and the acquisition of virtuous motivation

So case histories can play a role in the acquisition of the capacity for correct judgement. But virtuous behaviour requires not merely correct judgements, but appropriate motivations. The third claim here is that case histories can also play a role in their acquisition.

Once again, the Aristotelian account of the acquisition of virtue provides a context within which this claim can be explained. As noted in the second chapter, the acquisition of the appropriate desires and emotions for virtuous action is also a matter of experience, in that it too depends on practice or habituation. In general, in the first instance a child's desires for virtuous action will be guided. The child will desire to be brave, or self-controlled, or just, for example, because a parent or teacher (say) advises it to act in that way. At this stage the child will want to do the brave act as the act his parent advises, but not because he (the child) sees anything intrinsically worthwhile in it. In due course, as a result of coming to see some point in the activity, the child may develop a different kind of desire for such an act, namely a desire for a worthwhile act of that sort because it is perceived to have some point. Such a development is only possible as a result of practice, since it is only through practice that the child can come to the internalized knowledge that the act has some point, as already discussed.

The child may then, as a result of further practice, come to desire an act of that sort as a courageous act. He may desire it for its own sake, because it is courageous. In this further development the child comes to see the perceived point as associated with his embryonic conception of courage. This further development of desire also depends on practice since it also depends on the child coming to see the act as courageous. This involves seeing the points of different activities as linked to a common concept. This is only possible along with the acquisition of *nous* which depends on practice.

However there is also a second way in which the agent's desires develop with practice. The effect of acting on a desire is to reinforce the motivational strength of that desire. For the motivational strength of an agent's desire can become detached from the agent's view of the importance of that desire and not develop to the same extent; this is what occurs in the weak-willed (*acratic*) agent. Acting on desires is, therefore, important in developing them in this second, motivational aspect.

In the light of this account it should be clear that case histories can also contribute to the development of an agent's motivational states. If the discussion already presented is correct, then *nous* can be developed through working with a case history. Thus a student can come to an internal appreciation of the ethical point of an action through the quasi-experiential engagement that is possible in a richly detailed and well-written case history, or perhaps through using a briefer case as the basis for creative and imaginative role play.

It follows that such a student's desires can also develop as a result of such study. Thus a reader might come to adopt the perspective of Lewis in the John Lewis case study. If he thereby comes to see the point of developing employees as John Lewis do, and perhaps to see that as part of distributive justice, the agent can come to desire that kind of distribution as just. This will involve a development of his conception of justice, but associated with that will be a development of desire, from simply desiring such behaviour as the way he himself would wish to be treated as an employee, to desiring it because it is just. This is quite a complex example. But the simple point is that since case histories can enable the agent to come to see a consideration as important, they can be instrumental in bringing about a corresponding change in his desire.

Can the study of a case history affect the motivational force of the student's desire? This will depend on the extent to which the case history encourages the reader to engage imaginatively with its protagonists. Clearly, this will once again be affected by two features of the case history. First, there is the degree of detail that is provided, and perhaps also the extent to which the subject matter draws the student in. And, second, there will again be the quality of the writing. The plausibility of the importance of such features of style and content can be appreciated by considering their role in literature. By the same token, the notion that imaginative engagement with a case can affect the strength of desire is also made plausible by considering the effect that a fictional story can have in that regard.[14]

In sum, a case history can affect the motivational force of a student's desires if the student comes to sympathize imaginatively with a personality, or perhaps even with an abstract perspective in the case. The effect may be to reinforce an already existing desire, which is perhaps most plausible since that may itself have some causative effect on the agent's sympathy. However, the quasi-experience might even be sufficient to give motivational strength to a novel desire. In the latter case, the student would not only come to see the point of some activity for the first time, but also acquire, also for the first time, a corresponding feeling of motivation. Imagine, for example, that a student comes to feel justified anger (justified as he sees it, at least) that the *Challenger* was allowed to launch. He might never have been in a situation like any of the engineers in that case but now, for the first time, feel motivated to do something about safety implications if and when in relevantly similar circumstances.

Conclusion

Case histories can be used in a number of roles in ethical education. They can have a theoretical role, and can be used to enhance a student's understanding of a theory. But they can also be used in a way which will affect the character development of the student. Thus, if the Aristotelian account of moral psychology is broadly correct, and if case histories can teach business ethics (or applied ethics quite generally), then it is foolish to think that courses in business ethics (or applied ethics quite generally) cannot or should not affect a student's behaviour.

Notes

1 The term 'behaviour', here and throughout, is meant in its sense of conduct, not simply physical movement.
2 One other way in which case histories can be used will not be analyzed here, so it will be mentioned only to be put to one side. It is often suggested that, when teaching applied ethics to students with no general background in philosophy, it is useful to begin with case histories since beginning with actual historical practice brings ethics closer to where the students are. Roughly speaking, the thought here must be that such students are free of any ethical theory, and that for such students the case can work as a stimulus, or introduction, to ethical thought. Whether a student capable of studying ethics really can be entirely free of ethical theory, and thus exactly what role the case history thus used has in the development of ethical thought, will be left aside here. There are further complex methodological issues as to the study of ethics here, on which Aristotelian ethical theory for one has something to say. See, for example, my 'Aristotelian Ethics' in R. Chadwick (ed.), *The Encyclopaedia of Applied Ethics* (Academic Press of America, San Diego, CA, 1997) vol. 1, pp. 212–13.
3 *NE*, V, 3–4, 1131 a10–1132 b14.

4 Aristotle's main discussion in *NE* is in Book VI, esp. chs 5–9 and 12–13. In what follows I am also indebted to M. Nussbaum, *The Fragility of Goodness*, (Cambridge University Press, Cambridge, 1986) pp. 298–306, though my concern here is not with the relevance of rules to Aristotle's understanding of practical wisdom, which is Nussbaum's focus there.
5 *NE*, VI, 8 1142 a23–9, in Nussbaum's translation, *op. cit.*, p. 305.
6 *NE*, II, 2 1104 a2–10.
7 *NE*, II, 9 1109 b20–23.
8 M. Nussbaum, *op.cit.*, pp. 302–4.
9 M. Nussbaum, *op. cit.*, p. 305. As noted, Nussbaum presents this view in the context of arguing that Aristotle is a moral particularist. Whether that is right or not, this account gives some flavour of the nature of *nous*, intellectual perception.
10 *NE*, VI, 8 1142 a12–16. Nussbaum, *op. cit.*, p. 306, also notes a similar passage at *NE*, VI,11 1143 a25–b14.
11 *NE*, II, 1 1103 a36.
12 The variety of circumstances that can be encountered, and of considerations of importance in those circumstances, is one of the main reasons why ethics is such a hard subject.
13 *NE*, I, 3 1095 a6. Such childlikeness will be a reflection of bad upbringing, lack of good guidance.
14 This is not to say that a case history need only be used like a work of literature. There may be other ways in which it may be used in teaching, as was suggested with reference to the Rick and Bianca case, for example. It is only to make plausible the fact that it can affect the force of an agent's motivations.

Index

absenteeism 139
ACAS (Advisory, Conciliation and Arbitration Service) 129
accountability 13, 32, 33, 104
advertising 13, 142, 149, 150; in Third World 141, 143, 146
Advertising Standards Authority 149, 154
advice lines 99
ADW (Third World Working Group) 145
agent, weak-willed 172
AIDS 148, 155
Aldrich, Arnold 120
Allen, James 23
Altair (Greenpeace ship) 64
American Board for Engineering and Technology Code 119
Angel, Martin V. 62, 69, 76–7, 81; 'Brent Spar: no hiding place' 88–90
Anti-Bribery Convention 105
applied ethics 2, 23–4, 161; *see also* business ethics, study of
Aristotelian virtue theory 3, 4, 5, 24, 39–53, 161, 162, 164–73; acquisition of virtue 44, 52–3, 171–3; *acrasia* and *encrateia* 52; courage 45, 46, 47, 48, 172; definition of virtue 43; desire 44, 45, 46, 52, 171–3; doctrine of the mean 45, 46; *eudaimonia* 40–2, 46, 49, 50–2; experience 167–70, 171; and goal of business 49–52; good judgement 165–6; *hexis* 44; human nature 42, 49, 50; implications for business ethics 47–9; justice 48–9, 162; key questions of 40; nature of virtue 43–6, 48; *nous* 166, 167, 168, 169–71, 172; *phronesis* (practical wisdom) 46, 165–71; potential for virtue 43; practice (habituation) 43–5, 52–3, 168, 171–2; *prohairesis* 43, 44–5; rationality 42, 43, 45–6; rules of friendship 48; temperance 48, 52
Aristotle: as basis for Sternberg's theories 4, 25–6, 38–9, 41; on imprecision of ethics 166–7; on purpose of ethics 23; on purposes of human activities 25–6
Aston Business School 127
Atlantic Ocean 59, 60
auditors 14, 101
Auken, Svend 84
AURIS 69, 70
Australia 104
autonomy 156

Baby Food Action Network 153
Baby Friendly Hospital Initiative 147
Baby Killer, The (Muller) 145
Baby Milk Action 149, 158
baby milk substitute *see* infant formula milk substitute
Ballarin, Oswald 145
Bangladesh 125–6
Bank of Credit and Commerce International 28, 101
banks, international 16
Barings 22, 28
BBC (British Broadcasting Corporation) 64, 67, 73, 74
BCCI *see* Bank of Credit and Commerce International
behaviour 23–4, 25
behavioural change 164–5
Bellamy, Carol 147–8
Ben & Jerry's 81

Benetton 13
Big Bang (City) 16
Bingham Inquiry 101
Biologist 88–90
Bjerregaard, Ritt 84
blackmail 100
Blair, Tony 124, 127
Blue Circle Cement 129
boards 12; independent members 13–14; of John Lewis 133; policy setting and enforcing 17
Bode, Thilo 78–9
Body Shop 81
Boer War 11–12
Boesky, Ivan 10
Boisjoly, Roger 111, 112, 115–16, 118
Bophal 9
Borden 142
Borrie, Gordon 24
BP 60
Brabeck, Peter 148
Breaking the Rules 1994 153
breastfeeding 142–3, 144, 146, 147, 148, 156; and AIDS 148; research into 154
Brent Spar controversy 59–95; chronological sequence of events 91–5; cost of decommissioning 67; decommissioning decision and lack of consultation 60–3; dialogue issue 75–81; effect on industry 74–5; Greenpeace news releases 84–7; Greenpeace occupies rig 63–5, 84; Greenpeace's exaggeration of oil volume and radioactivity 65–7; public opinion 73, 76, 77, 79–80; recycling and re-use possibilities 72; re-use as Ro/Ro ferry quay 67; risks of land disposal 68, 70; role of media 63–4, 65–6, 67, 73–4, 77; scientific and ethical arguments 68–72, 87, 88–90; Shell's efforts to restore reputation 67; Shell's reversal of decision 65; social accountability analysis 79–80; types of contaminants present 68; *see also* Greenpeace; oil rigs, decommissioning of; Shell UK Limited
bribery: problem of defining 18–19; whistleblowing and 97, 100, 102–3, 104, 105
Burnyeat, M. 43
business ethics, study of 1–5, 11, 161–74; applying theories to case histories 163; understanding theories 162–3, 164; using case studies for comparison of theories 163–4; *see also* Aristotelian virtue theory; case histories; ethics; Sternberg, E.
buy.com 134–5

Cadbury, Sir Adrian 3, 24, 154, 155
Cadbury Limited 9
Cadbury Report *see* Code of Best Practice
Cape Kennedy Launch Complex 39-B 108
case histories 1–5, 161–74; and acquisition of *phronesis* and *nous* 165–71; and acquisition of virtuous motivation (link with desire) 171–3; and behavioural change 164–5; imaginative engagement with 172–3; quality of the writing 170, 172; theoretical purpose 162–4; varied length and depth 170, 172
Caux Round Table Principles 12, 155
CBI (Confederation of British Industry) 128
CD-Roms 3, 5
Challenger Flight 51-C 110
Challenger Flight 51-L disaster 108–22; as case history 173; confusion over temperature specifications 112, 118–19; design problems of solid rocket booster (SRB) 109–10, 111; inadequacy of lines of communication 120–1; initial launch delays 110–11; launch and causes of explosion 112–13; possible last-minute actions during countdown 120–1; pre-launch teleconference 111–12; Presidential Commission on 108, 116, 117–18, 119, 120, 121; problems of bureaucracy 115–16; reasons for hurried launch 110–11; safety programme 114–15; Seal Erosion Task Team 110, 111, 112, 115–16, 118, 119–20
Channel 4 73
charity 29–30, 137
China, People's Republic of 125–6
Church 145, 147; *see also* religion

City of London 14, 16, 129
civil service 125
Clarke, Tom 16–17
class prejudice 128–9
Coats Viyella 127
Code of Best Practice (Cadbury Report) 10, 13–14
codes 10–11, 155; four levels of 12; international 12–13, 154; national 13; personal 12; self-regulation 14–16; trade and professional 13; *see also* company codes
Columbia space shuttle 109, 114
'commerciogenic malnutrition' 144
Committee of Independent Experts (EC) 102, 105
communication channels 99, 102, 116, 132, 133, 135
community, concern for 137
companies: duties to employees 20–1; duties to suppliers 20; environmental policies after Brent Spar 74; framework of laws and regulations 12; three levels of responsibility 16–17; *see also* employment policies
company codes 13; conflict of interests 17–22; Shell's social accountability analysis 79–80
competition: global 123–4; in public sector 125
complaints procedures 102, 132, 133; *see also* whistleblowing
confidence 14, 21–2, 104, 138; public 101
confidentiality 100, 104
Conservative government: and Brent Spar controversy 62, 64–5, 67, 68, 69, 70, 76, 77, 79, 87
consultation: of workforce 124, 125, 127, 128–9
consumer choice: paternalism 156
consumer research 99
contracts 36, 48
controls 22
cooperation 155
corporate collapses 9
corporate responsibility, narrow perception of 75–6
corruption *see* bribery; whistleblowing
Corus 127
Council for Ethics in Economics 3
courage 45, 46, 47, 48, 172
Crippen, Robert 114

Daily Express 66
Daily Mail 66, 69
decision-making 11–12, 16–21; avoidance 21; in ethical theory 163; complex 11; effect of Brent Spar controversy 75; NASA and 120–1; *see also* ethical decision model; *phronesis*
Denmark: supports Greenpeace 64, 84
Department of Trade and Industry (UK) 62, 63, 71, 88
deregulation 129; of utilities 10
desire 44, 45, 46, 52, 171–3
Det Norske Veritas (DNV) 66
dialogue 59, 60, 156; lessons of Brent Spar controversy 75–81
dignity, principle of 155
directors: relationship with auditors 14; *see also* boards
disasters 9, 101; *see also Challenger* Flight 51-L disaster
Discovery space shuttle 109
discrimination 17
dismissal, unfair 124, 128
distributive justice 26, 35–8, 162, 172
DNV *see* Det Norske Veritas
'dumping' 143

Ebeling, Bob 115
Economist, The 79
Edinburgh International Television Festival (1995) 73
Edmonds, John 24, 131, 139
education: humanistic 23; John Lewis and 135
efficient markets, theory of 102
Eggar, Tim 77, 87
electric shock experiments 123
Elkington, John 75, 79–80
employment policies 28–9; bonuses 132; communication channels 99, 102, 116, 132, 133, 135; consultation 124, 125, 127, 128–9; in EU 124, 125, 128; evidence of effect on company performance 127; global competition as excuse for inadequacies 123–4, 125; health and safety 135; importance of quality of staff 22; job losses 20–1; job insecurities and inadequate

conditions 123–4, 125, 126–7; of John Lewis 131–40; leisure pursuits 136; low pay 123–4, 125–6, 129; positive effect of security and good morale 129–30; profit-sharing 136; redundancies 37, 124, 129; training 124, 127, 128–9, 135; in UK 124, 125–30; views of managers and employees on 126–7; Warr's psychological perspective 135–6
Employment Relations Act (UK) 127
Engineering Ethics (Harris, Pritchard and Rabins) 119
environmental issues 29, 80–1, 137; *see also* Brent Spar controversy
equal opportunities 124
Erfjord 65
ethical audit 151
ethical decision model 33–8
ethics: applied 2, 23–4, 161; and behaviour 23; definition of 12; imprecision of 166–7; normative 2; purpose of 23; teaching of 23; *see also* Aristotelian virtue theory; business ethics, study of; metaethics
eudaimonia 40–2, 46, 49, 50–2
European Commission: financial misconduct crisis 101, 102, 105
European Space Agency 111
European Union: and workers' rights 124, 125, 128
experience 169–70, 171
Experiment in Industrial Democracy (Flanders, Pomeranz and Robins) 138, 139
Exxon Valdez 9, 59, 77

'Fairness at Work' (White Paper) 127
Fay, Chris 76
Feynman, R.P. 108, 117–18
finance industry: whistleblowing procedures 99
Financial Aspects of Corporate Governance, Committee on the 3, 10, 13–14
Financial Times 78
Focus on Food campaign 137
food industry: marketing 142; whistleblowing procedures 99; *see also* Waitrose
Ford, Henry 81
Foreign and Corrupt Practices Act (USA) 9–10
Fowler, Mary 69
France: HIV-contaminated blood scandal 101; workers' rights 125
free market 28, 150
free samples 143
Friedman, Milton 75–6, 139

Galileo probe 118
General Electric Company 18
General Synod of the Church of England 147
Geneva Convention on the Continental Shelf 61
Gerber 145
Germany: protests against Shell 63, 64, 78; role of Board 12; workers' rights 125
global code 12–13, 154
global competition: as excuse for job insecurities and poor conditions 123–4, 125, 126
global market 137, 141, 150–1
GMB 126
goals 49–52
governments 9–10; monitoring role 153; policing role 152; *see also* Conservative government; Labour government
Greenpeace 59, 62–71, 73–81, 84–91; apologises to Shell 66–7; and decision to decommission Brent Spar 59, 62–3; emphasis on moral stance 65; ethical arguments 70–1, 73; loss of reputation after release of incorrect figures 65–7, 73, 75, 77, 78, 85–6; manipulation of media 73–4; membership decline 63, 67; news releases 84–7; occupation of Brent Spar and protests against Shell 63–5, 78; opposition to Sustainability-Shell model 81; possibility of dialogue with 78; post-Brent Spar policy 78–9; 'precautionary principle' 69, 71, 73; and public opinion 73, 77; radioactivity and industrial wastes campaigns 68; and scientific arguments 68–70, 71, 77, 87, 88–9; as stakeholder representative 76; *see also* Brent Spar controversy

Greenpeace Germany 63, 64, 78
Guardian 66
Guinness 129

habituation *see* practice
Haiti 125–6
Halley's comet 111
harmony 138, 155
Hawkins, Peter 138
health 51; *see also* safety
health professionals 47, 156; education of 146; marketing to 142, 143–4, 146; use of free samples 147
Heinz 145
Hendricks, R. 145
hexis 44
Higginson, Richard 138
Holland 125
Horsman, Paul 79
human nature 42, 49, 50

IGBM *see* Interagency Group on Breastfeeding Monitoring
imagination 170, 172–3
India 153
infant formula milk substitute 141–58; conflicting evidence 153; confusion of local sales forces 153; dangers of and infant mortality 144; debate, boycotts and development of guidelines 145; end of boycotts 147; inadequacy of social obligation approach 149–51; language on packets 152–3; marketing strategies in Third World 142–4, 145–6; milk banks 143, 144; milk nurses 143, 144, 146; social responsibility approach 151–4; UNICEF and 145, 147–8, 152, 153, 154–5; WHO Code on marketing 145–6, 147, 148, 149, 152–3, 156; *see also* Nestlé
integrity 13, 138
Interagency Group on Breastfeeding Monitoring 148, 153
Inter-Faith Declaration 12
international codes 12–13, 154
International Paediatric Association 148
internet 3, 5; Greenpeace and 63, 67; John Lewis and 134–5; Shell and 67
Isle of Grain refinery 60
Italy 125
ITN (Independent Television News) 73

Japan: nuclear leak 101
Jelliffe, D.B. 144, 146
jobs *see* employment policies
John Lewis Furnishings 137
John Lewis Partnership plc 131–40; attitude to suppliers 137; as case history 172; Charitable Trust Fund 137; communication channels 132, 133, 135; concern for community 137; constitution and management structure 133; and education 135; emphasis on responsibility 136–7; fulfils Warr's criteria for satisfied workforce 135–6; growth and performance 134–5, 138–9; history 131–3; in-house journal 132; and integrity and harmony 138; Learning Centres 135, 138; low absenteeism, labour turnover and pilferage 139; negative aspects of system 139; paternalism 139; principles 131–2, 134–5, 136, 138, 139; staff bonus 132
John Lewis Partnership Trust Ltd 133
Johnson, Douglas 146
judgement, good 165–6
justice 48–9, 141, 151, 154, 168, 172; distributive 26, 35–8, 162, 172

Kennedy, Edward 141
Kennedy Space Center 109, 111, 120
Kilminster, Joe 112
Kohl, Helmut 64
Kraft 145
kyosei see harmony

Labour government: and ocean disposal 73; and workers' rights 124, 127–8
'law of effect' 44
Lewis, John Spedan 131–2, 133, 135, 136, 137, 138; *see also* John Lewis Partnership plc
literacy 128; in Third World 144
Lloyd, David 73–4
Lund, Bob 111–12, 119

McAuliffe, Christa 111
McDonald, Alan 111, 112, 118
McIntyre, Alastair 69–70

Major, John 64–5, 67
management: as block to communication chain 99; contrasting attitudes in Britain and Scandinavia 128–9; at John Lewis 136; lack of knowledge of wishes of employees 126; perceptions of failure 129–30; *see also* boards; employment policies
market testing 125
marketing: by MNCs (in Third World) 141, 142–4, 146; WHO code on 145–6, 147, 148, 149, 152–3, 156
Marks & Spencer 125, 138
Marshall Space Flight Center 111, 112, 114, 115, 118, 119; criticism of 120–1
Mason, Jerald 112, 119
mathematical skills 128
Maxwell, Robert 9, 28, 101
May, William 115
Mead Johnson 142
mean, doctrine of the 45, 46
media 10; role in Brent Spar controversy 59, 63–4, 65–6, 67, 73–4, 77; whistleblowing to 98, 100, 103–4, 107
medical profession *see* health professionals
Melchett, Peter 74, 85–6
metaethics 2
Methodist Task Force 146
Milgram experiments 131
Miller, Bernard 138
Minimum Wage, National 127
Minnesota Principles 12
MNCs *see* multinational corporations
Morely, David 145
MORI surveys 77, 126
Mortensen, Peter Sand 84–5
Morton-Thiokol Industries (MTI) 109–10, 111–12; bureaucracy of 115–16; and confusion over SRB's temperature specifications 112, 118–19; contact with NASA 119; inadequacies of decision-making process 120–1; inadequacies of risk evaluation 118; pressures on 117; Seal Erosion Task Team 110, 111, 112, 115–16, 118, 119–20; *see also* *Challenger* Flight 51-L disaster
motivation, virtuous 171–3
MTI *see* Morton-Thiokol Industries
Muller, Mike 145, 150
Mulloy, Lawrence 112, 120
multinational corporations 9, 10–11; and Caux Round Table Principles 155; global financial power 150–1; importance of reputation 156; social responsibility of 151, 152, 156; and Third World marketing 141, 142–4, 150; *see also* Nestlé
Muskie, Edmund 146
Muskie Commission *see* Nestlé Infant Formula Audit Commission

NASA (National Aeronautics and Space Administration) 109, 110; confusion over SRB's temperature specifications 112, 118–19; inadequacy of decision-making and communication processes 120–1; involvement of its own engineers in *Challenger* disaster 116, 118–19; pressures on 110–11, 117, 118; reaction to concerns of engineers 112, 116; safety programme 114–15, 117–18, 119; *see also* *Challenger* Flight 51-L disaster
National Environmental Research Council 71–2, 87
National Space Transportation System 108; competition to 111; orbiter space shuttle project 109; *see also* *Challenger* Flight 51-L disaster
natural world 41–2
Nature 69
NCCN *see* Nestlé Coordination Center for Nutrition
NERC *see* National Environmental Research Council
Nestlé 141–57; ASA ruling against 149; boycott of products leading to conspiracy allegations by company 145; as case history 170; development of infant formula 142; inadequacy of social obligation approach 149–51; marketing strategies in Third World 142–4; neglects to replace Muskie Commission 153, 154; new policy on free milk supplies 154; obtains clarification of law on packeting language 153; removal of boycott

against 146, 147; role of dialogue 156; social responsibility approach 151–4; social responsiveness approach 154–5; sues ADW 145; tries to enlist academic support 148–9; tries to improve PR 145, 146; and UNICEF 147–8; WHO code accepted by 146, 147; *see also* infant formula milk substitute
Nestlé, Henri 142
Nestlé Coordination Center for Nutrition 146, 147, 154
Nestlé Infant Formula Audit Commission (Muskie Commission) 146, 147, 152, 153, 154
Nestlé UK 149
New Internationalist 145, 150
New Scientist 74
New Zealand 104
Newton, Lisa 3
NGOs (non-governmental organizations) 145, 151, 152, 153, 156; accountability 154
Nicomachean Ethics (Aristotle) 23, 40, 41–2, 43, 48, 49, 162, 165–9
Nisbet, Euan 69
normative ethics 2
North Feni Ridge 62
North Sea 59, 60; industrial fishing 79; *see also* Brent Spar controversy
North Sea Decommissioning Group 75
Norway: and Brent Spar 65, 67, 68, 70, 75; Det Norske Veritas 66
nous 166, 167, 168, 169–71, 172
Nussbaum, M. 167, 174
NVQs (National Vocational Qualifications) 128

Oakeshott, Robert 139
obligation 163, 164
Observer 69
OECD (Organization for Economic Cooperation and Development) 105
oil rigs, decommissioning of 59; Brent Spar as test run 62; Labour government's policy on 73; moratorium on seabed disposal 67, 70, 87; oil and gas industry sets up discussion group 74–5; regulations 60; *see also* Brent Spar controversy
openness 13, 19–20, 101, 104; John Lewis and 138; NASA and 121; Nestlé and 147; Shell and 73, 76, 78
'ordinary decency' 26, 35–8
organic food 137
Oslo and Paris Commission 67, 87
Oslo Convention 62
OSPAR 60, 70
Oxford University 149

Pagan, Rafael 146
paternalism 139
pay: executive 34–5, 37–8; 'going rate' 37–8; low 123–4, 125–6, 129; statutory limits 36, 127
peer pressure *see* self-regulation
Peter Jones 131, 132, 133
Pettersson, Pelle 84
pharmaceutical industry 49, 142
phronesis (practical wisdom) 46, 165–71
phronimos 43, 165
Plato 23, 40
Politics (Aristotle) 49
Polly Peck 28
practice (habituation) 43–5, 52–3, 168, 171–2
Presidential Commission on the *Challenger* Disaster 108, 116, 117–18, 119, 120, 121
pressure groups 74
Pridham, Jack 69
private sector: as initiator of good practice 99
problem-solving: by consensus 129
professional codes 13
profit-sharing 136
'Profits and Principles – Does There Have to be a Choice' (Shell) 79–80
prohairesis 43, 44–5
'Public consequences of private action' (Sethi and Post) 149
Public Finance Initiative 125
Public Interest Disclosure Act (UK, 1998) 105
public opinion: and Brent Spar controversy 73, 76, 77, 79–80
Public–Private Partnerships 125
public services 128; tendering for 125
Purcell and Kessler 129
purpose of business 25–7, 47, 49–52

radioactivity 66, 68

Rainbow Warrior 62
rationality 42, 43, 45–6
Reagan, Ronald 111, 113
redundancies 37, 124, 129
religion 12, 104, 145, 146, 147
reputation 21
revisionism, historical 60, 74
risk-benefit analysis 76, 78
Rockall Trough 70
Rockwell 117
Rogers, William Pierce 113
Roland, Alex 114
Rose, Chris 87
Ross Laboratories 142
Rothermund, Heinz 76
Rover 127
Rudall Blanchard Associates 61

safety 135; *see also Challenger* Flight 51-L disaster
Sainsburys 138
Sambrook, Richard 74
Sangeorge, Robert 74
scandals 101–2
Scandinavia 128–9; *see also* Denmark; Norway
science: and Brent Spar controversy 59, 64, 65, 66, 67, 68–72, 77, 87, 88–90; contested use of 59
Scottish Association for Marine Science 70
seabed: geological structure 62
self-regulation 14–16
Selfridges 134
Shalom 138
shareholders 12, 20, 21, 30, 32, 76
Shell Austria 64
Shell Germany 64
Shell UK Limited 59; decision to decommission Brent Spar 61–3; estimated levels of contaminants 65–6, 71; failure to consult 62, 63, 75; good environmental reputation 61, 62, 64, 76; postpones Better Britain awards 74; and privileged dialogue model 81; protests against 63, 64; and public opinion 73, 77, 79–80; reaction to Greenpeace occupation 63–5; reverses ocean disposal decision 65; and scientific arguments 65–6, 67, 68, 71; secrecy and openness 73, 76, 78; Social Accountability Team 79–80; tries to restore its reputation 67; *see also* Brent Spar controversy
Shepherd, John 87
Skills Task Force 128
Slaughter and May 15
small businesses 17
social accountability 79–80
social audit 151
social obligation 149–51
social responsibility 29–30, 151–4, 156
social responsiveness 154–5, 156
Socrates 23, 40
Solomons, Robert 138
South Africa: Protected Disclosures Act (2000) 104
stakeholder theory 30–3, 156, 163, 164; definition 152; employees 129; and environmental issues 59, 60, 62, 67, 75–6, 77, 78, 81; and international marketing 154; mutual responsibility concept 152; problem of defining limits 155, 164
Statements of Business Practice 13
Steam Loop affair 15–16
Sternberg, E. 24–39, 139, 150, 151, 156, 164; Aristotelian approach 4, 25–6, 38–9, 41; on distributive justice 26, 35–8, 162; ethical decision model 33–8; on executive pay 34–5, 37–8; on inevitability of business ethics 28–9; objections to social responsibility approach 29–30; on ordinary decency 26, 35–8; on purpose of business 25–7, 47, 50; on relationship of ethics with business success 27, 28–9; on stakeholder theory 30–3; on validity of business ethics 24–7
students: as opinion formers 148–9
Sullom Voe pipeline 60
suppliers 20, 137
SustainAbility 75, 81

Tawney, R.H. 132, 135
'Teaching of Ethics in Higher Education' (Hastings Centre) 23
temperance 48, 52
tendering 125
Tesco 138
Third World: AIDS 148; birth rate 142, 143; breastfeeding 142–3, 144, 146,

147, 148, 154, 156; health professionals 142, 143–4, 146, 147; hygiene 144; illiteracy 144; infant mortality rate 144; marketing by MNCs 141, 142–4, 145–6; poverty 144; suitability of free market concept in 150–1; urbanization 143; *see also* infant formula milk substitute
Thompson, Arnie 111, 112, 118
Time International 78–9
Times, The 69, 70
Titan missiles 109
Tomorrow 74
trade codes 13
trade unions 104, 127
training 124, 127, 128–9, 135
transparency *see* openness
Transparency International 12–13
'triple bottom line' 79–80
trust 22, 36, 104

UK: employment conditions and policies 124, 125–30; Nestlé boycott in 147; rules on duties of auditors 101; whistleblowing legislation 104, 105; *see also* Conservative government; Department of Trade and Industry; Labour government
UK Committee on Standards in Public Life 98–9
UK Offshore Operators Association 70, 87
UNICEF 145, 147–8, 152, 154–5; *Cracking the Code* 148, 153
Unilever 79
United Nations Protein Advisory Group 144
US Air Force 109, 114
USA: anti-trust laws 148, 155; role of law and regulation 12; whistle-blowing legislation 99, 104
utilitarianism 24, 163–4

Vane, Sir John 69
virtue ethics 154, 156; *see also* Aristotelian virtue theory
Vorfelder, Jochen 78

Waitrose 134; Organic Assistance Scheme 137; and small suppliers 137
Wall Street Journal 67, 74, 79
Wallace, Helen 87
Warr, P. 135
Washington Post 146
water companies 124
West, Michael 127
whistleblowing 48, 96–122, 164; aims of a good system 102–3; anonymity 100; bribery and 97, 100, 102–3, 104, 105; case histories 106–7, 108–22; consequences of current culture 101–2; definitions 96; external 100, 103–4, 107; importance of keeping records 116; internal 98–9, 102–3, 104–5, 106–7; legal position 100; legislation on 99, 104–5; negative attitudes of organizations 99; providing an effective system 103–4; as responsibility of whole organization 121; risks and perceptions of 96–7, 98; silence option 97–8, 102–3
WHO *see* World Health Organization
wisdom, practical *see phronesis*
Worcester, Bob 73
workforce *see* employment policies
'workforce and productivity, The' (West and Patterson) 140
World Health Assembly 145
World Health Organization 145, 147; Code on marketing 145–6, 147, 148, 149, 152–3, 156; and transmission of AIDS through breast milk 148
Worldwide Fund for Nature 74
Wyeth Laboratories 142

Young, John 114